The
POLTERGEIST PRINCE
of London

The

POLTERGEIST
PRINCE

of London

THE REMARKABLE TRUE STORY
OF THE BATTERSEA POLTERGEIST

SHIRLEY HITCHINGS & JAMES CLARK

The
History
Press

Dedicated to the memory of Harold Chibbett,
a real gentleman who became a dear friend.
Thank you for everything you did for us.

Shirley Hitchings

First published 2013

The History Press
The Mill, Brimscombe Port
Stroud, Gloucestershire, GL5 2QG
www.thehistorypress.co.uk

British Library Cataloguing in Publication Data.
A catalogue record for this book is available from the British Library.

ISBN 978 0 7524 9803 4

Typesetting and origination by The History Press
Printed in Great Britain

CONTENTS

FOREWORD

I am very grateful to Harold Chibbett for keeping such good records of Donald's haunting. Without his hard work this book could not have been written.

I was only a child when all this happened and I did not really know what was going on. At the time a lot was kept from me by Mr Chibbett and my parents, to protect me from harm or worry. However, I can honestly say that what is in the book is true and did happen.

I am now in my seventies and, looking back, my one regret is that Donald took my teenage years away from me.

I think Donald wanted his story told and I am glad at last of the opportunity to carry out his wish. Whoever or whatever he was, I would like to think that he was the French Dauphin, but you must decide this for yourself.

James Clark has been extremely patient and I thank him for his time in writing this book with me.

Shirley Hitchings, 2013

ACKNOWLEDGEMENTS

We are grateful to the following people who helped us during our research for this book: Peter Edwards, Helen Farnsworth, the late Andrew Green, the late Norah Green, Janice Holton, Kate Jarvis, Steve Jebson, John Kahila, Roberto Labanti, Joe McNally, Kieron McNulty and Robert Schneck, as well as all those others who asked that their names be withheld.

Special thanks also go to Jayne Ayris, for casting her expert eyes over more than one draft of this material and offering invaluable feedback, and to Alan Murdie for much help and encouragement and for enabling the reproduction of images owned by the estate of the late Andrew Green.

In addition, we owe a deep debt of gratitude to Harold Chibbett for documenting these events and to Shirley's father Walter (Wally) Hitchings for so conscientiously maintaining a journal recording what took place.

To anyone we have overlooked, we sincerely apologise.

INTRODUCTION

This story was very nearly lost.

Numerous newspaper articles appeared during the early weeks of these events and a few brief summaries of what took place later appeared in books about the paranormal. However, by far the most detailed reports were those made by the psychical researcher Harold Chibbett and his records were almost thrown away.

Chibbett died in 1978 and after his wife Lily followed him some sixteen years later their surviving relatives had no desire to hold onto his vast collection of investigation reports. Chibbett had always promised Shirley that the records relating to her story would one day be hers, so his relatives told her she could collect whatever she wanted before everything went to the rubbish tip.

Shirley and her husband Derek raced from the south coast of England to Chibbett's house in north London. There they discovered an Aladdin's Cave of paranormal papers, the repository of Chibbett's decades of investigation into esoteric subjects. It was clear, though, that the process of discarding material had already begun and that there would be no time for a return trip. As tempting as it was simply to grab the entire collection there was far too much to take with them, so with Derek's help Shirley set about looking for material relating specifically to her and rescuing as much as she could.

The papers she saved hold tantalising hints of Chibbett's other investigations (such as that into 'Charlie' the Basingstoke Poltergeist), the full details of which are gone now. But Shirley did find a vast amount – probably the majority – of the documents dealing with her story.

For more than a decade afterwards those papers gathered dust in her attic, incomplete, dog-eared and in no real order. By the mid-2000s, however, Shirley was contemplating using them to put her full story on record, largely to redress the way she felt some authors had, over the years, misrepresented what had happened. Working with James Clark, a writer who had recently looked into her story for a book titled *Haunted Wandsworth*, Shirley was able to reconstruct large parts of Chibbett's account from the scattered pages she had saved. These were then combined with other source materials such as contemporary news reports and the three surviving volumes of her father's diaries.

Another potential source of information was Shirley's own memories of the events which took place more than half a century earlier. However, memories fade and become distorted with time. Moreover, while these events were taking place Shirley was kept mostly unaware of what Chibbett and her parents discussed regarding her and 'her' poltergeist. In fact Chibbett was always wary that he might be dealing with the product of Shirley's subconscious mind and so he tried to avoid influencing her with his own speculations. Thus, much of the material that appears in this book was forgotten by, or new to, Shirley when we began to collate the records. As a result, presenting this story as a first-person account would have given a highly misleading impression. We have therefore deliberately written this book using the more detached third-person perspective, placing our emphasis on what was recorded at the time, rather than on what Shirley recalls now.

These records tell the tale of 'Donald', who has always been described as a poltergeist although this hardly seems an adequate label for the bizarre story which began to unfold in early 1956. It might also be an inaccurate description, given that we lack a universally accepted interpretation of what a poltergeist actually is. For simplicity's sake, we refer to Donald as a poltergeist; readers should make up their own minds as to who – or what – 'he' really was.

Readers should also bear in mind that much of the material Chibbett documented recorded events from the Hitchings family's point of view. That is to be expected because they were the people 'on the spot' at the time. But, because the family came to believe that Donald was a supernatural entity, they simply reported incidents by recording that Donald had, for example, banged on the wall at a particular time, without properly exploring any other explanation. Therefore, when we make a statement in this book along the lines of 'Donald banged on the wall' this should be taken as referring to a reported incident that was blamed on Donald, rather than necessarily indicating our acceptance of the original implication.

As will become clear, there has always been considerable debate as to what exactly was happening in Shirley's home and the story told here can be read in different ways. Readers of a psychological disposition will doubtless interpret what they read from a very different perspective to those who believe that poltergeist phenomena are evidence of currently unexplained powers of the human mind, while those who believe that poltergeists are discarnate spirit beings will have very different opinions again. Although our Discussion chapter towards the end of this book briefly considers various interpretations of this story, it is not our intention to persuade readers to interpret what happened in any particular way. As Harold Chibbett would have wanted, the purpose of this book is simply to describe what took place.

It is thanks mainly to Chibbett's hard work that the full story of Donald – the Poltergeist Prince of Battersea – can finally be told.

Donald's Spelling

Whatever else he may have been, Donald was a notoriously unreliable speller and his communications are littered with errors. In many cases, the original version of his message no longer exists and the transcript given in this book comes from a record made by (usually) Harold Chibbett or Walter Hitchings. They (Chibbett especially) often improved what Donald had written by correcting spelling and grammatical mistakes, changing the occasional French word to English, and so on, in order to make the messages easier to read. Where possible, however, we give Donald's original spelling so as to offer a more accurate representation of what was actually received: please assume that spelling errors in these messages are *sic* throughout.

Note also that Donald rarely used punctuation. In fact, his early tapped communications were delivered as continuous strings of letters without even any breaks between words. The dashes that appear in transcripts are used for the sake of clarity.

PART I

IT STARTED WITH A KEY

CHAPTER 1

It started with a key. Approximately 2 inches long and silver in colour, it was of the barrel type and probably designed for the sort of small lock that might be found on a desk or cupboard. The teenage Shirley Hitchings discovered it on top of her bed in No. 63 Wycliffe Road in late January 1956, but when she took it into the kitchen to ask whose it was nobody could identify it.

Her father walked through the house, testing the key in every door, desk and cupboard lock there was, but he was unable to find a match. Eventually he reasoned that, if it did not belong to anyone in the family it could not be important, so he left it overnight on a table in the kitchen. The next day the key was again found on top of Shirley's bed.

It was an odd but minor episode that would have been swiftly forgotten had it not been for later events. With the benefit of hindsight, the key's arrival signalled the start of something that would throw the family's life into turmoil for years to come.

Wycliffe Road lies in Battersea, south London, approximately 1 mile north-east of the busy Clapham Junction railway station.

Until the nineteenth century this was a rural area on the out-
skirts of the city but the opening of the station in March 1863
brought with it rapid commercial and residential development.
Wycliffe Grove, as it was originally known, was built in 1866 at
the junction with the main road (Lavender Hill). It was later
extended northward and in 1895 was renamed Wycliffe Road.
By this time the area had well and truly become a suburb of
the expanding metropolis.

At the beginning of 1956 Wycliffe Road was an unremark-
able street of terraced houses in an ordinary working-class
district of London. The city itself was a largely drab and grey
place, scarred by German bombs and still occasionally choked
by dirty 'pea-souper' smogs; just four years earlier, the 'Great
Smog' had caused thousands of deaths. But London was
recovering: steps were being taken to improve air quality,
the food and clothes rationing that had persisted from the
Second World War was finally over, optimism was growing
and Londoners were at long last leaving behind the grim years
of post-war privation and starting to look to the future.

Standing about a third of the way along Wycliffe Road –
as measured from Lavender Hill – was No. 63. It had for many
years been home to the Hitchings family and, behind its neat
little red curtains, the two-storey house was effectively divided
into two separate properties. Walking through the front door
took you into the passageway, where a staircase ahead led
up the left-hand wall onto the upper floor. The ground-floor
rooms were home to Walter (Wally) Hitchings, aged 47, his
51-year-old wife, Catherine (Kitty), and their 15-year-old
daughter, Shirley. Occupying the upstairs rooms were Wally's
73-year-old mother, Ethel, and 'Mark' (pseudonym), a male
relative in his twenties (little information will be given about
Mark because he later sought to put behind him the events
detailed in this book).

Along the right-hand wall of the ground-floor passageway,
the first door led into Wally and Kitty's bedroom, the bay

window of which looked out into the front garden. Next to their double bed was a small bed used by Shirley. It was a family secret that Shirley still slept in the same room as her parents since, from a very young age, she had been prone to sleepwalking and Kitty was so worried that Shirley might accidentally hurt herself while asleep that the bedroom door was kept locked at night. It was not a large room and the two beds together almost completely filled the floor space.

The next room was one the family sometimes called the 'back room' but, confusingly, also referred to as their 'front room' because it was the best room in the house. Either way, it was the room behind the downstairs front bedroom and it will be referred to here as the 'front room'. It was kept comfortably furnished with a three-piece suite, a coffee table and a piano, but was generally off-limits, kept in pristine condition for use only on special occasions such as a visit from the vicar.

At the end of the passageway two steps led down to a turning where a door to the right opened into the back yard, while another door ahead led into the kitchen. The kitchen was the main room in the house, used by the family as a joint living/dining room. As well as four wooden, leather-seated chairs and three armchairs, the crowded room contained a dining table, another table against one wall and a glass-fronted cabinet holding ornaments and a few of Shirley's childhood storybooks. Dominating one corner was a large television set. This was a real luxury item for Battersea in 1956 and it was a focal point for much of the family's day-to-day life.

Behind the kitchen, at the rear of the house, was the scullery. From here a window looked out into the back yard, where the family had converted an old air-raid shelter to keep chickens.

It was by no means a prosperous household but it was clean and tidy, comfortably furnished and, in Shirley's words, 'quite a nice home'.

Soon after the mysterious key's arrival, the noises began. They started in the downstairs bedroom at about 10.30 p.m.

on Friday 27 January, shortly after the family had retired for the night. Wally described the sounds as 'tapping as though water pipes bubbling'. They grew so loud that Shirley went upstairs to Ethel's room to try to sleep, but there she found that something seemed to keep pulling at her bedclothes. Nobody slept that night.

The tapping recurred the following night, and the night after, and so on. Soon, there was tapping during the day too. 'It would have a metallic sound,' Shirley recalls. 'An odd sound, a hollow sound.' Sometimes it would come from the head of Shirley's bed and at other times from her parents' bed. It also started coming from the floors, ceilings and walls. The furniture too became a source of the tapping, which was sometimes accompanied by a scratching like the sound of claws. Now and then the tapping was heard while Shirley was in a different room, but on the vast majority of occasions she was present. It quickly became apparent that whatever was causing the sounds was somehow connected with the teenager.

Born on 18 December 1940, Shirley had turned 15 only six weeks before. Slim and dark-haired, she was an only child, imaginative, and frequently described as 'highly strung'. Her school report cards depict a quiet, shy pupil who, although not especially gifted academically, was intelligent and always tried hard. Part of her difficulty with schoolwork stemmed from her problems with spelling and in fact when Shirley was in her thirties she would be diagnosed as slightly dyslexic. As a young girl, she would often sit with Ethel, watching her make lace, but despite her granddaughter's pleas Ethel refused to teach this skill to Shirley, saying that Shirley was 'too impatient'. Embroidery, on the other hand, was something that Shirley could and did enjoy. Her artistic nature also found outlets in dance (she took both ballet and tap-dancing classes), drawing and painting. Shirley believes she inherited her love of drawing from her father, who himself had a talent for sketching.

In all other respects, however, Walter Hitchings (born 27 October 1908) was a down-to-earth, practical sort who impressed all who met him with his obvious honesty. Over 6 feet tall and thin to the point of gauntness, Wally cut a striking figure. He had previously worked as a steam engine driver and he was now employed by London Transport to drive underground trains on the Northern Line.

His wife Kitty (born 31 August 1904) was 'a small, elderly, and somewhat faded lady' (Chibbett's description) whose chronic arthritis forced her to spend much of the time in a wheelchair or else rely on walking sticks to get about. Despite this, Kitty was fiercely house-proud, determined to ensure the family's home was always presentable. Her own parents had been reasonably well-off at one time, however her family experienced money troubles after her father was killed during the First World War and they had been evicted from their home. When Kitty was around 14 years old her mother had died and Kitty, along with her sister, had been sent to live with relatives. There, the girls slept on the bare floor with only a thin blanket for warmth. Kitty blamed this for her arthritis.

Both Wally and Kitty were staunchly religious, belonging to the Church of England and having little knowledge of – or time for – such subjects as spiritualism and ghosts. They felt sure that the strange noises would quickly turn out to have a natural explanation. They thought such sounds might be a by-product of the electricity mains supply but this possibility evaporated as it became clear the noises were connected with Shirley. They next wondered if Shirley was producing the sounds herself, so whenever either the tapping or scratching started while Shirley was in bed they asked their daughter to hold her hands above the sheets where they could be seen. Shirley would do so – and the sounds would continue without interruption.

Despite getting next to no sleep that first weekend, Wally went to work as usual on Monday 30 January. Word of the strange noises quickly got round and at Morden station Wally found that someone had left a note for him. It proved to be from a fellow underground train driver by the name of Henry (Harry) Hanks, offering his assistance. Hanks was a spiritualist who practised as a medium in his free time and he believed he might be able to drive away whatever was responsible for the disturbances. Being a good Church of England man, Wally was far from keen to become embroiled in the world of spiritualism, mediums and contact with the dead, but on the other hand he had a duty to protect his family. If Hanks could indeed help it would be foolish to ignore him. Cautiously, Wally invited Hanks to visit No. 63 on Sunday 5 February.

On that date the part-time medium arrived with his wife and his daughter and the three of them, accompanied by Shirley, held a séance in the downstairs bedroom. Soon after Hanks left, the tapping returned.

Ten days later, Hanks visited again. As the Hitchings family waited, uncomfortable with what was happening and unsure what to expect, Hanks put himself into a trance. An hour passed before he opened his eyes. Sadly, he admitted he had failed to make contact with whatever was there. He told Wally he might get better results if Shirley were to accompany him to his own house in a few days' time to take part in a proper sitting. Reluctantly, Wally agreed.

Tensions within the sleep-deprived household were increasing and tempers were becoming frayed. Attempting to lighten the situation, the family gave humorous nicknames to the strange force that had seemingly invaded their home, referring to 'him' as Charlie Boy and Spooky Willie. Meanwhile, the tapping was growing louder. One day, neighbours who had been disturbed by the noises late at night pointedly asked Wally if he had been taking up the floorboards. Another time, Wally and Kitty were visiting the Muslim family who lived next door at No. 65 when everyone present clearly heard a loud knocking coming from inside No. 63, where Shirley was alone with her grandmother. According to a report made by an investigator a few weeks later, such noises were sometimes so loud they could be heard outside in the street, several houses' distance away.

Fortunately for the neighbours at No. 65, the stretch of yard running between part of their house and No. 63 protected them from some of the tapping that continued to break out both night and day. There was no such escape for those living at No. 61, whose terraced house shared an entire wall with No. 63. Those neighbours received their first proper introduction to the unfolding story roughly three weeks after the tapping first began when, according to Wally, 'we could not stand it no longer & had to bring the man from next door in to see & hear for himself'.

One of the occupants of No. 61 was Shirley's 'Auntie Lil'. Lily Love had always been Shirley's 'Auntie', despite not actually being related to the Hitchings family. Lily and Kitty had known each other since schooldays and, with Kitty now largely wheelchair-bound, Lily often helped out with the washing and ironing, fetched bits of shopping, and so on. In mid-February, knowing how much of a disturbance the noises were causing, 'Auntie Lil' invited Shirley to spend a night in No. 61 so that the rest of the Hitchings family could get a good night's sleep. Unfortunately for Lily, the tapping followed Shirley. Afterwards, Lily told a reporter (*Daily Herald*, 20 February 1956), '[Shirley] spent a night with us but none of us got any sleep because of the noise. We were all scared.'

By now, news was beginning to spread.

CHAPTER 2

In 1956 Wycliffe Road was a little community of its own. Everybody knew everybody else's business and, as word got round of the peculiar goings-on at No. 63, more and more neighbours dropped by. Ostensibly it was for a cup of tea and a chat with Kitty, but really they wanted the latest gossip. Strangers, too, began to arrive, many drawn by nothing more than curiosity, others by the desire to help. The Revd W.E. Douthwaite, vicar of the nearby St Bartholomew's church, was one of those who called at No. 63 hoping to solve the mystery. Despite his best efforts he left as baffled as everyone else.

News, however, was not the only thing that was spreading. So was Spooky Willie's ability to cause mischief. The tapping noises now seemed to follow Shirley and sometimes when she travelled on a bus her fellow passengers heard the noises and cast odd glances in her direction. The problem even followed her to work.

Shirley was employed as a dress cutter in the Alterations Department of a large department store in London's West End. It was her first job since leaving school and she had only been there for around ten weeks. The mysterious tapping upset and even frightened some of her colleagues and, when the occasional pair of scissors started to go missing, blame inevitably fell on Shirley and her invisible companion. Everyone could see that Shirley was exhausted and distressed from severe lack of sleep, so she was sent to see the firm's doctor. He did not believe a word of her story, until he too heard the tapping. For the sake of her health – and no doubt to prevent further disruption at work – he ordered Shirley to take a fortnight's leave.

At home on Saturday 18 February, Shirley accidentally dropped a glove onto the floor. When she bent down to retrieve it, it flew up and hit Wally in the face. Sometime later, loud knocking interrupted the family's plans to watch television. The most dramatic incident (sensationalised by newspapers as a 'levitation') came after Shirley went to bed that night. Wally and Mark had stayed up to keep watch and they soon heard tapping from Shirley's bed. It went on for 'a long time'. Wally's account of what happened next was reported in *Psychic News* (25 February 1956): 'Shirley said the bedclothes were being pulled under her so we got hold of them and felt that they were being tugged by force. While this was going on we saw that Shirley was being lifted out of her bed. She was rigid and about six inches above the bed when we lifted her out and stood her on the floor.'

Wally later gave a more detailed account to author and journalist John Langdon-Davies, as follows. Hearing Shirley cry out that the sheet was being pulled from under her, Wally and Mark rushed into the bedroom. As they entered they saw the sheet at one corner of the bed slowly move away from Shirley as if it were being pulled by an invisible hand. To make sure Shirley was not somehow moving the sheet herself they made her place her hands on top of the bedclothes, then the two men pulled the corner of the sheet back. The moment they let go, it was pulled away again. 'It was just like a tug-of-war,' explained Wally, 'and in the end I said, "Oh, let it be".' He and Mark stood and watched the sheet slowly pull away from beneath Shirley. According to Langdon-Davies' summary of what Wally told him, when the moving sheet reached her back Shirley 'involuntarily arched herself into a bow' and then, in Wally's words, 'it was just as if her head was raised'. The rumpled sheet shot from Shirley's bed onto her parents' double bed. 'I'm all stiff,' complained Shirley. 'I can't sit up.' Wally and Mark, going to help her, found that her body was rigid and 'when they pulled her up by the arms she remained upright until vertical and then collapsed.' Afterwards, Shirley told reporters, 'I could feel a force pushing into the centre of my back and lifting me up.'

By now, the mainstream media had caught on to the story and the stream of visitors was swelled by reporters. Harry Hanks's mediumistic efforts had had little or no effect in dampening the situation and the reporters that visited over the following days were told of objects that had moved by themselves. A china ornament and an alarm clock, both of which had stood on the mantelpiece, and a table lamp, had fallen to the ground. Something had also thrown a chair. According to the *Daily Express* (21 February 1956), all five members of the Hitchings family, some of their next-door neighbours and even the family's landlord, had by now seen objects move. The visiting reporters did not witness any movements themselves but, while Shirley was telling James O'Driscoll from the *News Chronicle* about her recent 'levitation', her wristwatch slipped quietly from her arm and fell to the floor. 'There he is again!' she cried.

The *South Western Star* newspaper sent their reporter Ross Werge. When Werge arrived at No. 63 on Monday 20 February, he interviewed Shirley and her parents, then went upstairs to talk to Shirley's grandmother. Ethel Hitchings was Wally's mother. She had lived in the neighbourhood for many years and was widely known throughout the local community, who respectfully referred to her as 'Old Mother Hitchings'. She had been a district nurse and midwife for her entire working life and even in retirement she remained the first port of call for many locals seeking medical advice. Ethel was as religious as Wally and Kitty, although unlike them she was a devout Roman Catholic. Too ill now to visit church, she was visited once a week by her priest, who would administer the rite of Holy Communion to her in her room. In a very real way, Ethel had been and remained the head of the Hitchings family, both of the immediate family within No. 63 and of the families of Wally's sisters – Shirley's Aunt Nell and Aunt Gert – who also lived in Wycliffe Road. In the event of any family crisis, Ethel would summon everyone to her, and the adults would have no choice but to answer her call and abide by her decisions. Although she was now almost completely crippled by arthritis and able to move only slowly and with pain, Ethel remained a formidable presence. Of Irish ancestry, given to smoking a pipe, and inherently bossy, she was a tall and rather hefty woman. The extra weight she had put on as a result of her illness made her, if anything, even more physically imposing.

Werge found the redoubtable old woman sitting in a comfortable armchair before a fire. She quickly made her feelings clear to the reporter, declaring, 'It's a lot of rot.' It was a typical announcement from a woman who would never stand for anything she saw as nonsense – even if that meant ignoring the evidence of her own eyes. Ironically, Ethel was the only family member to claim any prior experience of the paranormal. Years before, when working in a hospital, she had been present when patients had died and Shirley remembers that Ethel claimed to have once seen a misty essence leave a patient's body at the point of death. According to one newspaper account (*Weekend Mail*, 1-5 March 1956), Ethel also claimed she had once 'seen the ghost of her dead husband at the bottom of her bed'. Despite her stubbornness, Werge persuaded Ethel to admit that 'slippers had flown over her head and clothes pegs she had secured seconds before had mysteriously detached themselves.' She also told Werge that, on another occasion, she had been mixing a pudding when a spoon suddenly jumped into the bowl.

Werge's most remarkable interview, though, came later that day and was not with Ethel but with Spooky Willie himself. At around 2.30 p.m. Shirley offered to demonstrate to the reporter the tapping sounds she said were generated by the poltergeist. She placed her foot on the seat of a hard wooden chair, Werge placed his hand next to her foot, and before long Werge felt and heard faint tapping for himself, apparently coming from the wood. Although he watched Shirley's foot intently he was sure she was not creating the sounds herself. He asked Shirley to move her foot to the edge of the seat but the tapping continued. Shirley walked across to a wall and leaned against it, and the tapping not only followed her but also became louder. She moved to the opposite side of the room and leaned against a cupboard, and the tapping sounded from there instead.

At some point, one of them had the idea to use the sounds to try communicating with Spooky Willie. Between them, Werge and Shirley agreed a simple code – one tap for 'No', two for 'Yes' and three for 'Don't know'. For the next three hours the reporter questioned the poltergeist.

'Are you evil?'
'NO.'
'Can we help you in any way?'
'YES.'
'Have you a message for Shirley?'
'YES.'
'Will you deliver it today?'
'NO.'
'Tomorrow?'
'NO.'
'On Sunday?'
'YES.'

Werge asked the poltergeist to tap out Shirley's age. Spooky Willie answered correctly with fifteen 'distinct thumps'. When asked about his own identity, however, he seemed less certain.

Somebody – probably Hanks – had previously suggested that the poltergeist was the spirit of an old man tapping with a stick, but Spooky Willie told Werge he was the spirit of Shirley's great-grandmother (Ethel's mother), who had died forty years previously. A little later, however, the poltergeist claimed to be a boy named Donald, who had played with Shirley when they were children.

In his subsequent article, Werge claimed he had been 'extremely sceptical' before his visit, but less so when he left. His report concluded, 'Perhaps there is a natural explanation, but it has me beat. And I take a lot of convincing.'

Another reporter who visited that Monday was Elizabeth Few from the *Daily Express*. Upstairs in Ethel's parlour, Few and Shirley sat at a table with Shirley resting her slipper-clad feet on an old wooden chair. Like Werge, Few interviewed the poltergeist by asking questions and receiving simple responses, although in Few's case a reply of two taps was interpreted as meaning 'No' rather than 'Yes'.

Few rested her hands on the chair and asked Spooky Willie if he was evil. He replied that he was not and Few 'heard the knocks distinctly' and with her hand 'felt them throb'. The atmosphere was light-hearted and the reporter and the teenage girl giggled as they questioned the empty chair. Shirley asked if the poltergeist meant her harm and was told, 'NO'. Few asked if he had been responsible for the key found on Shirley's bed: 'YES'. They learned that, 'YES', the poltergeist was guilty of throwing 'all those things' and, 'YES', he would do it again. Would he be a nuisance that night? 'YES.'

'Oh dear,' cried Shirley in alarm. 'No sleep again and more clothes pulled off the beds. Please go away.'

Three double taps followed: 'NO. NO. NO.' The poltergeist sounded another triple 'NO' later when Few announced it was time for her to go. The reporter made her excuses and left – 'thankfully', she later wrote.

During her visit, Few built up a similar picture to the one Werge had: that the poltergeist was claiming to be a boy named Donald (or possibly Ronald). The reporters understood this to be a particular boy who had regularly stayed at his nan's house in Wycliffe Road during the school holidays. His family and Shirley's had known each other well and, because Donald/Ronald and Shirley had been the same age, they had often played together as children. Two or three years before, Donald/Ronald's father had taken a job overseas and the family had moved abroad. Shirley had been most upset to see her friend go. He had promised to write to her, but never had.

It is no longer clear exactly why the poltergeist became identified with this boy and the issue is rather confused. Possibly, the idea was rooted in an incident involving a gold bangle belonging to Shirley. Donald/Ronald had often teased Shirley by stealing a particular bangle of hers and, some time prior to the reporters' visits, Shirley had discovered that this same bangle was missing. Few's article mentions that while she was interviewing Spooky Willie, Shirley asked the poltergeist, 'My gold bangle has disappeared. Have you got it, Donald?' The poltergeist confirmed that he had taken it and refused to give it back.

This seems to be the first recorded instance of anyone referring to the poltergeist as 'Donald', and the context does suggest that Shirley thought the poltergeist was connected with her childhood playmate. Shirley's own present-day recollection, however, is that the identification of Donald the poltergeist with her friend Donald/Ronald resulted from a misunderstanding made by the reporters. She believes that the first use of 'Donald' as the poltergeist's name took place before this, with her mother jokingly using the name in allusion to Donald Duck, and that the choice of name had no more relevance than did Spooky Willie or Charlie Boy. Yet despite Shirley's present-day conviction, some of the messages that would be communicated by the poltergeist over the early weeks and months of these events do clearly refer to the poltergeist wanting to renew the friendship between Shirley and her old playmate. (Fortunately, any initial worries the family had that Shirley's old friend had died and come back to haunt her were quickly dispelled: by the end of 21 February Ethel had contacted the boy's family and confirmed that he remained alive and well.) Regardless of how the early (mis) identification with Shirley's old friend came about, after 20 February 1956 the names Spooky Willie and Charlie Boy fell into disuse. Everybody began to refer to the poltergeist as Donald.

On Tuesday 21 February the family began to keep a journal of these strange events. It was a big day for Shirley because she was due to appear on national television that evening, to be interviewed on the BBC. Shirley wrote the first journal entries herself (although thereafter it was usually Wally who recorded brief notes) and her entry for that Tuesday was as follows:

2.00 a.m. Went to bed leaving mystery key on sideboard.

2.05 a.m. Father noticed key back on my bed. Tapping continues.

2.08 a.m. Gloves dropped. Inside one of them was my face cream.

2.20 a.m. We felt something lying across our feet. Tapping continued but fell asleep keeping light on.

8.30 a.m. No tapping but both sheets on bed begin to pull up. Dad and Aunt Gert come to watch as witnesses.

11.00 a.m. Newly made bed rumpled behind Dad's back while I was in kitchen.

1.00 p.m. Tapping gives me message from Donald. Didn't make sense.

1.30 p.m. Chair overturned upstairs in Grandma's room.

2.45 p.m. Tapping follows me into bedroom. Key still on bed.

4.45 p.m. Tapping follows me into Fleet-street shop.

The reporter Elizabeth Few was with Shirley in this shop. In a subsequent article Few confirmed that she had heard the taps referred to, noting that they apparently emanated from somewhere near Shirley's feet. Because the girl was wearing thick, crepe-soled snow boots Few was 'baffled' as to how Shirley could have been making the sounds herself.

Shortly before the family left for BBC Television Centre that evening, Shirley and Donald were interviewed by a reporter from the *Daily Sketch*. The crude and limited method of communicating with Donald via tapped responses of 'Yes', 'No' and 'Maybe' had already started to evolve. Hanks had suggested an idea inspired by that notorious tool of mediums, the Ouija board; if the poltergeist could tap in reply to a question, it should be able to tap to select individual letters of the alphabet. Wally would never allow an actual Ouija board into the house, so the next-best method was to write out the alphabet on a sheet of paper or card and invite Donald to respond to spoken questions as someone pointed to each letter in turn. Every time Donald tapped, the selected letter was noted down and in this way messages could be laboriously spelled out.

An even more elaborate method of communication would evolve over the following weeks. Drawing still further on the image of the Ouija board, this involved arranging separate cards for each letter of the alphabet in a large ring on a tabletop. To speed matters up, additional cards would be placed in the centre of the ring for common answers such as 'Yes' and 'No'. Somebody – often Mark – would point to the cards, moving around the ring as the poltergeist tapped to select letters. Sometimes a wine glass was moved around the ring instead, with the poltergeist tapping to indicate when the glass was in the correct place.

Wally and Kitty disapproved of such 'spirit games' as they called them, but reluctantly allowed these sessions to take place and sometimes even participated themselves. One detail that very quickly emerged from these sessions was that the poltergeist had difficulty spelling. This would be a consistent feature of Donald's communications over the years to come and it suggested a close connection between the poltergeist and the mildly dyslexic teenager.

With this evolution of communication methods, the newspaper stories began to change from the 'classic' poltergeist narrative of childish thumping and flying objects into something approaching a love story between a young woman and a disembodied spirit. Shirley insists that this romantic angle was nothing more than a fictional creation, or at least blown out of all proportion, by the media.

The *Daily Sketch* reporter present on 21 February was one of those keen on the concept of Donald as a ghostly suitor. Shirley had no boyfriend at that time and the reporter asked the poltergeist outright, 'Do you love Shirley?' A single tap sounded in response:

'YES.'

'Will you ever leave her?'

'NO.'

The reporter and Shirley then listened as the tapping slowly picked out letters, spelling, 'BE LOVING SHIRLEY – COME SOON.' Further tapping stated that Donald was 15 years old and had been born in Kent. Shirley's similarly named childhood playmate would also have been 15, and his family likewise came from Kent, although in a sinister addition Donald stated that he had not been born of flesh-and-blood parents.

Also describing Donald as Shirley's 'ghost admirer' was an amusing article by the *South London Advertiser*'s Joyce Lewis (23 February 1956). Lewis did not use the alphabet method of communication but the more basic 'Yes'/'No' system and she marvelled at how much expression could be conveyed through simple tapping. After cheekily proposing marriage to Donald (and being turned down) Lewis asked, 'Don't you usually like girls?' whereupon a single solid tap announced a definite 'YES'. Was Donald turning her down because she was too old (at 24)? 'YES'.

Shirley's television appearance that evening was on the BBC's topical magazine programme *Highlight*. The teenager described to the programme's viewers what had been happening at her home and maintained that before it had started she had never heard of poltergeists, let alone known what they 'normally' do. Unfortunately, Donald himself failed to put on a show for the cameras.

After Shirley returned home another journalist turned up at No. 63. According to Shirley's brief diary entry, he asked Donald to throw something for him. The journalist stayed for around two hours and saw nothing but as he was leaving shortly after midnight Donald threw a bottle top at (presumably) his back. Shirley did not record what his reaction to this was.

The situation in Wycliffe Road was becoming unmanageable. Shirley's television appearance and the many newspaper reports were drawing in the curious and the ghoulish, and the numbers of people passing by the 'haunted' house in the hope of seeing something were growing day by day. 'Judging by the uproar which has blown up over the poltergeist ... one might think it was the first phenomenon of its kind,' sniffed *Psychic News* (3 March 1956).

Neighbours found ever more inventive excuses to pop round and gossips merrily disseminated their findings. Neighbourhood children would sneak into the garden to peer through the window or listen at the front door and one newspaper reported that local children were scrawling the word 'Donald' on parked cars.

Increasingly, answering a knock at the front door would reveal a complete stranger, often somebody claiming to have psychic gifts and offering help. The more obvious 'nutters' were politely but firmly turned away, but many self-proclaimed mediums were allowed inside to give their opinions. Unfortunately, it was rare for any two psychics to reveal the same 'truth'. One would announce that the house was haunted by a little old lady angry at passing over before she was ready, while another would identify the spirit as that of a murderer denied entry to heaven. It all added to the general air of chaos and confusion.

Even the postal delivery became something to dread when begging letters started to arrive. Evidently, because the story was in the newspapers, the writers assumed the family was being paid vast sums for their interviews. This was far from the case. Although Shirley did earn three guineas for her appearance on the BBC, neither she nor the rest of her family had earned a penny from the newspaper stories. Over the coming months Wally learned to deal with the begging letters the best way he could – by throwing them onto the fire.

The greatest irritation was the growing army of reporters camped outside the house. Wycliffe Road was not especially wide and it was impossible to avoid the pack of journalists that descended upon anyone who called at No. 63, yelling out their questions and demanding to know what was happening. Under siege in their small home, life was becoming unbearable for the family. The stress affected everyone, but especially Wally. Soon the train driver started worrying that lack of sleep and the constant strain on his nerves was putting his passengers' safety at risk. The frustrations bubbling inside him occasionally escaped in flashes of temper and he would scream at the reporters to 'Go on! Piss off! Leave us alone!' Ethel, too – annoyed but also frightened in her upstairs rooms – desperately wanted the poltergeist to leave and for calm to return. 'I tried to get rid of him by putting a crucifix on the floor of my bedroom,' she told one reporter (*Daily Sketch*, 22 February 1956). 'Donald went mad. He nearly threw me out of bed and rapped so loudly that the neighbours complained.'

Family, media and public alike eagerly awaited the next big event, scheduled for the evening of Wednesday 22 February. Donald was going to be exorcised.

CHAPTER 3

The exorcism would be attempted by Wally's fellow underground train driver, the medium Harry Hanks. Hanks had convinced Wally and Kitty – who still distrusted spiritualism – that this could help Shirley. Some of the reporters also helped persuade Shirley's parents to allow the exorcism, although this was possibly less to do with helping Shirley than because they sensed an entertaining news story. As for Shirley herself, she was not sure she actually wanted to lose her ghostly companion but Wally put his foot down, stating, 'This nonsense has to stop.'

Hanks was to perform the exorcism at his home in Groveway, Stockwell, approximately 1½ miles (2.5 km) west of Wycliffe Road. Harry Hanks was in his early fifties and had worked for London Transport for just over thirty years. He claimed that he sometimes received messages from spirits while he was driving trains, although he stressed that these communiqués from the beyond did not affect his concentration and so did not interfere with his job. Outside work, he operated as a medium.

He had been born with his gift, he asserted, although he had been unaware of it until, aged 10, he saw the figure of a man emerge from his bedroom wall and walk across the room. In his early teens, shortly after the end of the First World War,

Hanks gravely informed his mother that another great conflict was coming and he claimed to have correctly predicted to within a year when this would break out. Hanks had become seriously involved with spiritualism at the age of 28, since when he had conducted numerous séances.

The setting for the exorcism was Hanks's first-floor sitting room, with its television set, knick-knacks and dartboard. A dog lazed in front of the fireplace, budgerigars and canaries watched from a birdcage, and a pair of unimpressed goldfish swam around inside their fish tank. The lighting was dim and dull pink, merging with the dying coals in the grate to cast a warm glow across the brown and orange wallpaper. Those gathered to try to drive Donald away from Shirley were Hanks himself; his 51-year-old wife Georgina; their daughter Dorothy who was in her early twenties; a clairvoyant named Mrs Daisy Bennett; and Mrs Ada Roden, a spiritualist. Shirley was accompanied by her father, who had not had time to change out of his work clothes. There were also many onlookers. Hanks had seen an opportunity to publicise the spiritualist movement and had invited numerous reporters, photographers and TV cameramen to cram themselves into the room.

Despite the cameras, Hanks refused to allow any photography or filming during the procedure itself because he felt it would interfere with the conditions needed. Although footage apparently showing the exorcism was later aired on ITV, the images shown were actually staged for the cameras after the real exorcism finished.

With everything set, the sitters joined hands. They sang 'Onward, Christian Soldiers', the reporters joining in as Mrs Ada Roden accompanied them on an upright piano. Mrs Roden then joined the circle as the company sang 'The Lord is my Shepherd', after which a period of contemplative silence was followed by a prayer.

Dorothy Hanks was learning the skills needed to practise as a medium and she now attempted to slip into a trance.

She 'shook convulsively' (*Daily Sketch*, 23 February 1956) but failed to achieve the correct state of consciousness. Her father was sympathetic and told not her not to worry, before closing his own eyes and successfully putting himself into a trance. As he sank under, wrote the same reporter, his 'face contorted and his hands waved.'

A hush enveloped the room as Hanks's breathing deepened. The next moment there was a hammering at the front door. As the dog barked excitedly and the startled birds squawked and flapped, Mrs Hanks hurried downstairs. From upstairs in the sitting room, she could be heard remonstrating with someone on the doorstep, refusing them entry. A few seconds later, Mrs Hanks came back into the room looking worried. She tried her best to inform her husband that the police were at the door – but there was no reply from the deeply entranced Hanks.

The police had been patrolling Brixton Road in their car when they received an order to go to Groveway. An anonymous informant had notified Scotland Yard that a 'black magic' ceremony was taking place there. Now two uniformed policemen came thumping up the staircase to investigate. Mrs Hanks did her best to explain that the event was a spiritualist meeting and perfectly legal. For a quarter of an hour, the police watched and listened to the proceedings before they finally left, satisfied that – whatever was going on – it was breaking no laws.

The sitters did their best to continue. 'We mustn't lose the power,' encouraged Mrs Roden, attempting to restore a suitably sombre atmosphere as Shirley did her best not to giggle at the turn of affairs. Eventually the exorcism was underway again and Hanks stretched out his hands to Shirley. He shook violently as his spirit guide – an African spirit named (with an utter lack of modern political correctness) 'Sambo' – spoke through him. In a deep voice, 'Sambo' declared that the exorcism had worked. 'It is free, my friend,' he boomed. 'The interference is from you. God bless you all.'

Hanks awoke from his trance, Mrs Bennett delivered a short prayer and the exorcism was over. Over cups of tea, Hanks explained that he and his guide had driven away the spirit that had taken possession of Shirley. He had then sealed her damaged aura and created a psychic barrier that should protect her from other spirits.

'I feel much happier,' Shirley said. 'I think the poltergeist has gone for good.'

The following morning, Hanks drove the short distance to No. 63 to check on Shirley. Before the exorcism he had been worried that the poltergeist, strengthened by all the recent publicity, might have been too powerful for him. 'Poltergeists like to be the centre of attention,' he had warned. 'The more fuss they get the stronger they become.' He was therefore delighted to learn there had been no trouble from Donald overnight. Unfortunately, a short while later the actions of two reporters from the *Weekend Mail*, keen to find their own solution to the story, seemed to upset whatever delicate balance had resulted from the exorcism.

They called at No. 63 around noon and persuaded Wally and Kitty to let them take Shirley with them. They explained they would take her to be examined by a medical professional. First, however, they drove Shirley to the newspaper's Fleet Street offices where she was plied with sweets and fizzy pop in an effort to, in Shirley's words, 'butter me up'. They encouraged her to demonstrate the poltergeist's tapping sounds and when the noises started they examined Shirley closely. The resulting *Weekend Mail* article (1-5 March 1956) stated that they went so far as to have a female reporter strip Shirley (although Shirley does not remember being searched in this way), looking for some type of concealed 'clicking instrument'. They found nothing. Later, the reporters asked Shirley to remove the winter bootees she was wearing, suspecting she might be clicking her toe or toes. At this point, it appeared that Donald became tired of being tested because the noises stopped.

Afterwards, the reporters drove Shirley through London's West End to a large private house in an expensive district. Although Shirley had no idea where she was, the house evidently had connections with the medical profession: a long-needled instrument reminding her of a dentist's drill hung from one wall while a nearby cabinet was full of medicine bottles. A man entered and greeted Shirley, speaking with some sort of foreign accent. The newspaper article described this stranger as a member of the Medical Hypnotists' Association with a 'wide reputation for psychiatric work'. He spent most of the rest of the afternoon attempting to hypnotise the teenage girl, who did not understand what was happening. Frightened, Shirley refused to obey the man's requests for her to relax and focus her attention on the pen moving back and forth in front of her eyes. When she was instructed to stare into a glass ball, Shirley again refused, fidgeting and patting her face to keep herself alert. Despite the exasperated doctor's efforts to calm her, she would not keep still and time and time again asked him to stop and pleaded to be taken home. At last the doctor gave up in frustration.

The journalists had little choice but to drive Shirley back to Wycliffe Road. She arrived home six hours after she had left, upset and distressed. That night, to the despair of Wally and Kitty, the poltergeist disturbances started again.

The tapping noises came first, growing louder as the evening deepened into night. Then, at around 11.20 p.m., a photograph in a glass-fronted frame flew from the mantelpiece and struck Kitty in the back. The noises continued throughout the night and the family got little sleep.

When the tapping had started again, Harry Hanks had been deep underground, driving his train through the tunnels beneath London. He would later claim that he had sensed something had gone wrong in Wycliffe Road and that when he returned to his home in Stockwell, he, his wife and his daughter felt compelled to pray for Shirley.

On Friday morning Wally telephoned Hanks. 'Come quickly,' he said. 'It's begun all over again.' Less than thirty minutes later, Hanks was at No. 63, listening to a scared Shirley explain that not only had the poltergeist come back but now the noises were louder than before. Hanks believed that the actions of the two journalists the day before – no matter how well-intentioned they might have been – had demolished the protective aura he had put in place around Shirley. The only thing he could do was repeat the exorcism. He asked Wally to allow him to take Shirley away for a few days and not to tell anyone where she was. Wally gave his consent and once again Shirley was taken out to a car and driven away.

Hanks took Shirley to his home in Stockwell. He felt it important to perform the second exorcism as soon as possible but, given how pale and exhausted Shirley was, she first needed to regain her strength. The Hanks family spent much of that weekend praying for their guest, to 'surround Shirley with power'. Shirley remained indoors in the room that would be used for the exorcism, shielded from visitors and watched over by Hanks's daughter, Dorothy.

For Shirley, it was a pleasant few days. Hanks insisted she had nothing to fear from Donald, that he (Hanks) was controlling the poltergeist now and that Shirley should simply 'be a child'. Much of the time, Shirley did not understand what the spiritualist was talking about and she privately believed Donald was simply hiding from Hanks, letting Hanks fool himself that he was in charge. Nevertheless, she felt deeply peaceful in Hanks's home and was quite happy to let him continue doing whatever it was he was doing.

Several days earlier, Donald had informed the *South Western Star*'s reporter that he would deliver a message on Sunday. If the poltergeist had ever truly intended to deliver that message, his plans were presumably interrupted by Shirley's staying with Hanks because no such message came. On Sunday evening, Hanks made his second attempt to drive Donald away. Most of the people involved were the same as before: the three members of the Hanks family were joined by the two experienced mediums Mrs Daisy Bennett and Mrs Ada Roden, and an uncomfortable Wally was again present to make sure Shirley was safe. The difference was that, this time, the proceedings were private. The only journalist allowed to attend was Mr W. Neech, a sympathetic reporter for the spiritualist newspaper *The Two Worlds*. (Hanks had contacted Neech on Friday to let him know Donald had returned and to arrange for him to meet Shirley. Neech, accompanied by two acquaintances, had won the teenager's confidence and both Shirley and Hanks felt comfortable enough with all three to let them participate in the exorcism.)

Just before the exorcism began, according to Neech's later article, there was an abrupt drop in temperature and the sitters felt 'icy breezes' flow across their hands. Shirley 'shivered and hunched herself up, wide-eyed and silent' as she sat opposite Hanks. Mrs Roden stood and led the circle in an opening prayer. They sang a few hymns and Hanks closed his eyes, breathed deeply and entered a trance. Soon, 'Sambo' spoke through him, telling Shirley not to be afraid. Hanks's eyes opened and 'Sambo' gazed out at the girl, who looked back and smiled. 'The little star, she shines much brighter,' announced the spirit guide through Hanks's mouth. A pressure seemed to lift and Shirley laughed as the exorcism was concluded, apparently successfully.

Shirley stayed with the Hanks family for several days more, enjoying what was essentially a relaxing holiday. Meanwhile, Hanks was working behind the scenes to do whatever he could to ease her eventual return to everyday life. He informed her doctor of what had happened (although quite what the doctor made of it can only be imagined) and talked to the staff manager at the West End store to arrange for Shirley's transfer to another department when she returned to work in around one week's time. But Hanks remained slightly worried. He still felt that his first attempt to drive the poltergeist away had succeeded but that the journalists' actions the following day had broken down the protective psychic barrier he had erected around Shirley. In fact he felt certain that Shirley was a natural medium whose undeveloped powers had then attracted a *second* earthbound entity to her and that this was why the disturbances had started up again that evening. Shirley thought otherwise. In her opinion there had been no new entity – just Donald, the same as before – but Hanks believed the later incidents had been caused by the spirit of a woman who had committed suicide in Wycliffe Road years before. He was confident that he had now 'rescued' this second spirit, but he urged Shirley to be careful. She had an innate psychic ability, he warned, and this might yet attract further trouble.

CHAPTER 4

John Langdon-Davies was a well known and respected author and journalist with an interest in unexplained phenomena. On Tuesday 28 February 1956 he visited No. 63 and Wally and Kitty apologetically informed him that Shirley was not at home (they did not say she was with Hanks, claiming instead that she was staying away for a few days on the advice of her doctor). So Langdon-Davies interviewed Wally and Kitty instead. The following details come from his record of that evening, a copy of which was kept by Harold Chibbett.

Langdon-Davies spoke mainly to Wally. Kitty was present, but spent the entire time watching television, only turning away from her programmes now and again to offer additional information or correct her husband if he got a detail wrong. The couple made a favourable impression on Langdon-Davies who described them both – but particularly Wally – as 'very sensible and indeed "superior" types' whose attitude towards what was taking place was 'philosophical' and whose main desire was simply for life to return to normal.

When Langdon-Davies asked for details of what had happened so far, Wally related one episode after another, 'almost without stopping', giving so much information that it was impossible for Langdon-Davies to record more than a fraction of what he was told. With a few exceptions where phenomena had taken place in the bedroom, everything described had happened in brightly lit conditions. In addition to those incidents already mentioned in the present book, Wally told Langdon-Davies how on one occasion the tapping noises had become so maddening that Wally had placed a crucifix close to the apparent source of the sounds. As had happened when Ethel had tried the same tactic, the problem was only exacerbated. The volume of the noise increased, and in Wally's words, 'you would have thought it was annoyed by the crucifix and was telling you to take it away.' When he removed the crucifix the noises calmed down. The suggested implications must have troubled the deeply religious man.

Wally also commented on how Shirley often seemed to know when the taps were coming. It was as if she was physically in contact with the source of the noise (as if the sound came from the floorboards on which she was standing), Shirley sometimes claimed she could feel the vibrations moving from the external world into her body shortly before the tapping began.

Langdon-Davies learned that the previously mentioned bangle of Shirley's that had gone missing had later been rediscovered, 'much tarnished', next to a piece of soap in a pink plastic box on a table in the kitchen. He was also given further information about the incident when Shirley's wristwatch had come undone and fallen to the floor in front of several reporters, an incident that had obviously left a deep impression on Wally and Kitty. Wally told how Shirley had picked the watch up and put it back on her wrist, only for it to fall off again. One of the reporters 'then took the watch, strapped it on [to Shirley's wrist] and passed the strap end over and under. In view of them all, the strap was seen to unwind itself, the buckle to loosen and the watch to fall once more.' Wally then told Shirley to put the watch in her pocket, which she did, but a short while later it was again found on the floor.

By the end of February, noted Langdon-Davies, there had been many incidents involving the mysterious movement of objects. He recorded a few of the incidents Wally described, although unfortunately not in great detail.

On one occasion, Shirley had been sitting on a chair in the kitchen when a small exercise book that had been on top of a pile of books on another chair 'was heard to whiz through the air and seen to land behind an ornament of the glass case' on the opposite side of the room.

On another occasion, a locked case containing theatrical make-up had been resting at one end of a table in the kitchen when somebody (unnamed) heard an object fall. The sound came from a corner at the opposite side of the room from the table. Investigation revealed a small stick of red grease paint (used by Shirley in her ballet dancing shows) lying in the corner. The stick was known to have been in the case earlier, and was put back inside. Later 'another object was heard to fall in the same place and was found to be a blue grease paint from the same box.'

Another incident involved an empty half-pint milk bottle that had been on Ethel's upstairs landing. Kitty was standing in the kitchen near the door leading to the scullery when the bottle flew past her. It was seen (by an unidentified resident) to land in the back garden and did not break. Its assumed flight path from the upstairs landing would have 'involved a turn of 180° and the negotiation of two (presumably) open doors'.

In a further instance an unnamed person saw a chair in Ethel's room slowly tilt and fall over.

Another time, Wally had just poured himself a whisky and placed the bottle's cork on the kitchen table. When he looked for the cork a moment later there was no sign of it. For Wally to drink whisky was such a rare act for the almost teetotaller that he felt it necessary to apologise to Langdon-Davies for the indulgence, explaining that it had been a bitterly cold night and the family had had very little sleep over the previous week. While relating this tale, Wally overlooked some minor details and Kitty interrupted to remind him of them. Langdon-Davies was impressed by the couple's 'keen desire to get the details right'.

Regarding another incident, Langdon-Davies noted only very brief details, stating that strips of carpet had been 'drawn along the floor with more than one person looking.' On yet another occasion Wally had been standing in the back yard when he was hit by a small tea strainer that had flown at him from the scullery. On two other separate occasions, three objects that had been hanging on walls or standing on tables had been found 'placed on the floor symmetrically'.

Langdon-Davies ascertained several general points regarding the movement of objects. First, Wally assured him that objects had actually been seen to 'describe an arc through the air and come down slowly on the floor.' In other words, their motion could not be explained by assuming somebody had simply thrown them. Second, although objects had been seen in flight, nobody had so far seen any object actually start on its journey: the first warning that something had happened was often when someone heard something 'whizzing past'. When objects landed they did so quietly but not silently and, with only one exception, the objects had not been broken. Finally, nobody had yet been hurt by any object, even when they had been hit.

Based on the testimony he heard, and with the important caveat that his report was nothing more than notes based on a single conversation, Langdon-Davies concluded that 'we have a classical poltergeist case, that it has the advantage of being admittedly associated with the 15 year old girl, but that, if we are to accept the evidence of a number of very different people, the phenomena in most cases cannot be attributed to her normal physical action.'

In fact, the overall picture was so similar to the stereotype of a poltergeist case that Langdon-Davies 'carefully investigated [during his chat with Wally] the possibility of someone connected having read up an account of poltergeist activities.'

He decided that this was unlikely. He did, however, appear to have overlooked the fact that between November 1927 and January 1928 there had been a well-publicised poltergeist case in Eland Road, Battersea, no more than a ten or fifteen minute walk west of Wycliffe Road – see *Haunted Wandsworth* by James Clark for further details. In March 1956 Ethel told at least one newspaper reporter that she remembered the Eland Road poltergeist well.

Based on what her parents had told him, Langdon-Davies noted that Shirley was a 'healthy and happy and unfrustrated' teenage girl. He was able to speak on the telephone to Shirley's doctor but there was little the doctor could tell him because the Hitchings family had only recently transferred to his practice. The doctor confirmed that although Shirley was naturally rather frightened by what was happening, she was generally healthy and had given 'no sign of any neuropathic condition'. Nevertheless, the doctor intended to advise Wally to take Shirley to the Maudsley Hospital to be examined by specialists in psychiatry.

In Langdon-Davies' opinion, Wally and Kitty were motivated by neither fame nor fortune. As for their thoughts regarding what was happening, they seemed reluctant to accept at face value any of the theories that had been put to them by reporters, police and spiritualists. Indeed, they were not particularly interested at all in *why* it was happening; their overwhelming desire was simply that 'it' – whatever 'it' was – should be got rid of as quickly as possible.

For a while it seemed they had got their wish.

CHAPTER 5

February gave way to March and life remained peaceful. Shirley had been staying with the Hanks family for an entire week now and nothing unusual had happened in that time, either at No. 63 or at Hanks's house. Then, as had happened after Hanks's first attempted exorcism, something reignited the situation.

That something was the publication of a sceptical newspaper article, written by the two journalists who had taken Shirley to visit a hypnotist. 'SPOOK WAS IN GIRL'S BIG TOE!' screamed the title in the *Weekend Mail* (1-5 March 1956), and the article boasted that the newspaper had 'solved the tapping mystery'. The authors told how newspaper staff had noticed the way the tapping seemed to emanate from the vicinity of Shirley's feet and had ceased when they made her remove her bootees. Looking at her feet they had discovered a minor deformity: a hammertoe affecting the big toe of her right foot, the very slightest movement of which, they claimed, caused the joint to crack, making a sound 'exactly like a ghostly tap'.

The journalists stated that they had then taken Shirley for a medical examination, writing that as the doctor held Shirley's right big toe and gently moved it up and down, it clicked. After speaking with Shirley the doctor concluded that shortly after

receiving her new winter bootees Shirley had started to make
the tapping noises in this fashion – without realising she was
doing it herself. The noises had been attributed to a supernatural agency, the seeds for which belief had, in his opinion,
been accidentally sown by Ethel with her tale of her deceased
husband's ghost appearing at the foot of her bed. The doctor
further claimed that (contrary to Shirley's testimony on the
BBC's *Highlight* programme) Shirley was a fan of television plays
with 'weird or even horrific subjects'. There was thus, he said,
a fertile ground for ideas about the supernatural to take root and
grow and, when apparently strange happenings had focused
interest on Shirley, she had welcomed the attention because of
the excitement it brought to her 'quiet life'. The doctor stressed
his belief that Shirley had never intended to hoax anybody
and that she was not consciously aware of making the sounds
herself. The journalists agreed with his verdict.

It was not the first time someone had wondered whether the
answer to the tapping might be found inside Shirley's footwear.
When the *South Western Star*'s Ross Werge had 'interviewed'
the poltergeist on 20 February, he had thought the tapping
came from somewhere close to Shirley's foot. However,
he had therefore watched her foot closely but reported that
it 'didn't move an inch.' Similarly when the *Daily Express*'s
Elizabeth Few heard the tapping while she and Shirley were in
a shop on 21 February, Few noted that the sounds came from
'near Shirley's feet', although Few felt Shirley could not have
been making the sounds herself because of her 'thick, crepe-
soled snow boots'. On 22 February, several reporters had
visited No. 63 and given Shirley what one called 'the biggest
gruelling [*sic*] since the days of the Gestapo' (*Clapham Observer*,
6 April 1956). For two hours they asked questions such as
'How many people are in the room?' and 'What is the number
of this house?' and listened as the tapping sounds replied
'like a demented Fred Astaire'. When they noticed that the
tapping appeared to be coming from the floorboards beneath

Shirley, two reporters lifted her into the air. The tapping continued and a third reporter bent down to listen more closely, before announcing that the sounds were 'coming from her right bootee' (*Daily Sketch*, 23 February 1956). They made Shirley remove her bootees and asked Donald yet more questions, but received no further replies. 'You've annoyed him,' Shirley had explained. 'He's tired.'

Of course, the clicking of Shirley's big toe could not account for the alleged movement of objects. Shirley recalls today that when the journalists took her to be hypnotised, Donald not only produced the tapping sounds in the doctor's office but also made papers fly off the doctor's desk. The newspaper article made no reference to this. In fact, those reporters did not believe Donald had ever paranormally moved anything. They even quoted an (unnamed) eyewitness as saying of one incident, 'I thought Shirley herself threw the box of make-up which I saw flying through the air.' In the doctor's opinion, it was perfectly possible that Shirley had moved such objects herself without realising it. 'In her present condition,' he stated, 'she would be quite capable of moving something and forgetting that she had done so.'

Not everyone was impressed by the *Weekend Mail*'s ideas. The spiritualist newspaper *The Two Worlds* responded that there was no conceivable way in which the cracking of a big toe could have been heard in another room, as had been reported, and denied that the suggested explanations were sufficient to explain the reports of flying objects and levitation.

Shirley herself is to this day annoyed at the way the *Weekend Mail* journalists lulled her into what she sees as a false sense of security before 'tricking' her into taking off her bootees and holding them up for the camera. She states that although her toe was indeed slightly deformed through ballet dancing it was not a 'hammertoe' and that her toes 'did not and do not click on their own or with help'. She strongly denies that this was the source of Donald's tapping.

The timing of the article was disastrous. As had previously been arranged, Shirley returned to No. 63 on Saturday 3 March but, instead of coming home relaxed after her 'holiday', she was thrown into a situation where she found herself accused of faking the whole furore. Yes, the claim was that she did not *consciously* realise what she was doing, but to the highly strung teenager this sounded as if she were being called crazy. Almost as soon as she walked through the door, the tapping started again. It continued at intervals throughout the day and grew louder around nightfall. At some point the tapping communicated a message, which Shirley took down one letter at a time:

I AM FIVHTEEN – I COME FROM FRANCE – LOST IN CHANNEL – CANNOT REMEMBER NAME – I HAD A GIRL LIKE YOU – DONALD IS NOT AWARE OF ME – I WANT SOMEONE TO TELL HIM – I WANT HAPPYNESS BETWEEN YOU TWO – WONT GO TILL MADE IT SO – LET ME GO HAPPY BY TELLING RONALD OF ME BUT NOT TELL HIS FAMILY – HE MUST KEEP ME A SECRET BETWEEN YOU AND ME AND TO HIMSELF – GIVE THIS TO KERCH – LET NO ONE SEE IT – GET KERCH YOU BUT KEEP SCRET AND TELL [MARK] – IF GIVE TO FAHTER I BE ANGRY AND SET FIRE.

'KERCH' referred to Michael Kirsch, one of the many reporters who had been calling at No. 63. Shirley remembers finding him friendly to begin with but later deeply sceptical about events at No. 63. There may also have been an initial spark of attraction between Shirley and the young man ('He was really nice looking ... I fancied him,' recalls Shirley now), although it is far from clear whether this was reciprocated.

Although nobody realised it, Donald's message hinted at the strange path this story would later take. For now though, all attention was on the noises, which became so disruptive that Saturday that somebody (probably Kitty) telephoned the local police station for help. The police contacted Wally at work and persuaded him to return home but this failed to stop the tapping. The noises continued late into the night.

After they eventually ceased the family tried to sleep but, at around 1 a.m., Shirley called out from her bed to say her wrist-watch had disappeared. Wally asked the poltergeist to return it and the watch promptly fell to the floor by his feet. When Wally saw that some pieces were missing he warned Donald that he would call the police, at which the watch's missing glass front dropped to the floor. The strap and metal surround were still absent though, so Wally again threatened to call the police. The final missing pieces fell to the floor, but the metal surround was found to be badly bent.

A short time later, as Wally was out of the bedroom brewing tea, and Shirley and her mother were in their beds, both of the latter saw Shirley's bedroom slippers in mid-air near the bedroom door. The slippers were approximately 3 feet above the floor and had apparently appeared there just a moment earlier. As Shirley and Kitty watched, the slippers fell to the ground. Just at that moment, Wally returned carrying the tea and all three of them saw the slippers 'walk' forward four steps.

Sometime afterwards – still during the early morning hours – Shirley heard a metallic knock from her bed. Looking beneath the blankets she discovered a tin of cold cream that had previously been in a 'tallboy' chest of drawers. In a separate incident at around the same time, Kitty was lying in Shirley's bed when she felt what she described as 'fingers' touch her on the back. Soon, the tapping returned, and some-body used the alphabet code to transcribe the following message: 'GET KIRSCH — GET HIM OUT OF BED'. Shirley's diary note for this date also briefly mentions 'whirling winds' that rushed around the room and a brooch pin being 'bent like a coiled spring'. The activity paused at around 3 a.m. but a while later, as an exhausted Shirley and Kitty lay in bed, their bedclothes started to roll up from the foot of the bed.

The tapping began again soon after Shirley awoke on Sunday morning. Shortly after 1 p.m., the family jokingly asked Donald to fetch Shirley her handkerchief from her dressing table drawer. When the poltergeist did not oblige, Shirley went to get the handkerchief herself – and discovered that the drawer's contents had been tipped out. Later, there was another message asking for 'KERCH'.

The disturbances continued that evening and the following day. When Shirley got up at around 9 a.m. on Monday, and walked into the kitchen to join her father, a pen that had been sitting on a sideboard flew under the kitchen table. A little later a brooch was also taken from the sideboard and thrown towards the table although afterwards the brooch could not be found anywhere. By this time the tapping had started again and it would continue throughout the morning. At around 3.40 p.m. the poltergeist removed a shoe from Shirley's foot and threw it through the air. Later, Wally made himself a cup of tea and placed it on the fender beside the fire in the kitchen. After a short while a puddle of tea was noticed on a stool beside the fire but the liquid had evidently not come from Wally's teacup because that was still full. That evening, two more tapped messages ordered the family to 'GET KERCH' because the poltergeist needed to give him a message. ' ... DON'T PLAY ANY GAMES,' warned the second message, 'I WANT KERCH – IF YOU WONT – WELL'.

Just after midnight, several marks were found in the passageway by the downstairs bedroom. Wally discovered they smelled of perfume. Three large spots of the same scent were on Shirley's bed and as Wally examined those something hit the wall behind him. It was a small, empty glass bottle of violet scent that had been kept inside Shirley's make-up case in the kitchen. Then Wally's attention was diverted by tapping and scratching sounds under Shirley's bed; there was a bang and, the next thing Wally knew, the bottle was on the floor underneath the bed.

The poltergeist was well and truly back and disappointment made the renewed disturbances all the harder to bear. When there was a knock on the door that Tuesday evening it seemed inevitable that it would be another reporter, or another nosey neighbour seeking the latest gossip. But when Wally wearily answered it he found waiting on the doorstep a friendly looking gentleman in his mid-50s, whose unassuming three-piece suit, pipe and battered briefcase gave him an air of calm reassurance.

'Mr Hitchings?' asked the stranger politely, holding out his hand. 'Good evening. My name is Chibbett.'

CHAPTER 6

Harold Chibbett's father had been a dedicated Methodist and the strongly religious atmosphere in his childhood home doubtless helped prepare the way for Chibbett's subsequent fascination with the supernatural.

Chibbett was born on 19 February 1900 in Islington, north London. After serving in the army during the First World War, 'Hal' Chibbett took a job working for the Civil Service in London. By this time, he had become deeply interested in psychical research and spiritualism, a movement then undergoing a major revival as many struggled to cope with the loss of loved ones. His interest deepened as the years passed, and he began attending séances. His surviving papers show a willingness – perhaps even eagerness – to believe that spirits of the departed could appear to the living, yet this did not mean he accepted claims of the paranormal uncritically. During the interwar years, Chibbett founded a group called 'The Probe', which actively researched and investigated psychic and occult phenomena, and Chibbett made a point of continually questioning his own assumptions. His agile mind was not restricted to psychical research. In around 1937, for example, he joined London's first science-fiction club and he was for many years a writer of science-fiction stories and enthusiastically and actively involved within science-fiction fandom. But a vast amount of his spare time and money would always be devoted to investigating unexplained phenomena.

When Chibbett first heard about the poltergeist in Battersea he was living in Bowes Park in north London and working for the Tax Office. It was a mundane job that counterbalanced his more exotic interests, but it was perhaps suited to his temperament. Despite his keen desire to explore mysteries, Chibbett saw his primary role less as an investigator than as a recorder of events. 'As I see it,' he wrote in his notes on the Wycliffe Road poltergeist, 'my function is to record alleged facts as accurately as may be, and to comment on them later in the light of my experience in psychic matters.'

When Chibbett first visited No. 63 on the evening of Tuesday 6 March he was invited into the kitchen to chat with Shirley and her parents. He got the sense that the family was 'becoming accustomed' to their strange situation and were clearly 'convinced of the reality of the phenomena'. His initial impression of Shirley was that she was a likeable but 'precocious child [who] because of this is likely to be a source of irritation to some people'. Although other observers had considered Shirley to be terrified by the poltergeist, Chibbett felt that the teenager was 'not at all perturbed by the disturbances', noting that these 'nearly always take place in her presence, although her father alleges that *some* incidents have occurred when she was not there' (emphasis in the original). Chibbett suspected that Shirley had a tendency to 'exaggerate a little, and it is noticeable that it is often Shirley herself who draws attention first to things which are happening.' Yet this was 'not to say that she was the direct cause of the phenomena, but [rather] that the strange events lent her the sort of glamour which adolescents appear to treasure.'

After a while, Mark joined everyone in the kitchen. He told Chibbett that, although he had initially thought Shirley was playing games, he now believed the poltergeist to be real. 'I am inclined to give some weight to this gentleman's opinion,' noted Chibbett, 'because he appears to be a rational type.' Shirley's grandmother Ethel also joined the gathering for a short while but did not stay long enough for Chibbett to form an opinion of her.

Chibbett stayed for around six hours, hoping to see or hear something for himself, but it seemed that Donald was resting that evening. So Chibbett spent most of the time interviewing the family about the events of the previous few weeks. 'The type of phenomena appears to be no different from those usually reported in poltergeist disturbances,' he noted afterwards, commenting that the general state of 'alarming confusion' had been caused not so much by the phenomena themselves as by the 'constant intrusion into the [family's] home of experts of all descriptions'.

At around 7 p.m., John Langdon-Davies paid the family another visit. To pass the time, Langdon-Davies produced a pack of ESP (extra-sensory perception) cards and conducted an impromptu experiment with Shirley. ESP (or Zener) cards were designed to test for ESP in a manner that lends itself readily to statistical analysis. Each pack consists of twenty-five cards divided into five sets of five symbols: star, circle, square, wavy lines and cross. A participant attempts to identify one by one which symbol is present on a card hidden from view. All other conditions being accounted for, there is a 20 per cent (1 in 5) chance of getting each answer correct by simply guessing. So a result of five correct answers in each run of 25 cards should be expected purely by chance but unusually high deviations from this norm might provide evidence for ESP. Chibbett noted that out of each run of 25 cards, Shirley 'scored guesses respectively: 10, 9, 8 ... falling eventually to the norm of 5'. A number of parapsychologists over the years have noted an apparent tendency for participants' hit rates to tail off after initially high scores. Chibbett's brief description of Shirley's results appears to match this observation so well it is a pity this experiment was not recorded in greater detail. Unfortunately, to achieve statistically meaningful results with ESP cards lengthy runs are needed to smooth out naturally occurring peaks of correct and incorrect guesses, and experimental conditions need to be strictly controlled. It is a shame that a more rigorous set of experiments was not conducted with Shirley.

Just before Chibbett left, more visitors arrived. This time it was a pair of reporters from the *South London Advertiser* newspaper, one of whom was Joyce Lewis, who had established a good rapport with Shirley during her first visit and had been given permission to sleep over at the house. Shortly after midnight (the second reporter having presumably left), Lewis and Shirley retired to Shirley's parents' double bed while Wally and Kitty spent that night in the 'front room'. Almost immediately after they settled down, Lewis was startled by a noise. The following extract comes from Lewis's subsequent article ('A night with a poltergeist', *South London Advertiser*, week ending 17 March 1956) and is reproduced with kind permission of *South London Press* (1865) Ltd:

> Suddenly I almost shot from the bed. Such a fearful and terrifying scraping noise was coming from under it.
>
> 'Don't worry,' said Shirley calmly. 'This is just the beginning!'
>
> Stifling thoughts of rushing out and hailing the nearest taxi home, I swallowed hard and declared I was quite calm.
>
> The time: 12.15.
>
> And here is the rest of the timetable of that night:
>
> 12.17: I feel the undersheet slowly but firmly come up and up. I push it down frantically only to feel a terrific tug as it rises again. This little game continues some minutes. Then I get out and re-make the bed.
>
> 12.22: The scraping becomes more violent, this time from the wooden head of the bed. My spine chills as the blood-curdling noise moves to a spot under my pillow.

12.30: Still holding Shirley's feet between mine, I am acutely aware of an icy draught passing over them. 'He's on my foot,' whispers Shirley. 'Can you feel him?' Before I can reply the bedclothes are whipped off again. Grimly I get out and re-make the bed.

12.48: A scratching noise is coming from the eiderdown. I feel quite faint as something passes across the bed close to my face.

1.00: I smell a pleasant perfume – something like violets. Then in a flash it changes to a burning rubbery smell. We check the fuses and electrical points but can find nothing wrong. Settle down again.

1.20: Shirley shrieks: 'Something has clawed me!' In a flash we are out of bed and I examine the marks on her leg. The skin is reddened and there are four distinct marks – like those of a nail or claw. I have been holding Shirley's hand [*sic*] and feet all the time.

1.35: I am almost paralysed by the most awful bang on the bed just by my nose. Shirley mutters sleepily as the bed starts to bounce up and down as though shaken by a giant hand.

2.05: Donald tickles my ankle. I think this is going a little far and my comments are brief but distinct. In reply he pulls up the bedclothes.

The bed is now in complete chaos. Even the mattress is a bunch of knotted lumps. I remake it.

2.30: Shirley has fallen asleep exhausted. I lay [*sic*] watching, listening to the appalling scratchings. Then I am startled to feel Shirley's arm slowly go out of the bed. I pull frantically, but the force pulling her is too powerful for me. When the girl awakes shuddering she is halfway out of bed.

2.45: Scrapings, bangs, tappings and games with the bedclothes continue. And it is an exhausted household that decides to break for tea and biscuits, just after 4.00.

4.30: Shirley is again pulled out of bed. This happens regularly at intervals of a few minutes until 'It's got my toe,' shouts Shirley. 'There's something on it.'

She lifts her foot out of bed and for the first time that night we burst into laughter as we see that Shirley's big toe of her right foot has been neatly tied up with a small piece of string.

Accompanying Lewis's report was another article, describing how a team of reporters from the same newspaper had investigated the poltergeist story (the date of their investigation was not given but it was probably carried out at around the same date as Lewis's night at No. 63.) After a trip to the newspaper's office, with Donald tapping away both at the office and in the car, Shirley was driven home and three *Advertiser* employees – chief reporter Norman Rogers accompanied by Gwen Farnham and Joyce Lewis – and a 'ghost hunter' named John Heel, spent approximately five hours with her. To guard against the possibility that Shirley was producing the tapping herself, Heel secured Shirley's hands and feet with insulating tape, and the five of them sat around a table, calling on Donald to make himself known. There was a sound Farnham described as 'like the noise a creaking joint would make if muffled by cotton wool'. Then Rogers's hat 'shot off' a bookcase and hit the table. The reporters thought it might simply have fallen or perhaps been thrown but noted that 'nobody was near it at the time'.

Shirley told them how that morning she had smelled a scent that at first resembled violets but slowly changed into a 'foul stench'. That was typical of poltergeist cases, replied Heel. Shirley reacted with surprise, but an unnamed man (possibly Mark) told the reporters that a previous visitor had mentioned this same fact a few days before. Shirley responded that she had not heard anyone say this and, in any case, had first smelled the scent of violets prior to that particular person's visit.

When Shirley was released from the insulating tape she, Lewis and Farnham moved to another room, leaving the men behind. Now Donald tapped out a message; he told Lewis and Farnham that he did not like being investigated and warned them not to play any tricks. After Heel and Rogers re-joined them, everyone sat around a dressing table and Donald tapped some more. Heel said that he felt the table vibrate, describing the sensation as 'like an underground train going by.'

'The setting is right for a poltergeist,' concluded Heel afterwards. 'We have a 15-year-old girl, highly strung, artistic. There is an atmosphere about the house.' Heel was inclined to believe that Donald the poltergeist was genuine, although it was 'too early to be certain.'

Returning to the events of 6/7 March 1956, Joyce Lewis eventually left shortly after 4.30 a.m., 'exhausted' by her night at the house. Shirley and her parents returned to bed to get what sleep they could before daybreak. They would need as much rest as possible because things were to take a sinister turn.

CHAPTER 7

When Shirley awoke on Wednesday morning (7 March 1956) she discovered that her wristwatch, on her bedside table, had been crushed as she'd slept. A little later, the tapping started again; it would continue all day. Kitty noted that a 'clock & two pictures [were] found in front of fire on mat in the kitchen' and that Shirley saw 'a ball thrown in the air'. By nightfall the tapping – accompanied by 'heavy' scratching – was so insistent that the family worried it was building up to something worse.

By this date the family were sometimes sleeping on cushions on the kitchen floor, where Donald tended to be less active than in the bedroom. They would take turns to stay awake and nervously listen out for the tapping. 'Sometimes [Donald] insists on talking to us until dawn,' Kitty told one reporter (*The People*, 11 March), 'and if we take no notice he starts throwing things at us'.

At around 11.15 that Wednesday night, Donald started to tap out a lengthy message. He apologised for his absence during Chibbett's and Langdon-Davies' visit the previous day (tapping 'I AM SORRY I GO WHEN PEOPLE COME BUT I AM AFRAID') but insisted yet again that the reporter Kirsch be summoned to the house. 'THERE WON'T BE A TOMORROW FOR KIRCH IF YOU DON'T,' he warned. 'HE IS IN DANGER'.

Not having the reporter's contact details the family did not try to get in touch with him. At 4.30 on Thursday morning the poltergeist repeated his demand. Presumably Wally then telephoned the newspaper office because Kirsch did visit No. 63 later that day. What happened while he was there was not recorded and after he left there was only a little tapping. However, at around 2 a.m. Donald demanded, 'GET KIRCH – I LIKE TO GET KIRCH ON HIS OWN – I'D TEACH HIM A LESSON – I POKE HIM – I COME WITH MESSAGE LATER – I GET REVENGE ON KIRCH – SUF-FOCATE HIM TONIGHT – SAVE HIM IF YOU LIKE […] I WARN YOU – GET HIM TONIGHT FOR SAFETY'.

After that, Donald was quiet again, until Friday. 'A few taps and he lifts the poker on hearth in kitchen, about foot off it,' recorded Wally. He added that a gold cross and chain which belonged to Shirley (and which had vanished some days before) were discovered hanging on a dog ornament on the sideboard, and that the carpet 'came up in middle [and] rose about 1 inch to 1½ inches'. Shirley told her father that a basin flew out of a cupboard as she was getting some biscuits. There was also more tapping asking for Kirsch.

The family went to bed at about 11 p.m., when (recorded Wally) Donald 'started his nonsense again in the bedroom but he liked to tap out music so we hummed it to him and gave him some sums to do & [he] got them all right. A few more tunes & some very hard bangs on bed & scratches. He made the bed rock. It was awful & he seem[ed] to go after a few more taps of music. Otherwise from 12.30 a quiet night.'

The tapping resumed at 9 a.m. on Saturday. That morning, a pen belonging to Shirley went missing. Just after midday, about 3 shillings' worth of sixpenny savings stamps were found beneath a chair. After they went to bed that night, reported Wally, there was the 'usual nonsense'.

Then Donald turned his attention to another reporter. This time it was Ronald Maxwell, one of the journalists who had co-written the *Weekend Mail*'s 'big toe' article. At 1.30 on Sunday afternoon, Donald tapped out, 'GET MAXWELL – KIRCH IS NO GOOD'. There was another demand for Maxwell that evening, then (at 8.50 p.m.) Shirley took down the most threatening message yet: 'I WILL SET HOUSE AFIRE IF YOU DON'T GET MAXWELL – SO TAKE CARE.'

Shortly before midnight, as Shirley and Kitty were getting ready for bed, Shirley spotted three green balls of light – roughly the size of ping pong balls – in the air. She only had time for a brief glimpse before they vanished. Moments later, Ethel heard a match being struck, and watched in amazement as a lit match slowly floated through the air towards Shirley. As it passed over the girl's head it dropped to the floor, catching Shirley on the way down and slightly singing her eyebrow. Too frightened to sleep, the family was still alert when the poltergeist began tapping again a few minutes before 1 a.m.: 'GET MAXWELL – I JUST GIVEN YOU TASTE OF WHAT I AM GOING TO DO – SO GET MAXWELL – I WARN YOU NO ONE WILL STOP ME'.

There was another message later that Monday morning: 'GET MAXWELL – OR I SET FIRE TODAY – SO DO AS I SAY – GET HIM – OBEY – IT IS YOUR MASTER.'

Sometime later Shirley was on the upstairs landing outside Ethel's room when she saw a green flash and smelled smoke. Wally was not due to begin his next shift on the trains until later that day and was downstairs in the kitchen when he heard Shirley cry out. He rushed to investigate and saw smoke coming from the downstairs front bedroom. There he found the bed sheet and the almost new eiderdown on fire along the edge nearest the door. He immediately began to beat out the flames, burning his hands and forearms.

As Wally dragged the still smoking bedclothes out into the road, next-door neighbour Lily Love ('Auntie Lil') noticed what was happening and telephoned the fire brigade. Four fire engines soon arrived, swiftly joined by police officers and an ambulance. Wally was taken to St Stephen's Hospital in Fulham, south-west London. The back of his left hand had been badly burned by a piece of melted fabric which had stuck to the skin, and his hand had to be heavily bandaged. The burns would take many months to heal. The police and firemen did their best to establish the cause of the fire but were unable to ascertain exactly how it had started. Sitting in the kitchen later with her parents and grandmother, Shirley told reporter Elizabeth Few that she knew people suspected that she had started the fire herself but she insisted it had been the poltergeist. Shirley's family took her side.

The combination of sleep deprivation and constant anxiety was taking a toll on everybody. Wally feared that his daughter was heading for a nervous breakdown and he himself – already worried that the situation was putting his passengers' lives at risk – was suffering so badly from stress that he had lost half a stone in weight. Because of this, coupled with his injuries from the fire, his doctor ordered him to take a fortnight's sick leave.

The situation was causing work problems for Shirley, too. She was originally supposed to have returned to her job at the department store in early March. When March arrived, Shirley had been staying with Hanks and the medium had talked to her staff manager who had agreed to transfer Shirley to another department upon her return. By mid-March Shirley had still not gone back to work and, at the store's request, she now formally resigned.

The family had no idea what they should do next. The police were as helpful as they could be but obviously did not truly believe in Donald. Even if they had what could they have done? And the family's recent experiences with mediums, spiritualists and other assorted 'experts' had been mostly disappointing.

One of their few visitors who had not claimed to know all the answers from the outset was the quietly spoken psychical researcher who had come to see them the previous week. On Monday evening, after Wally returned from hospital,

Harold Chibbett visited No. 63 again. As during his first visit, Chibbett reassured the family that they were far from the only people ever to have had their lives upset by the mysterious happenings referred to as poltergeist phenomena. He explained that he had acquired a great deal of personal experience of similar cases over the years; if the Hitchings family was happy for him to do so, he offered, he would be pleased to work with them to try to understand what was happening here. Wally in particular was still a little wary of Chibbett but, as the days and weeks passed, Chibbett would earn the entire family's trust. He provided them with something they desperately wanted: a calm, understanding and patient presence who was prepared to listen to them.

Shirley slept in her grandmother's bedroom that Monday night and, to everyone's surprise, the night passed peacefully. The next day, however, was filled with tapping and after the family retired to bed (Shirley again went upstairs to Ethel's bedroom) loud tapping and scratching sounds kept everyone awake. Small objects were thrown about inside Ethel's bedroom and at one point something unseen tore Shirley's nightdress. When Ethel and Shirley smelled burning they called out for Wally who hurried upstairs to find what he described as a smouldering 'stain' (perhaps a scorch mark) on the landing. Everyone moved downstairs and a short while later they found another 'stain' in the kitchen.

The next day (Wednesday 14 March) one of Wally's sisters threw the family a lifeline. Aunt Nell lived at the Lavender Hill end of Wycliffe Road with her husband Bill and young daughter, and she invited Shirley to stay at her house for a short while. The tapping that had again started in No. 63 that morning ceased when Shirley left to visit her aunt. At Nell's house, the day passed peacefully. Shirley shared a room with her younger cousin and rested. Later, however, Nell started to hear occasional tapping and scratching sounds – these continued until around 3 a.m. Two hours later, they started again.

Nell took Shirley back to No. 63 on Thursday. At 2.30 that afternoon a very loud burst of tapping indicated that Donald had something important to say: he wanted Shirley to go back to Nell's. Shirley was allowed to return to her aunt's house and on Friday Nell telephoned Shirley's parents to let them know that the night had passed without incident and that everyone – Shirley included – had had a good sleep. Later that Friday, however, the tapping noises again began to sound in Nell's house. At 10.30 that night Nell used the alphabet system to take down a message from Donald. Nell's family was not to fear him, said the poltergeist, he was there to guard them.

A little later, Aunt Nell and her family got a full taste of what it could be like to live with Donald. The tapping continued relentlessly, objects were thrown and bedclothes were pulled from Bill and Nell's bed as they tried to sleep. Before long, they had had enough and at around 2.45 on Saturday morning Shirley was taken back to No. 63 in a police car. Her forced return angered Donald who immediately began tapping threats, demanding that he be taken back to Nell's house or he would start another fire. Nell refused to allow Shirley back. She had had her fill of Donald.

While Shirley was staying with Nell her parents got rid of reporters who wanted to see her by claiming their daughter had gone to stay with relatives in the countryside, on doctors' orders. They kept up this pretence for a while after her return, but the following week they allowed Christopher Riche-Evans, a reporter for *Psychic News*, to visit the house three times. On one occasion he stayed for around eight hours. His subsequent article (*Psychic News*, 24 March) described Wally and Kitty as 'a sincere, pleasant couple' who were 'genuinely anxious to rid themselves of the nuisance which has been interfering with their sleep, and affecting their health'. Riche-Evans described Shirley as likeable and imaginative, with a sparkling personality, and (like Chibbett) felt she had come to treat Donald 'as a joke rather than a nuisance'. Riche-Evans did not personally experience anything strange during his visits but he recorded details of the family's experiences up to this time. In addition to incidents already mentioned in this book, these included instances when family members had seen various objects (including a pillow, an article of clothing and a lighted scrap of paper) 'float through the air'. There had also been mysterious draughts, sudden drops in temperature, and strange whistling and hissing noises.

On the evening of Sunday 18 March, Harold Chibbett visited No. 63. Donald began to tap at around midnight and Chibbett took the opportunity to question the poltergeist. Remembering how Donald had stated (on 3 March) 'I COME FROM FRANCE – LOST IN CHANNEL', Chibbett asked if Donald knew the meaning of 'La Manche' (the French name for the English Channel). Tapping spelled out 'ENGLISH CHANNEL'. A little later Chibbett asked if Donald knew any alternative meanings to the word 'Manche', whereupon Donald tapped 'HOSE' and (correctly) 'SLEEVE'.

Donald's next message was, 'I WILL DO HARM TO ANYONE WHO DON'T BELIEVE IN FLYING SAUCERS'. The subject of flying saucers (today more commonly referred to as UFOs) had probably come up in general conversation during Chibbett's previous visits, as it was among the researcher's various passions. Keeping an open mind as to what Donald actually was, Chibbett was prepared to entertain the possibility of the poltergeist being some form of discarnate but superior intelligence, so he seized the chance to ask whether Donald could reveal anything about space travel. In 1956, the prospect of space travel was the subject of much public speculation but had yet to become reality and nobody knew for certain whether humans could survive the stresses that would be involved. If the poltergeist revealed information about space that was then unknown to any living human – information that could later be verified as scientists gained new knowledge – that would be very interesting indeed.

'I CAN TELL YOU WHAT YOU PEOPLE HAVE NOT LEARNT,' came the poltergeist's unhelpfully evasive reply. 'YOU GOT A LONG WAY TO GO.'

'Does life similar to human beings exist on any other planets?' asked Chibbett. 'NO,' replied Donald, but he did go on to claim that there were 'things' up to 8 feet tall out there and that life of some sort existed on Jupiter, Mars, Saturn, Mercury and Pluto, although not on Venus or the Moon. When Chibbett asked where Donald himself came from, he was told, 'I COME FROM THE ATMOSPHERE'.

'I COME TO LEARN YOU ALL ABOUT SPACE AND IT IS CHILD'S PLAY,' announced Donald at 11 a.m. the next morning (Monday 19 March). He did not reveal any cosmological wisdom, however. Instead, at 12.25 p.m. he tapped, 'I WILL SET FIRE TO NAN'S BED IN NIGHT – I DON'T JOKE – GET READY FOR FIRE – YOU DON'T THINK I DO IT'.

Between 5 and 7 p.m. there was a great deal of tapping and scratching from the kitchen table and the electric stove was twice found to have been switched on. Concerned, Wally turned the electricity supply off at the mains. It was just as well he did: at 1.15 on Tuesday morning, as Shirley lay on the kitchen floor trying to sleep, there was a violent tapping and Wally discovered that the electric rings on the stove had been switched on again.

CHAPTER 8

Chibbett called at No. 63 on Tuesday evening (20 March). He visited long enough only to arrange to stay overnight on Thursday, but before departing he left three questions for the family to ask Donald the next time the poltergeist began tapping. The questions related to flying saucer research and could only be answered by someone with quite specialised knowledge, knowledge unlikely to be exhibited by a 15-year-old schoolgirl.

Donald did not appreciate this attempt to test him. After Chibbett left, he tapped, 'YOU MADE ME ANGRY – I SET FIRE – YOU CAN'T STOP ME – YOU ALL MUST DIE – NO ESCAPE NOW – I DO NOT KID – GET OUT OF HOME FOR TONIGHT I SET ATOMIC GAS OFF'. Later that night, some blue eye make-up went missing from Shirley's make-up case and a stick of her perfume was broken. The cloying scent filled the house, but at least it wasn't 'atomic gas'.

As arranged, Chibbett returned at 8 p.m. on Thursday, looking forward to spending his first full night inside No. 63. Shirley, Wally, Kitty and Ethel were all there to meet him, and Mark joined them later. They told Chibbett what had happened since Tuesday evening. Donald had begun tapping away again on Wednesday morning and at around 10.30 he had switched off the electric stove. Later, while Shirley was digging in the back yard she had complained that Donald had thrown earth at her. Wednesday afternoon had passed peacefully (Shirley had visited the Muslim family who lived at No. 65) but after her return that evening pieces of burned paper were discovered under the table in Ethel's room upstairs. Splashes of water were also found (probably in the same room) and Shirley claimed that while she was in Ethel's room the poltergeist threw a glass milk bottle at her. She had been lying on the mat in front of the fire, by Mark's knee, at the time. Mark corroborated the general details of her account, but when Chibbett questioned him more closely Mark conceded that he could not be absolutely certain the bottle had been out of Shirley's reach. It was possible, he admitted, that the bottle had been on a table by the fireplace (which would not have been unusual) and that Shirley had taken the bottle and thrown it herself without his noticing.

Between 11.30 and just after midnight, Donald had repeated his demands for the reporter Ronald Maxwell to be summoned and for Shirley to be allowed to sleep in Ethel's room. Meanwhile, at 1.15 on Thursday morning, something was found to have been scrawled inside a notebook (the circumstances – who found the notebook, where it was found, etc. – were not recorded). The scrawl, although barely legible, proved to be writing and had apparently been made with a blue ballpoint pen. Shirley denied writing the message and the family believed Donald was the culprit. The message, which read 'Shirley I come … my Shirley', was presumably written across two pages, but only one – showing the first three words – has survived. Wally recorded that there was also 'a drawing of face to shoulders & other writing', although he did not go into further detail.

Written messages, allegedly physically written by Donald himself, would later become a major feature in this story. For now, though, the majority of Donald's messages continued to be communicated by tapping out letters of the alphabet. Some messages were tapped while Chibbett was there on Thursday.

At 10.30 p.m. Donald again asked that Shirley sleep in Ethel's room that night ('ONE MUST GO WITH NAN THE GIRLY'), repeating his instruction at a quarter past midnight ('NAN TAKE TO BED GIRLY – I AM HERE TO HELP – OBEY'). Wally asked if Donald would allow his mother and daughter to sleep and the tapping merely replied, 'OBEY YOU'. A few minutes later, Donald again demanded that the reporters Maxwell and Kirsch visit him. At half past midnight Donald tapped, 'I TELL YOU IN FRENCH – GET DICTIONARY – ABI IS KAEM KIP KEER.' Although the meaning (if any) was unclear it was another hint that France was somehow relevant.

Shirley and her grandmother did as they had been told, while Chibbett remained downstairs to spend an uncomfortable night on a mattress on the kitchen floor. Wrapped only in his overcoat for warmth, it was a long and cold vigil – during which precisely nothing interesting occurred.

Chibbett had yet to experience any 'physical phenomena' (i.e. objects moving) himself. Nevertheless, reports from witnesses such as the reporter Joyce Lewis, as well as much of the family's testimony, left him in little doubt that amid incidents that might be 'attributed to malobservation and "jitters" [there was] a residue which cannot be explained away'. The one phenomenon Chibbett had directly experienced was Donald tapping out messages, and what he had observed persuaded the researcher that this case was no hoax:

> These characteristic percussions are heard nearly always in the immediate vicinity of Shirley, and appear to be within rather than on the floor or carpet. Indeed, the vibration can sometimes be felt some distance away. Mr Hitchings keeps a notebook with the alphabet written down; he points to each letter in turn, and the raps sound as the selected letter is reached. [...] I cannot see that Shirley can possibly be consciously responsible for them, because she cannot be aware from her usual position which letter Mr Hitchings has reached on the alphabet.

A week or two earlier, Shirley's parents had made arrange-
ments for her to be examined by a specialist in psychiatry.
It was around now that Shirley was taken to the Maudsley
Hospital in Denmark Hill, south-east London.

A sceptical article in the *South London Press* (27 March) alleged
that Wally had only consented to this after being pressured to
do so. The article (Wally later ascertained it had been written
by Kirsch) stated that police officers told Wally that if Shirley was
not examined then she might be taken before a juvenile court
to decide whether she should be taken away from her parents.
Although this was accurate (and Kitty had persuaded Wally
to allow the examination on the basis that they had nothing
to hide), Wally was furious that it should have been made public.

At the Maudsley, Shirley was given a thorough examination. The original medical records no longer exist, however,
and the results that appear here are taken from a report in the
South London Press (30 March). Apart from observing that Shirley
appeared very nervous, the doctors could find no mental or
physical abnormalities. They instructed Wally and Kitty to
watch her at all times to ensure she got the rest she needed,
and not to let her sleep alone. Shirley remembers that they also
prescribed some tablets that were intended to calm her. Knowing
what these tablets contained might offer further insight into the
doctors' opinions but unfortunately there is no record of what
they were and all Shirley can recall is that the tablets were blue
and large 'like balls'. Whether they would have had any effect
on Donald is likewise unknown because Shirley never took them
(something that relieved Kitty who had been far from keen to see
her daughter on medication). Soon after the family returned to
No. 63, a sulphurous smell drew Wally and Kitty to the kitchen
where they found a large pudding basin on the table. It was full
of water in which was dissolving the entire supply of tablets.
Soon all that remained of the medicine was a nasty smell.

As if the situation was not already strange enough, it now began to seem that there was more than one 'entity' inside No. 63. Since the early confusion as to who/what the poltergeist was – the spirit of a boy Shirley had once known, the ghost of Shirley's great-grandmother, the spirit of an old man with a stick, or whatever – the Hitchings family had grown to accept the presence of a supernatural being they called Donald. But on Friday 23 March, Donald intimated that there were further entities around. At 9.30 p.m. he warned that the family was in danger, adding at 10.20 p.m. that 'THEY WILL [start a] FIRE' and referring to a 'TIME BOMB HIDDEN'. Donald continued to tap warnings, telling the family that 'THEY' called themselves Miky and Dopy, and that because these entities somehow obtained their power from Donald he was forced to go away when they arrived. 'I AM GOING NOW,' he tapped. 'THEY ARE AROUND.'

There was no fire, no bomb went off during the night and Donald was back the next morning. Early that afternoon he tapped, 'I THINK GOT RID OF THEM – MIKY AND DOPY – THEY GONE FAR FROM HERE – THEY TOOK MY POWER'.

At 6.45 that evening Donald ordered the family to summon 'Evans' (presumably Riche-Evans). They did not and four hours later Donald warned: 'I AM GO TO BE BAD TONIGHT – HA', and shortly after that, 'NON[e] WILL SLEEP – SET FIRE UNDER FLOOR – YOU WON'T [k]NOW.'

'Who is this [trouble] all over?' asked Wally, to which Donald replied, 'ERIC'. This may have referred to Eric Davey, who will be encountered shortly. Like Hanks, Davey was an underground train driver and a part-time medium. He was known to Wally and had almost certainly been among the many recent visitors to No. 63. Why Donald should have taken exception to him is unknown.

'Why did you come to us in the first place?' asked Wally.

'TO DESTROY HOUSE – I WON'T FAIL THIS TIME.'

There was a whistling sound, then a muffled whispering as if somebody were having difficulty speaking. Among the moans and wheezes, the only distinguishable words were 'yes' and 'no', whispered in reply to further (unrecorded) questions.

Donald spoke again (and even tried to sing with Shirley!) at around 10.30 on Sunday morning (25 March), according to a frustratingly brief diary note by Wally. At noon, he spoke again. Aunt Nell was visiting No. 63, having earlier found a pair of her husband's cufflinks that had been missing for a while. She asked Donald if he had been responsible for their return and a ghostly whisper replied, 'Yes.'

Then he reverted to tapping. That evening Donald again demanded that Shirley sleep in Ethel's room, but Ethel, not one to let a ghost intimidate her, refused to answer him. At 10.30 p.m. the poltergeist tapped: 'I WON'T GO IF NAN DON'T DO AS I SAY – SORRY [...] WALLIE – FOR NAN'S DISOBEYMENT TIP HER OUT OF BED [...] LET'S GO AND GET SILLY OLD COW UP – SILLY OLD BUGGER – SHE IS OLD BATTLEAXE – FACE LIKE NOSE OVERGROWN BEETROOT.'

Wally chose not to record other parts of this message because they were too rude about his elderly mother. 'He [Donald] seems not to like her much now,' he commented. This was probably – at least in part – due to Ethel's refusal to do as Donald told her. When the argument over Shirley sleeping upstairs was repeated on Monday night, the old woman stood her ground again. Donald's exasperation is evident in one of the messages he tapped that night: '[9.55 p.m.] SILLY OLD COW DO AS I SAY – SHIT PAN – MONKEY CHOPS – WINDBAG – BUMFLUF – SHIT YOU SHIT [unclear] – SHE LET HER GO BED OR SHE CAUSE HARM – TIP HER OUT OF BED – I GO TILL MORN IF DO AS I WILL.'

Despite Donald's bluster, nothing happened.

❖

During a visit on the evening of Tuesday 27 March, Chibbett took down one of Donald's tapped messages himself. He sat at the table, opposite Shirley, quickly moving his pen across the alphabet card to point to each letter in turn. From Shirley's viewpoint any letters she might glimpse were upside-down and Chibbett moved the pen so rapidly he thought it 'very unlikely indeed' she could work out what he was pointing to. Yet at 8.35 p.m., the tapping spelled out: 'COLLEY ZIBER – DURRY LANE'.

'What does this mean?' Chibbett asked.

'THEATRE MANAGER.'

'About what date?'

'1720.'

At 8.50 p.m. a further series of tapping spelled out names:

'NANCY MAINFIELD – SIR RICHARD STEEL – JOHN HALL – ACTORS.'

'Were all these actors at the time of the theatre manager, at Drury Lane?' asked Chibbett, referring to the famous London theatre.

'YES.'

Further responses announced that whoever was tapping had been born in 1653, had died in 1753 aged 100, and had been an actor at Drury Lane. As Chibbett jotted down notes, Shirley recorded another message at 9.20 p.m.: 'KITTY RAFTER OR CLIVE'. Questioning elicited the answer that this was the stage name of an actress who had been alive during this period.

Chibbett decided to look into these claims later. In the meantime, could Donald provide information only Chibbett would know? 'Can you tell me my Christian names?' he asked.

'YES – HENRY EDWARD JAMES.'

In fact, Chibbett's Christian names were Harold Stanley Walter but he did not argue. Instead, he asked, 'Can you tell us anything not known to anyone present, but easily verifiable by me?'

'YES – GET KERCH OR I SET FIRE BED.'

After that, Donald would only repeat that Shirley was to sleep upstairs or else Ethel's bed would be set on fire. 'YOU CANNOT STOP MY POWER,' he warned. At 11.15 p.m., after Chibbett had left, Shirley complained that her feet had been tied together using some of the material that had bandaged Wally's burns of a fortnight before. That night, recorded Wally, there were 'bad scratchings & bumpings', although no fire.

At work the next morning, Chibbett was eager to follow the clues Donald had given him and he asked his colleagues at the Tax Office for assistance. One colleague happened to own a copy of W.J. McQueen Pope's book, *Theatre Royal, Drury Lane*, which he loaned to Chibbett the next day. In this, Chibbett quickly discovered many references to a Colley Cibber, who seemed to match Donald's description of a 'theatre manager' in 1720. 'Nancy Mainfield' was not mentioned but Anne – or Nance – Oldfield, a beautiful leading lady at Drury Lane during the period in question, was. Sir Richard Steele, too, was mentioned, described as an actor and playwright. There was no direct reference to 'John Hall' but the name Mr Hall was included among a company of actors. As for 'Kitty Rafter or Clive', Chibbett identified this as a reference to Katherine Raftor, an actress who first appeared at the Theatre Royal in 1729, and later married the barrister George Clive, becoming Kitty Clive.

'This case,' wrote Chibbett in his notes, 'is now beginning to be interesting.'

CHAPTER 9

It might have been 'interesting' to Chibbett, but to the Hitchings family it was maddening. Throughout Wednesday 28 March Donald tapped along to music playing on the wireless and made repeated demands (in vain) that Kirsch be summoned. One of the family asked what Donald looked like and was told simply, 'POLT'. Donald expanded this description a little later: 'BIG CLAWS HAND AND FEET – MEN'S BODY.' At 10.30 p.m. he again insisted that Shirley sleep in Ethel's room.

A few minutes later, the medium Eric Davey arrived, Wally having agreed to let him try to drive the poltergeist from the house. Donald fell silent, but before long there were tapping and scratching sounds. The family's diary records that just after 11 p.m. they heard, 'Two small murmurs. Crying out (three times)'. Then Donald tapped a message asking Davey to stop: 'DON'T DO IT – ME NOT HURT ANYONE HERE'. Donald continued tapping and Davey kept going.

Unfortunately, whatever Davey did had little effect. At 4.30 p.m. the following day, while Shirley was visiting a friend's house in nearby Clapham Junction, the girls heard tapping at that address. At 8.20 p.m., back at No. 63, Donald again demanded that Shirley sleep upstairs, giving

Ethel until 10 p.m. to agree. At 9.30 p.m., recorded Wally, 'Donald made some paste with soap powder & put it on floor.' The 10 p.m. deadline passed uneventfully, but an hour later the poltergeist reminded them he was waiting for an answer: 'IS NAN MIND MADE UP? IF NAN TAKE BED I GO.' Ethel complied and the family was permitted to sleep peacefully.

Eric Davey was due to visit No. 63 again on Friday evening (30 March). Donald was not pleased. 'I DO NOT LIKE HIM – ERIC NO GOOD – HE ONLY TAKE ME FROM YOU TO USE AS POWER,' he complained at 6.35 p.m. Half an hour later he told Shirley, 'I AM HERE TO GUARD YOU FOR EVER GIRLY'. The evening wore on with no sign of Davey and at 11 p.m. Donald tapped, 'NAN WILL TAKE GIRLY BED – ERIC DID NOT COME – WHY NOT?' Just then, Davey arrived. The medium was soon asking Donald questions, to which the poltergeist replied that he had been born in the year 1798 and (again) gave his age as 15 years old. After Davey left, the night passed quietly.

At noon the next day, Donald returned to make an announcement. He had decided to reveal his true identity and the reason he had come – although he would not tell his story to just anyone. He wanted a reporter and his first choice was Ronald Maxwell, one of the journalists who had written the sceptical 'big toe' article: 'ERIC WAS RIGHT – I [am] FIVETEEN – I COME HERE BY LOVE – I WANT TO MAKE [up for something?] THAT I LOST WHEN I GOT DROWNED – [Shirley's childhood friend] IS NOT AWARE OF ME – I COME TO LOVE – IF YOU GET MAXWELL TONIGHT I TELL ALL ABOUT ME AND WHY I COME'.

At 1.20 p.m., Maxwell having failed to come running, Donald offered 'EVAN' (Christopher Riche-Evans from *Psychic News*) as an alternative. Wally telephoned the reporter who agreed to visit soon.

Sunday started with Donald tapping along to music on the wireless and television but, as the morning passed and still with no reporter having arrived, the poltergeist lost patience. At 1.45 p.m. talcum powder was found sprinkled across the top of the piano in the 'front room', with marks resembling arrows and flame-like swirls drawn in the mess. At 3.15 p.m. Donald tapped, 'HELP ME I IMPLORE – GO TO [full name of Shirley's childhood friend] – I COME HERE TO MAKE A LINK OF HAPPYNESS OF TWO PEOPLE – MAKE HIM AWARE OF ME – GO IN ROOM – I TELL ALL ABOUT ME – I AM FIVEHTEEN – I LOST IN CHANNEL MY LIFE I KNEW [...] I COME TO LINK HAPPINESS I DID NOT LIVE TO ENJOY – WRITE TO [location of Shirley's friend] – I WANT TO BRING HAPPI-NESS TO SHIRLEY – I GO WHEN I SEE SHIRLEY HAPPY WITH HIM'.

That evening Donald explained that the flame-like draw-ings on the piano were a warning that the family should 'GET EVANS' before it was too late. He implied that Ethel was particularly at risk and Donald again insisted that Shirley should sleep in her grandmother's room: if not then 'THEY' – presumably Miky and Dopy – would cause trouble. By Monday evening Donald had changed his mind about the still-absent Riche-Evans and decided that he wanted to tell his story to Kirsch instead. The house was loud with tapping throughout Tuesday and at 9.15 p.m. Donald warned he would 'BE NAULTY TONIGHT' if the family didn't do as he said. Two hours later, still waiting for a reporter to attend to him, Donald made a bizarre announcement, 'I TALK TO YOU IN MARSON [Martian]', before tapping out an unintelligible string of letters: 'GILBOARTEMNRYLCHETY-MARESASRISIEFDRDKAPLAIETOEKEERKIM'. When the family eventually went to bed, Donald made so much noise that they left the bedroom and spent the rest of the night on the kitchen floor.

At 11 a.m. on Wednesday morning Kirsch did call at No. 63, but Wally – still angry with the reporter over his published comments regarding Shirley's hospital visit – denied him entry. Donald angrily demanded Kirsch be brought back. Wally refused and that night Donald again commanded the family to 'GET KERCH' and ordered Ethel to let Shirley sleep upstairs. 'Donald said he [would give] us a taste [of what to expect if they continued to disobey him],' reported Wally afterwards, 'and did, throwing things about the kitchen.' A red electric lamp of Chibbett's and a torch belonging to Ethel were both broken, and in the end 'Nan took Shirley to bed with her & we had a quiet night.'

Throughout Thursday there was 'tapping as usual' and at some point two groups of (unspecified) objects were discovered laid out 'in circles on floor in kitchen.' Soon after the family went to bed, wrote Wally, 'Donald done some damage ... up in Nan's bedroom. He threw a water jar, clock, shoes & other things.' Having got the family out of bed, Donald tapped out another message demanding they summon Kirsch so that Donald could reveal why he was here.

On Friday afternoon, wrote Wally, Donald 'threw a box at my wife because she would not take [a] message.' Between further demands for Kirsch on Friday was a message that night insulting Ethel, who had left the room: 'NAN HAS GONE – SILLY OLD COURPS [corpse] – NUT CASE – SHOW UP TO THE COURT OF FRANCE'.

Another message received that night is preserved in Wally's diary in its originally recorded form, as a piece of paper on which a long string of letters were written and later divided into words. Although not particularly interesting in itself, it can be seen that this message started as a nonsensical jumble of letters that only gradually began to form any sense. Shirley remembers that this was typical of the early weeks and months and so this is probably more representative of the early messages than the cleaned-up versions usually recorded by the family and Chibbett:

[10.35 p.m.]: ATCTEGIV – GAS – FAST – HVDIDXDAOFVBUE...
I VLOE [love] SHIRLEY – DO – NAILEG – IS A GIRL – I LOVE
YO – MUST YOU NDED STAND I TELL TRUHT [truth]
AND I DO – NAN – I LO LOVE SHIRLEY – G – EVER SINCE
THEY PLAYED – ASK I DSRITEL – TRUTH – I AM SHIRLEY
DONALD – IIV – I'VE WINEALANGEULD – COME TO MAKE
THAT LOVE – I WANT SHIRLEY – KERCH – TO TRY THIS
ON THE REOWNON [reunion?] COFFEE TABLE TOMOR-
ROW – I GIVE THEM ALL I KNOW WHUI [oui?].

By midnight on Saturday the poltergeist had decided that
Joyce Lewis could be the reporter to receive his story. In a
lengthy message he also made further references to France,
while mentions of 'Donald' here seemed to refer to Shirley's
childhood friend:

LOVE SHIRLEY – I COME TO MAKE LOVE BETWEEN
SHIRLEY AND DONALD – JOYCE – I GOT TO GIVE THIS
MESSAGE TO DONALD – DONALD IS NOT AWARE OF ME
– I WANT JOYCE TO TELL OF ME – KERCH MUST COME
TOMORROW – GET HIM YOU MUST – [MARK] DON'T
BELEAVE I MOVE THE GLASS – TELL HIM I THINK HE IS
BRAIN IS A BIT OF WOOD COMPARE WITH MY OWN –
HE MUST NOT INSULT MY POWER – REST – THIS IS NOT
LIKE THE PALACE IN FRANCE – SHIRLEY MUST DRESS
LIKE A LADY OF THE LADY OF [sic] COURT – GET HER
DRESS SKIRT BLOUSE COAT SHOES AND DON'T WORRY
ABOUT BANK MONEY – GET SOME OUT MONDAY – DO AS
I SAY – SHE CANNOT LOOK LIKE A SERVANT – SHE IS
MY GIRLY.

There was a great deal of scratching and banging on Sunday.
At around noon, at Donald's repeated insistence, Shirley tried
to telephone Kirsch at the newspaper office but there was no
answer. That evening the 'front room' coffee table and chair

were turned upside down, and a bottle of cleaning fluid was found to have been knocked over in the scullery. That night was a difficult one, judging by Wally's brief diary statement that 'Donald seemed to have someone else with him & played us up.'

Christopher Riche-Evans finally visited No. 63 on Monday (9 April), but Donald refused to reveal his story to him. That evening the family took down a by-now familiar message, this time via the 'Ouija-board' glass on the coffee table: 'GET [location of Shirley's childhood friend] – DONALD LOVES MY SHIRLEY – QUIET MY LITTLE ONE – I WANT KERCH'.

By early April public interest in Donald was waning, although the poltergeist himself showed no signs of leaving. In addition to Eric Davey's efforts at exorcism, a Mrs W.M. Durrant (described by *Psychic News*, 31 March 1956, as a 'well-known healer') had spent an evening at the house attempting to contact Donald. She said she had been distinctly aware of 'a presence' but was unable to resolve the issue.

Donald continued to interrupt the family's daily life with his frequent tapping and sometimes more disruptive activity. And every now and again a scrap of paper would be discovered inside a drawer or in Ethel's workbasket, with only occasionally legible marks scrawled across it. As with the writing discovered on 22 March, these marks were apparently made using a blue ballpoint pen and the family held Donald responsible.

Wally was due to return to work after his time off, but both he and his London Transport bosses agreed that the train driver's shattered nerves made it dangerous for him to continue in his old job while things at home remained as they were. Wally was given less onerous duties, such as collecting tickets, and he readily accepted the considerable reduction in wages this entailed.

Harold Chibbett was now a frequent visitor to No. 63. He would call at the house once or twice a week to make a record of all the latest goings-on, and his supportive manner had by now won him the family's trust. Yet Chibbett's calm words of reassurance covered the fact that he was baffled as to what was happening. It seemed unlikely to him that Shirley was perpetrating a hoax, but Chibbett could not decide 'who' Donald really was – or even whether Donald was alone. After all, the poltergeist had mentioned other entities called Miky and Dopy, and the 'Colley Ziber' messages – if taken at face value – appeared to be communications from the spirit of someone who had lived in around 1720. Were all the messages actually coming from Donald himself, or were some from at least one separate spirit? Was it possible that Shirley was somehow 'tuning in' to different psychic wavelengths and 'receiving' different spirits? Harry Hanks had suggested something broadly similar; in his opinion, Shirley was a 'natural medium' whose undeveloped psychic powers were attracting earthbound spirit entities to her.

Chibbett also wondered whether there might be some relevance in the coincidence of some of the names involved: was there a clue in the correspondence between Shirley's mother's name – Kitty – and the name of the actress Kitty Clive? Was the fact that Shirley referred to Ethel as 'Nan' relevant with respect to Nan-cy Mainfield/Nan-ce Oldfield? And – if there was any relevance to this – did it point towards some mechanism underlying the tuning-in of the postulated supernatural 'radio', or did it instead suggest that the characters originated within Shirley's subconscious?

In general, Chibbett was inclined to believe that genuinely paranormal phenomena were taking place at No. 63 and that 'more than one influence' was involved. Moreover, some of the poltergeist's messages suggested to Chibbett that a new personality was emerging as the main 'communicator'. In retrospect, the first hint of this had come on 3 March with the words,

'I AM FIVHTEEN – I COME FROM FRANCE'. Consequently, Donald had on 18 March correctly replied to Chibbett's question that the French phrase 'La Manche' referred to the English Channel. On the night of 22–23 March, the poltergeist had claimed that an apparently random jumble of letters was written in French. On around the same date, according to Riche-Evans in an article in *Psychic News* (31 March 1956), the words 'dauphin' and 'dolphin' had appeared in the poltergeist's messages; dauphin is the French word for dolphin and was also the royal title given to the heir apparent of the French throne. A message on 30 March had stated that the communicator was 15 years old and had been born in the year 1798. At noon the next day a further message stated, 'I [am] FIVETEEN – I COME HERE BY LOVE – I WANT TO MAKE [up for something?] THAT I LOST WHEN I GOT DROWNED'. On 1 April, Donald had stated, 'I AM FIVEHTEEN – I LOST IN CHANNEL MY LIFE I KNEW', the odd phrasing of which struck Chibbett as sounding foreign. On 6 April Donald had referred to the 'COURT OF FRANCE', and on the night of 7–8 April, part of a message had complained, 'THIS IS NOT LIKE THE PALACE IN FRANCE'.

Kitty was unsure. 'We don't think it is another one [i.e. a new entity],' she told the *South London Press* (10 April 1956). 'Donald has told so many lies already.'

But the repeated references to France and to drowning in the English Channel, together with the 'Shirley I come' writing found scrawled inside a notebook on 22 March, all contributed to a growing feeling shared by Chibbett and most of the Hitchings household. It seemed as if something new were emerging – and that whatever it was had a connection with France.

CHAPTER 10

There was certainly a French feel to some of Donald's messages of Saturday 14 April 1956 and just after noon he tapped, 'FAIRA SHUKER FAIRA SHUKER DOM AVOW SELAMENA DING DONG DAM'. Despite the eccentric spelling this was obviously the French song 'Frère Jacques', the melody (although probably not the words) of which dates back at least as far as the late eighteenth century. Later that day, another message contained the phrase, 'GOOD BY OR SHALL I SAY ORAWAR?' That was evidently an attempt at spelling 'au revoir'.

The following night, Donald gave the first clue as to what he had looked like during his lifetime: 'I COME TELL WHAT I LOOK LIKE – FIVE FOOT HIGH – FAIR HAIR – BLUE EYES – THIRTY FIVE WIDE'. The last phrase was assumed to mean measuring 35 inches around the chest.

Throughout April and May the idea that the poltergeist might be the spirit of a Frenchman became increasingly accepted by both family and investigator. In the meantime, though, Donald continued his usual tricks. First thing each morning there would be a burst of tapping the family took to mean 'Good morning'. Throughout the day there would be other periods of tapping, often in time to music playing on the wireless or television; the poltergeist was particularly

keen on the television series *The Adventures of Robin Hood*.
If Donald wanted to deliver a message he would tap loudly
a few times to get the family's attention and someone would
fetch the necessary pens and paper. Donald persisted with his
occasional requests for Kirsch or others to attend him. On
10 April he commanded the family to, 'GET KERCH – IF YOU
[don't] I WATER THROW', but when Kirsch arrived the next
morning Donald refused to 'talk' to him.

At 10.30 p.m. on Wednesday 11 April, Donald warned
that another entity was around and looking to cause trouble.
On the poltergeist's advice the family spent the night on the
kitchen floor. At 11 p.m., wrote Wally, 'the fun started'. There
was 'heavy blowing of wind over Shirley's head', Donald
'put green stuff on her legs – looks like paint' (from Shirley's
case of art materials) and 'threw [a] thimble at us.' After
around forty minutes Donald tapped, 'I SILENCE HIM IF
I CAN – WAS IT A FLY? – IT IS BAD MAN'. Then all was quiet
again – briefly.

Early the next afternoon Wally found what looked like a
large footprint in some white powder that had been spilled
across the floor. At midnight Donald's tapping kept everyone
awake. At 4.30 p.m. on Friday 13 there was an ominous discovery when cinders from the fireplace were found beneath a
nearby mat. Five minutes later more cinders were discovered
in the same place.

It had all became too much for Ethel. For almost three
months, the old woman had begrudgingly coped with objects
disappearing, turning up in unexpected places, getting broken
and being thrown through the air; with the thumping and
endless tapping that kept everyone awake; with sheets being
pulled from beds; with exorcisms that made her nervous and
offended her religious sensibilities; with journalists, spiritualists and assorted strangers invading her home; and with the
chaotic atmosphere of fear, despair, excitement and at times
near-hysteria that had become the family's daily life. There

was also the very real danger from fire, and Ethel seemed to be a particular target because Donald had taken to setting fire to the contents of her 'pig bin'. Despite the smell, Ethel preferred to keep her bin – used for collecting food scraps – indoors on the upstairs landing. However, on several occasions the contents had been found alight, forcing Wally to don thick gloves and take the burning material out to the garden. With her discomfort magnified by the unremitting pain from her arthritis, the situation had become unbearable for the cantankerous matriarch. In mid-April, she lost patience with the entire affair. The final straw was one of Donald's frequent blackmail demands, promising everyone a peaceful night's sleep on condition that Shirley slept in Ethel's room. On this particular night, Ethel had reluctantly given in but, when Donald failed to keep silent, she lost her temper and verbally let loose at him. The poltergeist responded angrily. 'I peeped out from under the bedclothes,' Shirley said afterwards, 'and all sorts of things were flying about – water bottles, tumblers, lamps.' Enough was enough. In the morning Ethel packed her bags and left to stay with one of her daughters who lived nearby.

On the evening of 13 April Donald demanded her return to No. 63. Shirley hurried out to fetch her, but Ethel refused to go back. Donald's reaction was reasonably muted: when Shirley and her parents went to bed that night, Wally noticed that his daughter's legs were smeared with blue paint, the used tube having been left under her sheets. Otherwise, the night passed peacefully.

Unconcerned by the effect his antics were having on other people, Donald decided it was time the family learned about life elsewhere in the solar system. As Shirley and Mark took down his messages on 16 April, the poltergeist referred to what seemed to be a being living on Mars who went by the name of Monga or Mongia. There were also, the poltergeist informed them, tall beings that lived on Saturn and (contradicting a statement he had made the month before) on Venus. He even passed on examples of extraterrestrial languages. One, allegedly in 'Marson'/'Marsion' or Martian, ran, 'MONGIAGIBBOARTEMNRYLCHETYMARESASRIS-IFFDRDKAPLAIETOEKEERKIM'. (This was almost identical to the 'Marson' message he had tapped out on 3 April.) Another was supposedly in Venusian: 'LOBLOFOLINGLINGHADOW-ERMOQEIHEJA'. A third contained what Donald claimed was the language of the planet Saturn: 'I AM HE WHO − RENEE − THEY TALK LIKE US − BMDDSRUNCMXEGUCNCT.'

The French-sounding name 'Renee' was directed at Shirley, whose middle name was Irene. As for the remaining content of these latest revelations, that remained a mystery.

On Tuesday 17 April Shirley refused to do as instructed when the poltergeist told her to write to her friend Donald/Ronald. 'YOU MAKE ME ANGRY' tapped Donald at 7 p.m. Wally summarised what followed:

> All bedclothes on floor, and a picture also. Both bedclothes on the mat in front of the fireplace. Then he broke a pint bottle of milk in the scullery, and emptied two kettles of water about and over Shirley. Then he turned on the electric stove and oven full & burnt the tea towel. He also turned on the water tap and filled the sink up after putting the plug in. He opened the scullery window and threw things out of it − all because Shirley would not do as he asked.

'I HUMBERLEY OPLAJISE FOR LAST NIGHT,' tapped Donald some twenty-seven hours later, 'BUT YOU MADE ME ANGRY'. He went on to explain that he wanted (with Kirsch's help) to reunite Shirley with her childhood friend, again strongly suggesting there could be a romance between the pair. Why Donald should have believed this has always baffled Shirley but Donald was insistent.

On Friday the emerging French aspect of Donald attempted to pull rank: '[6.30 p.m.] I STILL LOVE YOU SHIRLEY – BOTH OF US – RONALD HIM IS STILL WELL – TELL KERCH TAKE CARE – I ANGRY – I HAVE HIM GILATINED [guillotined] – I DOLEFIN [dauphin] PRINCE STILL.'

As this message continued Donald seemingly revealed more about himself: 'DONALD – SISTERS NAME IS ANNE AGE 9 YRS – BROTHER NAME IS PHELP AGE 12 YRS – HIM AND BROTHER DROWNED TOGETHER – FATHERS NAME LOUIE – I COME TO MAKE HAPPY – YOU RONALD – HE I SO LIKE HE – YOU WOULD LIKE ME IF YOU COULD SEE ME – HAIR THE SAME AS RONALD – PARIS BORN – SIR PERCY BLAKNEY – SCARLET PIPENELL – [H]IS CLOTH[E]S SILK SATIN VELVET LACE – HE WAS DROW[N]ED 12 OC [o'clock] AT NIGHT – THE MAINSALT [mainsail] HIT ME AND PHILP OR PFELP ON HEAD'.

Despite receiving a direct order from a dead prince, the family made no attempt to contact Shirley's old friend. Annoyed, Donald threatened several times that weekend to set fire to Ethel's bed, but by Monday he was proclaiming his innocence, blaming those messages on another entity. This was not one of the previous entities he had called Miky and Dopy but a newcomer he named Shagy Roots (or Shaggy Roots).

(Oddly, when the present authors were discussing these events in December 2007, Shirley was absolutely certain that Shagy Roots had not been an entity at all but rather an insulting nickname Donald gave to Ethel on account of the hairs growing out of the old woman's chin. Wally's diary and Chibbett's contemporary records make it clear, however, that in 1956 Shagy Roots was considered to be an entity in the same vein as the Miky and Dopy characters. As with them, Donald considered Shagy Roots a threat to the family, able and willing to start fires. Whereas Miky and Dopy had allegedly drawn their energy from Donald himself, Shagy Roots supposedly drew his from Ethel, who, it became apparent, 'he' did not like at all.)

'I WARN YOU HE POWERFUL,' tapped Donald at 10.30 that Monday night. 'LOVES TO PLAY WITH FIRE.' A quarter of an hour later (after Wally had presumably shut off power to the electric cooker) Donald added, 'YOU FORGOT HE CAN TURN ON GAS AT METER – HE CUT PIPE GAS – HE TURN ON GAS TAP – PUT AIR INTO PIPE – LIGHT – BLOW'.

There were numerous disturbances over the next few days. Small items – including spectacles and sticks of Shirley's make-up – were thrown around, Shirley's newly washed clothes were tipped onto the floor, a kettle of water was kicked over, and so on.

'Donald played about with Shirley this evening in the scullery,' wrote Wally on Tuesday 24 April, 'throwing things about [including] milk tops in a paper bag. The water tap was running and he put what we think [was] his finger over the flowing water and made a splash. [He] threw a tin bottle top in kitchen, a dish swab on a stick … came flying [into] the kitchen'. He also tipped a packet of soap powder onto the scullery floor, spilling the contents.

There were continued warnings/threats of fires, such as the following on Wednesday evening: 'OLD SHAGY ROOTS IS HERE – HE BURN UP THE HOUSE – BE BIULDING [H]IS SELF UP – I TELL TRUTH – I WARN YOU IT IS NO GAME BELEAVE ME – I AM HERE TO GUARD YOU'.

On Friday Donald once again demanded an audience with Kirsch and, when he grew frustrated, he created havoc. In the 'front room', furniture was upended and piled – together with objects from the mantelpiece – in the centre of the floor. Just after 11 p.m. Donald began tapping and scratching again, and the entire contents of one of Shirley's tubes of paint were squeezed out onto her arm. Then, reported Wally, 'he tied Shirley's foot up with a sock tight' and pulled the bedclothes from her bed before smearing her legs with first her blue and then her green make-up. A doll belonging to Shirley was thrown to the floor. When Wally told Donald to stop, the poltergeist replied that it was not him but Shagy Roots doing this.

By 9 a.m. on Saturday Donald was again demanding the family summon Kirsch. 'DON'T BE FOOLS,' he warned. Shirley went to buy a drink from a local shop and returned to find a face towel beginning to burn on the stove. Wally, who had a cold, had not smelled it. There were also smouldering cinders – apparently from the fireplace – on the kitchen floor. At 1.45 p.m. Donald tapped out another order: 'GET HIM – GET KERCH – IF NOT YOU MAKE ME ANGRY – I SET FIRE TO YOUR HOUSE AND KERCH HOUSE'.

'I WARN YOU,' he added an hour later, 'I NOT FOOLING – I DO IT.'

CHAPTER 11

For Chibbett – an enthusiastic psychical researcher – one of the most exciting episodes so far had been the apparent verification of details in the 'Colley Ziber' messages of 27 March. In late April, his acceptance of that material was heavily dented.

On 20 April, his Tax Office colleague Mr Irvine passed him a copy of the new *Radio Times*, indicating that the BBC was to broadcast a television play the following Tuesday. The title was *Kitty Clive*, one of the names in the 'Colley Ziber' material, and a look through the magazine showed that the play included characters named Kitty Clive, John Hall, Colley Cibber and Nance Oldfield – all names that had appeared in the messages. Moreover, a note at the bottom of the listing stated that this play had originally been broadcast on 27 March, the very day the messages had been received.

Sir Richard Steele (one of the other names Donald had given) was not listed but Chibbett made sure to watch the play when it was re-aired on 24 April and discovered that Steele was indeed mentioned. So were other details in the messages such as the facts that John Hall was an actor and that Colley Cibber was the manager. 'At first sight,' wrote Chibbett in his case notes, 'it looks as though fraud was operated here.'

On the evening of 26 April Chibbett visited No. 63 intending to challenge Shirley on this matter. Before he could utter a word both Shirley and Kitty told him they had seen the *Radio Times* listing. When Chibbett pointed out that the play had originally been broadcast no more than a few hours before the messages, they seemed 'genuinely surprised' but quickly explained that they could not have watched it because 'owing to a fault, their set could not pick up the BBC programmes'. The entire family, Ethel included, assured Chibbett they had not watched the play and the researcher believed them. 'I can myself confirm,' he wrote years afterwards, 'that at no time in the years 1956 to 1958 did I ever see a BBC programme on their set. The fault in the set was not rectified until 1959.'

When Chibbett asked whether the messages had actually come from Donald rather than 'Colley Ziber', the poltergeist tapped to say yes. 'Why?' asked Chibbett. Donald did not reply.

When he had sat with Shirley, listening to 'Colley Ziber' – or, as it now seemed, Donald – tap out responses to his questions, Chibbett had found it hard to believe Shirley was perpetrating a deliberate fraud. He still felt the same, but if not fraud what other possibilities were there? Chibbett considered three. The first was that the apparently supernatural Donald had communicated the details after seeing the play himself. The second was that Shirley had seen the play (perhaps at a friend's house) and held the details in her unconscious mind, and that these details then emerged through whatever mysterious power enabled her (in this scenario) to create tapping sounds. The third possibility (also involving Shirley somehow causing the tapping herself) was that her unconscious mind had psychically read the details in a nearby television listing.

Evidence to support Chibbett's growing suspicion that Shirley (and/or Donald) was able to pick up information psychically came later that same evening. At around 8 p.m., as Chibbett was recording letters being tapped out by Donald, he 'became aware that replies were being made to my (as yet) unspoken questions.' This realisation prompted Chibbett to conduct an impromptu experiment:

I told Shirley to write a short word of her own choice on a piece of paper, without telling anyone what it was or how many letters were in it. She did so. She was sitting on a stool opposite to me and about three feet away. I tilted my writing pad so that she could not possibly see what I was doing. Then I pointed at the printed alphabet letters in the usual way and the following was spelled out: I L A M P. After 'P', the raps went several times in rapid succession – the usual signal that the message was concluded. As the result did not make sense, I asked – mentally – whether there was a correction to be made. A rap indicated that there was. Again the same message was spelled out, but this time the letter 'I' was omitted, leaving the word: LAMP. I turned my paper face-downwards and then asked Shirley to reveal what she had previously written. To our astonishment, the words were identical!

The important point to note here is that during the whole experiment *I did not utter a single word!* Under the conditions I had imposed, it was impossible for Shirley to have seen either the printed alphabet or what I had written. […] But what impressed me most, was the immediate response to my mental questions; as for instance, I would indicate a letter and ask mentally: 'Is this correct?' and 'Donald' would reply by raps: 'Yes' or 'No'. There was no hesitation, and the general effect was as though someone were looking over my shoulder and seeing the alphabet as clearly as I was doing, besides being able to perceive what I was thinking about at the same time!

'Are you going to be good today?' asked Wally on the morning of Sunday 29 April. Donald tapped twice: 'NO'. Just after 11 a.m., Donald warned, 'GET MAXWELL – I DO THE SAME – FIRE BED – IF YOU DON'T GET MAXWELL THEN GET KERCH – I WARN YOU […] I MEAN WHAT I SAY'.

Before Wally left the house he switched off the mains supply to the electric cooker. This was fortunate because while he was out the cooker's electric rings were switched on. Twice Donald threw bedclothes onto the floor in the downstairs bedroom, and he did the same with items belonging to Shirley in the 'front room'. He also made what Wally later called 'a real right mess' of the three upstairs rooms, which were now vacant because Mark had decided to follow Ethel's example and leave No. 63 for a while. (Chibbett was shown these rooms a few days later, recording, 'The bedclothes had been pulled back and disarranged, heavy clocks overturned, and ornaments scattered about. In the [upstairs] kitchen, considerable soot was bestrewn on the mantelpiece. In one bedroom the bed still held the impression of a human form, as though someone about five feet in height had lain there.')

That evening, Donald continued his demands for Kirsch. Then, at 1.15 p.m. on Monday, he delivered his final ultimatum: 'GET KERCH – IF YOU DON'T I SET FIRE'.

Wally left for work at 1.50 p.m., again taking care to switch off the electricity at the mains before he went, but somehow the supply was turned back on. So was the cooker. Early that afternoon several (unspecified) objects placed on the cooker caught fire and similar blazes continued sporadically all day. Two neighbours, Charles and Doris Baker, came to Kitty's assistance and Mr Baker helped Kitty extinguish the flames while his wife switched the mains supply off again. Donald switched it back on and set more objects alight, and so it continued. By late evening Kitty was exhausted. Her neighbours persuaded her to call out the fire brigade, and she reluctantly did so at around 9 p.m. Once again, police and fire investigators were dispatched to what many locals by now called 'the spooky house', where they were shown the charred remains of collars, shirts, tablecloths, brushes and towels in a bucket in the back yard and asked to believe that a poltergeist was to blame. Understandably, they found it easier to suspect

Shirley and questioned the teenager for almost an hour. She pleaded her innocence and Wally – who had been called home from work – and Kitty stood by her. The cause of the fires was never officially established.

The family was terrified there would be further fires. They were tempted to copy Ethel and Mark and leave No. 63 but, as Wally told the reporter Elizabeth Few, there was no guarantee this would free them from Donald: 'We would move too. But we know it would follow us … we don't know what to do. It almost rules us.'

'We keep having tapped messages warning us the fire will come again,' Kitty told Few, which inspired the reporter to try to contact Donald herself. She joined the family at the coffee table, around the edge of which had been arranged pieces of paper bearing the letters of the alphabet. An upturned wine glass was placed on the tabletop and everyone lightly placed a finger on this. But it did not move.

A short while later, after the family had left the room, Few tried again. This time she was accompanied only by her photographer and she later claimed they received the following message: 'FIRE ME DO – ME DO IT AGAIN'. When Chibbett learned of this he eagerly noted that Shirley could not possibly have been responsible for this message.

Neither could Shirley have been responsible for some of the tapping sounds now being reported from locations other than No. 63. According to the *South Western Star* (4 May 1956), two unnamed visitors to the house were 'followed by mysterious rappings' after they left. One man was described as 'an insurance agent' and had probably visited following the fires of 30 April. The newspaper claimed he 'heard strange knockings in his home' after his visit. The second visitor – probably Eric Davey – had been 'astonished to hear thuds coming from under his feet when he hopped on a bus after a recent visit.'

❖

Wally thought that Donald's tapping the morning after the fires (Tuesday 1 May) seemed 'angry'. The poltergeist was again calling for Kirsch, whereas the medium Eric Davey was most definitely not wanted. 'IF ERIC COMES AGAIN I KILL GIRLY,' tapped Donald at 4.15 p.m. This was probably a statement to Shirley that Donald intended to kill Davey, rather than a threat to kill Shirley, but without punctuation it was impossible to be certain. Either way it was chilling.

Kirsch and Davey both visited No. 63 that evening. Placing his hands on Shirley's head, Davey went into a trance and announced that his spirit guide – a 7-foot-tall Indian named Harpet – had come to defeat the poltergeist. But, as Davey worked, Donald continued to tap away, and the exorcism had no noticeable effect. Kirsch watched these proceedings closely. To the cynical journalist the tapping seemed to come from the vicinity of Shirley's feet, and Kirsch afterwards stated that Shirley's foot appeared to him to 'throb slightly' in time with the sounds. Moreover, he claimed that when Shirley spotted him looking at her foot the tapping paused and only started again when he looked away. Afterwards, Kirsch wrote a measured article for the *South London Press* (4 May 1956) that was sceptical regarding Donald while simultaneously sympathetic towards Shirley. Kirsch suggested that the affair was being perpetuated by the very people who believed they were helping the family; he proposed that if only all the mediums, spiritualists, etc. would leave Shirley alone the situation would calm down and life return to normal. His call was ignored.

CHAPTER 12

It had been around a month and a half since Shirley had lost her job, and her parents felt it was time she found herself another one. On Friday 4 May 1956 Wally took Shirley for an interview to work at a bank. 'Donald tapped there,' Wally recorded, but fortunately 'nobody noticed anything.'

The poltergeist was relatively subdued for the next few days, but as time passed with no return visit from Kirsch, Donald's patience ran out. Just after 10 p.m. on Thursday 10 May Donald tapped: 'I WANT KERCH – IF YOU DO NOT [fetch him] I PLAY HELL TONIGHT […] ELECTRIC WIRES UNDER BEDROOM FLOOR – YOU CANNOT GET UNDER BOARDS.' After the family went to bed, wrote Wally, 'D started to scratch on Shirley's bed and seemed to be angry. I had to get up and take message. 3 words, KERCH GET KIRSCH.'

Donald continued to call for Kirsch throughout Friday. Also that day, something (unspecified) was scrawled on the scullery door, the key to the downstairs bedroom wardrobe went missing (it was later discovered hanging from the kitchen lampshade), and all of the family's freshly laundered clothes were taken out of that wardrobe and scattered around the room. That night Donald claimed burglars were prowling around outside and would break in at 2 a.m. They didn't.

The demands kept coming, combined with threats as to what would happened if Kirsch were not summoned. At 2 p.m. on Saturday 12 May, for example, Donald tapped, 'LIKE BEFORE – ONE BE IN HOME WHO CANNOT RUN – I WARN – I BURN YOU DOWN'. The one 'who cannot run' was clearly Kitty, whose arthritis made even walking difficult. Late on Sunday night Donald tapped, 'TONIGHT – HELL – TO SHOW POWER – I WARN,' after which Shirley cried out that Donald was pulling at her bedclothes, biting her and pulling her legs. The chaos continued for around an hour.

Why was Donald so determined for Kirsch to visit him? Chibbett decided to find out. Unable to travel to No. 63 as often as he would have liked, the researcher instead posted a list of questions to the Battersea house. The family read them aloud to Donald on the evening of Tuesday 15 May.

'Why do you continually ask for Kirsch?'

Donald simply replied, 'I WANT KIRSCH'.

Because Donald obviously wanted Kirsch to get in touch with Shirley's childhood friend, would Donald object to Chibbett writing to the friend instead?

'NO.'

Chibbett's questions also investigated the confusing connection between Donald and Shirley's similarly named childhood friend. (By this time the Hitchings family felt that Shirley's friend's name had probably been Ronald, rather than Donald, but they couldn't quite remember for certain, and the names used for him remained interchangeable in the poltergeist's messages.) Many of Donald's messages referred to this boy, for example the following, both communicated on 26 April, (1) 'DO YOU WANT RONALD [and] SHIRLEY TO BE FRIEND[s] – THAT IS WHAT I COME HERE FOR – SHIRLEY RONALD I MAKE HAPPY – PLEASE I COME HERE FOR ONE REASON ONLY SHIRLEY – NOW WHEN RONALD WENT YOU GOT ME BUT I GO THE INSTANCE SHIRLEY MEET RONALD AGAIN'; (2) '... I LOVE GIRLY – I GOT A SECRET FOR YOU

– DONALD OR RONALD LOVES YOU – HE'S NOT A AWARE
– I WANT YOU MEET HIM VERY SOON FOR A WEEK TO
MAKE HIM HAPPY AND LET ME SEE HOW IT WORKS OUT
– IF YOU LIKE HIM LIKE YOU DID THEN I GO AND LEAVE
YOU HAPPY […].' To Shirley's bemusement, it seemed that
Donald wanted to kindle a romance between the two teenagers.

'Have you any intimate connection with Ronald [surname]?'
was Chibbett's next question.

'YES.'

'If so, what is it?'

'I WANT HIM TO BE HAPPY – YOU GIRLY WHEN [you]
PLAY[ed with him?] YOU WERE HAPPY.'

A researcher more minded towards a psychological interpretation of poltergeist cases might have wondered about
the possible romantic fantasies of a teenage girl. Chibbett,
however, was inclined towards a spiritualistic framework in
which the poltergeist might be the discarnate spirit of someone
who had died many years ago and who was for some reason
interested in a romance between Shirley and Donald/Ronald.

Shirley responded to this notion of a potential romance on
16 May. The poltergeist evidently wanted her to meet her old
friend and so she asked, 'If I do not like Ronald, what then?'

'BUT YOU DO LIKE RONALD,' came the tapped reply.
'SILLY QUESTION!'

Then, pointedly turning away from the issue, the poltergeist
started to tap out only partially comprehensible questions,
occasionally adding his own replies: 'CAN YOU TELL WHAT
IS MYHOLIGHY – I TELL LATER MEANING – AND WHO
WAS CLARA PATTRA – HE CAME EGYPT – WOMAN NOT
MAN – AND DO YOU LIKE RONALD?' It was as if he were
parodying Chibbett's habit of asking him questions. Inter-
spersed among these messages were worries that 'Flannel Foot'
was in the vicinity. It was unclear who Flannel Foot was supposed to be – a burglar, perhaps, or another entity. Thankfully
he did not make an appearance.

The impression that Donald was actually the spirit of a deceased Frenchman had been growing over the last few weeks. On 2 May, Donald had described his clothing (which he apparently continued to wear after his death): 'SATIN – A TAIL COAT – KNEE BREECHES – HOSE – LACE – WAISTCOAT – BLACK BUCKLE SHOES – SOME [people] WORE WIGS'. He again claimed to have drowned in the English Channel, and added that his mother and father had been guillotined, which suggested some connection with the French Revolution. He also revealed that his real name was not Donald but Louis: 'I – LOUIS – KILLED BEFORE REVOLUTION,' he tapped.

This seems to be the first time Donald specifically referred to himself by this name, although on 20 April he had given his father's name as 'LOUIE'. Then a long message tapped out on 3 May included the phrase, 'I WAS THE CROWN'. The implications intrigued Mark who, while visiting the house that evening, sketched a fleur-de-lis (the stylised flower device long associated with French royalty). Mark asked Donald if he knew what the sketch represented. The tapping responded, 'FLELIR DE LIS'.

On 7 and 8 May, several of Donald's messages included the word 'CHERRY'; for example: '[8 May, 8.20 p.m.] TONIGHT I STAY HERE – BAD I AM – I NO GO CHERRY.' This was evidently intended to be the affectionate French form of address 'mon cheri / ma cherie'.

As if playing a supernatural version of the '20 Questions' game, Chibbett had been piecing such clues together and he now believed he knew who the entity was claiming to be. Among the aforementioned list of questions Chibbett posted to the Hitchings family was, 'Were you the first son of Louis XVI?'

The family read this out to Donald on 15 May. The tapping returned a simple answer: 'YES.'

When Chibbett visited No. 63 on the afternoon of Friday 18 May he found Donald unusually willing to communicate with him. The poltergeist was still prepared to allow Chibbett – rather than Kirsch – to write to Shirley's old friend Ronald and, when Chibbett asked for the overseas mailing address of Ronald's family, the poltergeist happily tapped out the details. Chibbett asked what he should write in the letter and Donald replied, 'TELL HIM OF ME'. When Chibbett pressed for more, all Donald would say was that he wanted a 'RENUIEON' (reunion) between Ronald and 'Ireney' because this would make them happy.

In the end it was agreed that Chibbett should write to Ronald's parents rather than to the boy directly, explaining the circumstances as well as he was able and asking them to permit their son to reply to Shirley if he so wished.

In return, Chibbett asked Donald to cooperate in an experiment similar to the 'I L A M P' experiment that had suggested that Shirley and/or Donald could read Chibbett's thoughts. The poltergeist agreed. Chibbett reported:

> So I concentrated mentally upon the name of a [spirit] Guide I am supposed to have, and Shirley took down the messages spelled out by raps. 'Donald' made several valiant efforts [to read what was in Chibbett's mind], coming up with: 'YOUR WIFE'S NAME – YOUR DAUGHTER – NO – A CLOSE FRIEND'. Finally, he got annoyed, and tapped out '(Y)OUR CAT'. But of course, none of these was correct. Thereupon I reversed the direction of the experiment, told Shirley to write down beforehand a word of her own selection, and in silence spelled out myself the letters of the alphabet as the taps indicated. I got: RONALD. Shirley turned up her pad. The word she had previously written was: RONALD.

On Friday 1 June (following several impatient reminders from Donald) Chibbett wrote to Ronald's parents. After summarising the story for them Chibbett concluded, 'it is possible that [these disturbances] might cease if your son Ronald were to write a friendly letter to his old playmate Shirley – who says that she would like to hear from him anyway…'

Ronald never did write back. Chibbett sent his family a second letter on 27 December, but there was no response until May 1957 when the family wrote not to Chibbett but to a relative of theirs living in London who contacted the Hitchings family on their behalf. That relative made it clear that Ronald's family wanted nothing whatsoever to do with the affair.

On the afternoon of Saturday 19 May, Shirley's friend Marge visited No. 63. As the two girls 'talked' to the poltergeist Donald told them who he really was: 'I AM DONALD IN THIS AGE – I AM ARIDGENLY [originally] LOUIE SEVENTEENTH SON OF LOUIE THE SIXTEENTH OF THE HOUSE OF LOUIE MON LION HA'. He stated the same thing the following day.

The poltergeist had now claimed (on 15 May) to be the 'first' – i.e. eldest – son of the French king Louis XVI, and also to be Louis XVII. As will become clear later, these claims could not both be true. Readers familiar with French history might also have realised that Donald's claims to have been born in 1798 and also to have died before the French Revolution of 1789 cannot be reconciled. At this stage, however, neither Chibbett nor any of the Hitchings family had ever had any reason to study French history, so such inconsistencies in the poltergeist's developing story passed unnoticed for now.

By the end of May 1956 Donald had essentially taken control of life inside No. 63. He dictated when the family could go to bed and gave instructions for Shirley to sleep upstairs whenever he felt it appropriate. He would often wake people by pulling off their bedclothes in the early hours of the morning, and/or tapping out urgent warnings that someone was lurking in the garden, that the house was about to be burgled, etc. And the tapping was never silent for long.

Donald would tap greetings when the family awoke each morning, tap greetings to Wally when he came home from work, tap along to music, and tap to tell the family to get pen and paper ready because he was about to tap another message. He frequently tapped out his unsolicited thoughts on whatever happened to be taking place in No. 63 at that time, not hesitating to complain if details were not to his liking. He might opine, for example, that Shirley should wear less make-up or finer clothing. He was forever insisting that particular people (notably Kirsch) be summoned into his presence, and he continued his ultimately doomed attempt to reunite Shirley with her friend Ronald. Simply ignoring the poltergeist's messages was inadvisable because behind the endless demands, instructions and pleas for attention was always the threat of another destructive tantrum or even another arson attack.

Even important life decisions were now under Donald's control. Shirley's job interview of 4 May had been successful and she was due to start her new career as a bank clerk on Monday 28 May. But at 7 p.m. on the Sunday evening Donald told Shirley: 'I WARN IF [you] THINK OF GOING TO WORK MONDAY I BREAK EVERY BIT OF BANK UP – I BREAK THE HOME UP TONIGHT IF [you] GO TOMORROW – I KNOW WHAT IN YOUR MIND – I JUST WARN I WILL NOT STAND FOR BE A GOOD BOY – I VERY BIG ANGRY – I AM GOING TO RIP UP ALL CLOTHS.' Within an hour, Kitty was so upset that she telephoned Wally at work to ask him to come home. Shirley's clothes had been thrown around the bedroom, recorded Wally afterwards. The 'front room' was 'also in a bad state' and Donald had 'set two dusters alight on the grill in [the] scullery'.

That night Donald threatened to 'GIVE YOU A NIGHT OF HELL' and 'BURN YOU DOWN'. After the family went to bed, wrote Wally, the poltergeist '[t]ore Shirley's undersheet and threw things about and put scissors in [Shirley's] bed.'

At 7 a.m. on Monday morning, Donald began scratching at Shirley's bed, then tapped, 'YOU HAVE MADE ME ANGRY'. Kitty discovered that her house keys were missing. Also missing were the keys for the wardrobe and the large key for the 'front room' door, and freshly laundered clothes from the wardrobe were found strewn around the bedroom. In the end, wrote Wally, 'Shirley did not go to work for fear of what he would do.'

'PROMISE ONE THING,' Donald tapped that night, 'THAT MY IRENEY DO NOT GO TO WORK […] I THINK I BAT YOUR HEAD IN FOR YOU KIT – DO NOT FEAR GIRLY – IF SHE KIT SEND YOU AWAY SHE HAVE ME TO RECONSIL WITH – I KEEP YOU SAFE.' Then, wrote Wally, 'Donald played about again in bedroom and threw something of Shirley's and banging and scratching on Shirley's bed and pulling her bed-clothes up. About 12.30 a.m. all went quiet.'

The next morning, while Wally and Kitty were in the kitchen, three large crosses appeared on the bedroom wall above where Kitty slept, another on the headboard, one on the pillow and one in the bed. They were drawn in black lead – a ubiquitous household substance in the 1950s, used to polish and protect fire grates – and proved impossible to erase.

The character of the on-going drama was changing. The idea of Donald as 'merely' a poltergeist was fading into the background as it was overtaken by the more romantic idea of Louis, the ghostly son of an eighteenth-century French king.

Occasionally, Donald's messages contained details that seemed deliberately anachronistic, intended to remind the family that he was from another century. One such example was the way he referred to coins as 'silver pieces'. A few weeks earlier, Shirley's pet pedigree rat Mabel had died and Donald was keen for Shirley to have a new pet. He announced his plan on Saturday 26 May, tapping it out to Shirley at the 'front room' coffee table on which were sitting ten silver-coloured shilling coins belonging to Wally: '[11 a.m.] THAT TEN SILVER PEACES [pieces] – CAN YOU PROMISE ME – WILL YOU SAVE LIFE OF AN ANIMAL? – I KNOW WHERE WANDSWORTH PET SHOP YOU GOT ALL FISHES FROM […] THERE IS A ONE ALL ALONE WAITING FOR YOU – LOOKS SO SAD – BUY HIM FOR ME AND YOU CALL [him] PINKY.'

Two hours later came another message: 'I TAKE FOUR TO KEEP FOR PINKY'. Four 'silver pieces' were now missing from the coffee table. Donald told the family he would only give the money back if they 'GET PINKY'. Shirley replied that she did not want a new pet, protesting that if the money had to be spent on something she would rather it were used to buy her some face powder. 'YOU DO NOT WANT MAKE-UP – IT SPOILS FACE – NO ONE HAD IT IN THE COURT – I WILL LOVE PINKY,' replied Donald. Eventually, Wally gave in. He promised to buy Pinky, who turned out to be a hamster, and the missing coins later reappeared.

Donald also made a point of drawing attention to his old-fashioned clothing. On Sunday 27 May, for example, as Shirley was carrying out household chores and presumably grumbling about the ironing, Donald told her, 'IF YOU HAD TO IRON THE SHIRTS I WORE WITH LACE FRILLS YOU WOULD MOAN'.

As June took over from May, more mysterious marks began to appear on the walls inside No. 63. Emphasising that the poltergeist's 'Louis' personality was in the ascendancy the new drawings were clearly representations of the fleur-de-lis.

CHAPTER 13

In a way, the drawings had been Kitty's idea. She had suggested that Donald 'do the florderly' for them, but when Shirley walked into the downstairs bedroom on the morning of Sunday 3 June 1956 she found that fleur-de-lis drawings now covered the walls there. There was another large fleur-de-lis, accompanied by a pair of crossed swords, drawn on a wall in the 'front room'. All had been scrawled across the wallpaper in long sweeps of black lead – not exactly what the house-proud Kitty had intended.

Donald wasn't the slightest bit concerned at the damage and distress he had caused. He acted as if he had a royal privilege to do whatever he wished. Two days earlier, he had reminded everyone that his father had been Louis XVI, king of France: 'LOUIS SEIZE – ROI AU FRANCE – IL MON PERE'; the French was less than perfect but the message was clear.

Further drawings would appear on walls and ceilings over the coming weeks and months: more representations of the fleur-de-lis, as well as of shields bearing that design. During this same period, Donald started to insist that Shirley play with her dolls in the 'front room'. Shirley was happy to do so. The poltergeist instructed her on how she was to dress one particular doll as Marie Antoinette. Whether it was coincidence or further evidence of an underlying connection between

Donald and Shirley, it happened that Shirley already had some interest in fashion and dressmaking. Therefore, with the help of her cousin Dolly, who was a dressmaker, Shirley was able to obtain appropriate scraps of material (Donald insisted upon silk for the gown). Apparently satisfied with the result, Donald promptly instructed Shirley to dress the other dolls as historical characters too, such as Elizabeth I and Anne Boleyn.

As Donald settled into his new pastime, Chibbett received a signed statement regarding phenomena that had allegedly occurred independently of Shirley, and for which she could not therefore have been responsible. The statement, which came from a friend of Mark and was given to Chibbett on 3 June, referred to tapping sounds during the time when Shirley had been staying at her Aunt Nell's house:

> On or about March 16th, 1956, I had just retired, when there were two distinct knocks on the bed by my feet. Another two followed by my knees, and a further two by my chest; and two more on the wood frame at the top end of the bed.
>
> Following this, there were several tappings on the wall, and after a few seconds the same thing repeated itself.
>
> Disturbed by this, I sat up and said: 'Is that you, Donald?' There was no reply, and all was quiet the whole of the night. I have heard nothing like it since.
>
> (Signed) J.A. C—
> 3rd June, 1956

Further confirmation that other people had experienced and were baffled by the bizarre phenomena reached Chibbett in early June when Joyce Lewis visited No. 63. Lewis was the reporter who had stayed overnight with Shirley on 6–7 March and had later written an article recounting how she had personally felt the bedclothes move, heard strange sounds, smelled a pleasant perfume that abruptly changed to a 'burning rubbery smell' and even felt the bed 'bounce up and down as though shaken by a giant hand'. Chibbett happened to be at No. 63 when Lewis arrived and he was able to speak to her.

'She confirmed everything which she had reported in the newspaper,' Chibbett wrote afterwards, 'which seems to absolve Shirley completely from any complicity in the phenomena. She [Lewis] referred especially to the scratching sounds she had heard, which she described as being "horrid". These I have not yet heard for myself, but they have been reported by several people.'

Chibbett also took the opportunity to ask Lewis about Kirsch and was told that the reporter had left the country. Lewis did not know when, or even if, he would be back.

Having failed to start her new job on 28 May, Shirley had been given a second chance. She was now scheduled to start on Monday 4 June. Unfortunately, Donald's attitude towards his 'Ireney' working had not changed.

At 6.30 on Monday morning, Donald tapped loudly to wake everybody. Wally later recorded, 'When the wife got up and came out to [the] kitchen and Shirley came out to [*sic*], Donald was up to his tricks in bedroom. He hid Shirley's best cloths [*sic*] and tipped the slop bucket over Shirley's under cloths [*sic*] which he put on [the] floor and the bucket he placed on top of wardrobe but still Shirley could not find her things so as she could get ready for work.' Donald also drew 'big crosses … with something black' (possibly the black lead again) in Wally and Kitty's bed and placed a face towel onto the electric stove. Luckily Shirley spotted the towel before it could catch fire.

As before, Shirley stayed at home instead of going to work. Donald continued to cause disruption throughout that week. On Friday, for example, the chairs in Ethel's room were found to have been knocked over, and the bedclothes thrown onto the floor. At around noon on Sunday, wrote Wally, 'Donald tied the kettle and pots to oven and to irony [*sic*] board.' 'I STOPPED YOU GOING WORK SO FAR,' Donald told Shirley at 4.40 p.m., following this with threatening messages such as: '[6.45 p.m.] I ANGRY – I PULL YOUR HAIR – HAVE YOU SEEN THOSE CHINESS [Chinese] FISHERMAN [sic] ALL ATMOIC ASH FELL ON THEM – ALL BURNT – SWOLLEN UP – THAT'S WHAT I CAN DO.'

That night, wrote Wally:

> Donald the polt was wild and when Shirley was in bed he started his games. Scratching was bad, and Shirley said to me Dad there's something hairy in my bed and when we looked there was bed stuffing and also her sheet ripped to sread [shreds]. I looked at her bed. It also was ripped. I change top one to the bottom and he also ripped that and the stuffing out of that and Shirley went to sleep in chair and Donald scratch[ed] on chair very hard. And then he through [threw] the sissor [scissors] at me while I was in my bed. [...] This is all over Shirley going to work ... which he is trying to stop.

The family later told Chibbett that the scratching sounds that night had been accompanied by what they described as 'rappings as though on metal'. Chibbett noted that the material found inside Shirley's bed was a mass of red flock roughly 6 inches (15 centimetres) in diameter and, when he examined her quilt, he found several small slits in the cover, seemingly made by a blade. Apparently the quilt's red flock interior had painstakingly been teased out through these slits.

Shirley refused to get back into her bed and after an uncomfortable night curled up in a wicker chair, she awoke on Monday morning (11 June) and started to get ready for work. 'Donald through [threw] two kettle [*sic*] at her,' wrote Wally. 'They were hot and a drop fell on Shirley and also he turn[ed] the back room upside down and also he took her money away from her that her mother gave her' (Wally later found the missing money inside a clock).

Kitty gave some replacement money to a friend of Shirley who was to accompany her on her journey. Soon after they left, Shirley telephoned home to report that she and her friend were lost and that her money had again vanished. 'As they headed back home,' recorded Wally, 'Shirley's friend was pushed nearly on the track and Shirley also at [Tottenham Court Road station].' When Shirley reached No. 63, Donald 'through [threw] a knife at Shirley' from the scullery into the kitchen. Wally found the blade stuck into the window frame.

Over the next few days Donald continued to make it clear that Shirley was not to go to work, repeatedly undoing Kitty's efforts to keep the 'front room' tidy. Before Kitty left to keep a hospital appointment on Wednesday (to receive treatment for her arthritis), Donald tapped out a chilling warning: 'I AM GOING TO THE HOSPITAL IN THE CAR WITH YOU KIT AND CAUSE IT TO TURN OVER'. Although he did not carry this out, Donald's threats were not taken lightly by the family; they remembered the fires. Shirley never did start her job at the bank.

The increase in violence was worrying, but Chibbett was growing ever more hopeful that Donald was genuinely the disembodied spirit of Louis, son of Louis XVI and Marie Antoinette. On 2 June he noted that recent messages conveyed 'an impression of a young boy, imperious in his demands on Shirley's time and attention…' Before long, though, Chibbett's optimism was severely dented.

Donald aka Louis was claiming: (1) to have been born in 1798; (2) to have drowned in the English Channel at the age of 15; (3) to have died before the French Revolution; (4) to have been the first-born son of the French king Louis XVI and Queen Marie Antoinette; and (5) to be entitled to call himself Louis XVII.

One major problem with these claims was that if Louis had really died before the French Revolution of 1789 then he could not have been born in 1798. Another problem now came to light. Eric Biddle, a friend of Chibbett, had been helping to look into the historical background of Donald's claims and what he was finding did not support the poltergeist's story. In a letter to Chibbett dated 11 June, Biddle noted three salient points his researches had thrown up: (1) King Louis XVI had had two sons; (2) the king's first-born son had died on 4 June 1789 at the age of 7, at Meudon in France after a long illness; and (3) the half-dozen or so books Biddle had consulted regarding the king's titular successor – Louis XVII – all 'seemed to agree that he [Louis XVII] died in prison […] His age was ten.'

'Though I can't remember just what the polt had to say on the subject,' concluded Biddle, 'what I have dug out does not, I think, tie up with his messages.' Indeed it did not. As well as the problem with the dates, it was clear that neither son had drowned in the English Channel. It was also clear that it had been the king's *second* son – not his first – who had become Louis XVII and so, whoever Donald aka Louis really was, he could not be both the king's first-born son *and* Louis XVII.

On 12 June Chibbett visited No. 63. He did not mention the holes appearing in Donald's story but a little before 7 p.m. Shirley spontaneously asked Donald to tell them again when he had been born. For some reason, the poltergeist now gave a different answer, tapping out, '1771 [or] 1772'. Asked when he died, the poltergeist now claimed, '1788 [or] 1789'.

This new year of birth would have been *almost* correct for someone who had died in 1789 aged 15, calculated Chibbett. (In fact, the year of birth was not correct for either of the king's sons but Chibbett was not aware of this yet.) There were still problems – for example, history recorded that neither son had lived to the age of 15 – but for now the new year the poltergeist was claiming for his death seemed 'near enough' to Chibbett. Yet why had Donald changed his story? Chibbett seems to have been oddly unconcerned by this. He was certain he had given no indication to either Donald or the Hitchings family that there were any problems with the poltergeist's story.

Had Shirley been carrying out her own historical research in the meantime and started to realise that Donald's dates did not fit together? Shirley is adamant this was not the case and that there was no easy way for her, as a relatively poorly educated teenager, to research historical information. Although at least one investigator who looked into this case at the same time as Chibbett remembered Shirley having a number of books concerning French history in her room Shirley denies that this was so. According to her, her parents were not great readers and the only books in No. 63 were a couple of children's storybooks and one or two junior encyclopaedias – basic reference works that did not contain much detail. Chibbett's contemporary notes back this up, stating that items of reading material 'in the Battersea house are few in number, and consist mainly of novels and magazines'. Moreover, argued Chibbett, Shirley was not a member of any library. As for the French words that occasionally appeared – with varying degrees of accuracy – in Donald's messages, Chibbett noted that 'Mr & Mrs H. are quite illiterate as regards foreign languages.' They also assured Chibbett that Shirley had not been taught any French at school (a detail confirmed in Shirley's school reports).

After questioning Shirley and Donald on 12 June, Chibbett was willing to accept that, despite the inconsistencies, the poltergeist's claims could still be essentially true. He even went so far as to describe the revised dates as 'the confirmation I was after.' Yet questions remained. Why had the poltergeist's story changed? How could 1798 have been mistaken for 1789? And Donald's troubling insistence that he was both the king's first-born son and the person known as Louis XVII would need to be addressed in due course.

For the time being, though, Chibbett decided to withhold judgement. He would simply continue his investigation – and wait to see where developments took him.

CHAPTER 14

On 20 June 1956 Shirley telephoned Chibbett to say that Donald had left a sealed envelope, addressed to the researcher, on the coffee table in the 'front room'. Previously reserved for important visitors, this room – the best in the house – was by now considered to be Donald's territory.

When Chibbett visited No. 63 that evening Shirley excitedly handed the envelope to him. Chibbett still had to wait for Wally to arrive home from work before he was allowed to open it – and even then the family obtained Donald's permission first. Inside was a newspaper cutting, referring to the case of a Battersea woman who had left her husband and young children. It had no apparent connection with events inside No. 63 but the envelope also contained a scrap of paper on which were the faintly pencilled words, 'I FORGIVE KIRSCH'. In the corner was a small, crude drawing of a fleur-de-lis. (Chibbett noted that it was similar to one Shirley herself had recently sketched.)

Then Shirley showed Chibbett another fleur-de-lis, this one marked on the shoulder of her 'Marie Antoinette' doll, saying that Donald had made the mark himself. A little later, everyone gathered in the kitchen. 'Shirley was standing by the fire-place,' reported Chibbett, 'and her parents were seated.' He continued:

All three were in full view ... when her mother exclaimed: 'What is that on your arm, Shirley?' On the upper part of her left arm was the imprint of a small, dark-blue fleur-de-lis. It ... looked as though it had been drawn or stamped with indelible ink. As far as I had noticed, Shirley had made no untoward movement to suggest that she had done it herself, although no doubt anyone versed in the art of illusion could have done it easily enough with a rubber stamp. However, I examined her closely to see whether there were any more impressions visible on her. There were none. I watched her movements closely thereafter, however, but a few moments later there was another similar impression – this time on the right side of her neck. I am reasonably certain that neither she nor her parents could have done this without my knowledge. Again I searched her immediate surroundings, but could find no trace of any rubber stamp or other instrument by which the impressions could have been made.

When Chibbett visited again one week later, he was informed that Donald had left another sealed envelope for him on the coffee table in 'his' (i.e. Donald's) room. Inside that room, noted Chibbett, 'Marie Antoinette was posed as though sitting on a throne, and the other dolls, purporting to be Lady Jane Grey, Anne Boleyn, etc., were placed round her in curtseying positions.' Shirley assured him that Donald had placed them so.

The new envelope contained a copy of a local weekly newspaper dated 4 May 1956. On page 9, Chibbett found some curious marks in blue ink that looked as though they might be some sort of writing. These were indecipherable at first, but when Chibbett turned the paper upside down and held it up to a mirror he saw that they read: 'OUT IN ONE MONHT – DON'T WORRY SHIRLEY [*sic*].'

Curiously, although the message was written in capital letters, Shirley's name appeared as if it were a signature, as if the message was *from* her rather than being addressed *to* her as everyone – including Chibbett – assumed. The signature did not match Shirley's own, however. The ink, meanwhile, was strangely smudged – possibly suggesting that the mirror-writing effect had been achieved by writing the message onto a surface using a fountain pen, then pressing the newspaper against this. In Chibbett's view, though, 'mirror writing' was 'a relatively common feature in written psychic communications' and, because the family was 'entirely unaware' of this, the message was further evidence that the paranormal was at work here.

As for the transposition of letters ('MONHT' instead of 'MONTH'), this was already a notable feature of Donald's messages. Chibbett referred to this peculiarity of the poltergeist's spelling as the 'reversal phenomenon'. Wondering whether Shirley's own spelling exhibited such reversals, he conducted some simple experiments, asking her to write out particular words for him. Afterwards he noted that 'Shirley ... does not make the same kind of errors.' (In fact, there is some evidence that Shirley did occasionally reverse letters, although by no means to the same extent as Donald did.) Chibbett also remarked that Shirley's handwriting was, to his eye, 'entirely dissimilar to that of "Donald"'. In his opinion, whatever was responsible for Donald's messages seemed to be entirely separate from Shirley.

Further messages increasingly included descriptions and incidental details of the life of 'Louis' in France at the close of the eighteenth century. 'Taking these messages together,' wrote Chibbett, 'one gets an oddly disturbing picture of a youth who might actually have experienced these things.' Chibbett referred to such details as 'the trivialities' and – although he acknowledged that they were far from being conclusive proof – he considered their cumulative effect to be suggestive evidence that the poltergeist truly was the spirit of the long-dead Louis.

These 'trivialities' carried much weight with Chibbett, especially in light of the seeming unlikelihood of Shirley obtaining such historical details from books. However, he apparently overlooked at least one possible source for the information.

This was a 1955 television series that was loosely based on Baroness Orczy's 'Scarlet Pimpernel' stories, about the daring English nobleman who rescued French aristocrats from the guillotine. Titled *The Adventures of the Scarlet Pimpernel*, this series originally aired on the ITV television channel in eighteen half-hour episodes between late 1955 and July 1956. This was during the very period that the 'Louis' personality was emerging. Shirley does not remember this series but Donald was evidently aware of it because on 27 July 1956 he would tap out a message asking Chibbett to 'GET ME MARIUS GORING'. Goring was the actor who played Sir Percy Blakeney, the starring role in this series.

On Saturday 7 July, Chibbett travelled to the Lake District for a fortnight's holiday with his wife. His next visit to No. 63 was scheduled for Friday 27 July but if he had hoped to forget about Donald until then he was out of luck. As he journeyed north Chibbett was wondering about a message Donald had tapped out on 28 June: 'CHIBBETT – HE GOING TO LAKE DISTRICT – BUT HIM NO SEE SAUSER [i.e. a flying saucer] – HE MIGTH HAVE A SURPIRSE THOUGTH'.

The Chibbetts stayed at a sheep farm near the small village of Torver, on the shores of Coniston Water in Cumbria. As they sat at breakfast one morning, Chibbett 'noticed something about the salt and pepper cellars. […] Each cellar had on it seven fleur-de-lis. When I saw these, it occurred to me immediately that this was perhaps the "surprise" to which Donald had referred.'

His hosts informed him that the cellars had been a wedding present and an inscription on the base of each showed that they had been manufactured in Jersey in the Channel Islands. Chibbett photographed the cellars and wrote to the Hitchings family to say he thought he had found Donald's 'surprise',

'I gave them *no further details*, but asked them to enquire of "Donald" whether his "surprise" was associated with a number; and if so, whether he could give further details.'

Donald did not reply, so when Chibbett visited No. 63 as arranged on 27 July he again asked the poltergeist to give a number associated with his 'surprise'. Donald tapped out, 'SEVEN.'

'How many objects are concerned in connection with that number?' asked Chibbett.

Two taps came in response.

'There were of course seven fleur-de-lis on each of the two cellars,' Chibbett wrote afterwards.

The researcher had brought along several of his holiday photographs:

> Of these, I selected three, one of which was a picture of the salt and pepper cellars, which had not been seen by the Hitchings, neither did they know the nature of the alleged 'surprise'. I shuffled the three snaps face downwards, so that I did not know the *order* in which they were. Neither, of course, did Shirley or her mother. I placed them, still face-downwards, under a copy of the T.V. Times. Then I asked Donald to indicate by raps which of the hidden three was the one relative to the 'surprise'. He tapped out '2'. I turned them up. The second snap was that of the cellars.

Next, Chibbett mentioned various locations from which the objects might have come and asked the poltergeist to indicate the correct one. Donald correctly selected Jersey. The researcher then asked whether Donald could persuade Shirley to draw him a picture of the objects shown in the photograph (which Shirley had still not seen). Donald 'would not, or could not, do this' but, as Shirley sat toying with her pencil, she glanced casually through the kitchen window and commented that she could discern the outline of a sword on the garden wall outside. Chibbett followed her gaze and 'sure

enough there was the faint resemblance of a hilted sword …
not so much drawn as outlined in paler brickwork against a
darker background.'

Did the image suggest anything to her, Chibbett asked. 'No,'
replied Shirley. Chibbett asked another question: had Donald
caused Shirley to receive a mental impression of a sword in
connection with the photographed objects? 'YES', came the
tapped response, followed by the phrase, 'THE ARM [*sic*] OF
MONACO'.

A few days afterwards Chibbett's friend Eric Biddle
managed to find a small illustration of Monaco's coat-of-arms
in an encyclopaedia. Corresponding by letter and relying on
the written word to describe this illustration, the two men
were initially excited by the possibility that this coat-of-arms
would resemble the crossed swords and fleur-de-lis design
that Donald had drawn on the 'front room' wall on 3 June.
It gradually became apparent, though, that any similarities
were only very general, and there was really little resemblance
between the two images. Much of what Donald had done that
evening impressed Chibbett, but the reference to Monaco was
– and would remain – baffling.

While Chibbett had been preparing for, and then enjoying,
his holiday, Donald had continued trying to persuade the
Hitchings family of his 'true' identity. 'I AM THE DOLFAN
[dauphin] OF FRANCE,' he tapped on the evening of 5 July.
'TELL CHIBB – I AM THE SON OF LOUIS OF FRANCE
– SOME TIME I WEAR A BLACK CAPE ON RIGHT SHOUL-
DER – THE CRUSADER'S CROSS – WEE – TELL CHIB – I AM
FRENCH […] I BELONG IN FRANCE – IT HAS CHANGE[d].'

On Monday morning (9 July) Shirley received a message
from Donald that was tapped out entirely in French. The brack-
eted guesses in what follows were added by Chibbett: 'JE ME

(? RAPPELLE LA) REINE ANTOINETTE – ET LE ROI A TOUS
DEUX – ET COMME MOI – J'AI (? ETE) LOUIS XVI – VOUS
ETIEZ A PARIS – BONJOUR JACQUES – VOUS VOYEZ
NOTRE STRATAGEME – CHARLOTTE CORDAY – MEUBLES
DU TEMPS DE LOUIS XIII – QUEL HOMME ETANT LE PLUS
FEROCE IL ES (EST) LE PLUS PUISSANT – JE ME RAPPELLE
ENCORE LOEUR (LEUR) COSTUME A TOUS DEUX'.

The French was far from perfect but with effort – and
some inspiration – Chibbett translated this message as,
'I (remember) Queen Antoinette and the King, both of them,
and (they were) like myself – I (was) Louis XVII – you were in
Paris – Good day, James – You see our stratagem – Charlotte
Corday – furniture of the time of Louis XIII – What a man
(!) being the most ferocious he is the most powerful – I still
remember the costume of both of them.'

(Charlotte Corday was the young woman who in 1793
stabbed to death Jean-Paul Marat – one of those responsible
for the French 'Reign of Terror' – as he sat in his bathtub.)

In his notes, Chibbett commented, 'This is extraordinarily
interesting – good French with only two trifling orthographical
errors. But it seems as though the sentences have been jumbled.'
Were the problems writing in French the result of some
supernatural method of transmission from the other side, or
did they instead betray the communicator's lack of familiarity
with that language? Sceptics might even wonder whether the
foreign words and phrases had been cobbled together from
sources such as French phrase books. Chibbett appears not to
have considered such a cynical option and, when he sent details
of the French message to Biddle, his friend was also impressed.
Had Donald continued to communicate in French it might have
become powerful evidence for his really being a French spirit.
Unfortunately, this type of message was to be rare.

Shirley spent much of the following afternoon playing in the
'front room' with dolls, including two dressed (in accordance
with Donald's instructions) as Louis XVI and Marie Antoinette.

At 4.30 p.m., Donald tapped out a message to her, announcing that he had altered the Louis doll's position: 'I PUT LOUIS CRYING BECAUSE MAIRE IS DYING – I AM ONLY PLAYING RENEE – I LIKE TO PLAY WIHT DOLLS OF MY OWN'.

An interesting feature of this message was the use of the somewhat French-sounding name 'Renee'. The poltergeist had called Shirley this at least once before (on 16 April), and had also referred to her as 'Ireney', after Shirley's middle name, Irene. As the Louis personality grew ever more prominent, the poltergeist increasingly called Shirley 'Renee'. When asked why (in April 1957) he simply replied, 'IT IS FRENCH AND I LIKE IT'. It is probably no more than coincidence that the name Renee happens to mean 'reborn' or 'born again'.

At 9.30 a.m. on Monday 30 July, Donald ordered Shirley to leave the house and not return until 11 because he wanted to have a conference with his 'statesmen' who, presumably, were also spirits. Kitty was already out (she had an appointment at the hospital) so when Shirley left to visit one of the neighbours she temporarily left No. 63 empty for Donald and his visitors. When she and her mother returned home later they found that the chairs in one room (possibly the upstairs kitchen) had been moved and arranged in a circle. Some of the house's few books (including the Bible) had been placed on the chairs, material had been draped over the room's mirrors, and the air was heavy with tobacco smoke. It was possible, commented Chibbett afterwards, that Shirley could have arranged everything in this way to be discovered later but 'the second episode is not so easy to explain away'.

At 10.15 p.m. Donald tapped that he was to hold another conference, this time in Ethel's old room. Before Wally went to bed he inspected his mother's empty room and found everything in order. Yet, recorded Chibbett, 'next morning the furniture had been rearranged ... and extra chairs added. If Shirley had been responsible for this, she would have had to get up during the night without disturbing her parents – remember, she is sleeping in the same bedroom [as them] – go upstairs, move heavy furniture about, and carry other chairs up the stairs from the rooms below. All this in the middle of the night without disturbing her parents, who are by now light sleepers anyway.'

In Chibbett's opinion, 'After some six months' study of her, Shirley seems to me to be ... incapable of the prolonged duplicity and skill which would be necessary' for her to be perpetrating a hoax. 'The alternatives left are either that Shirley is a schizophrenic, and does all these things unconsciously and with great cunning; or that genuine supernormal agencies are at work. At present, it seems to be a matter of taking one's choice. It is unproven either way.'

CHAPTER 15

On arriving home from work on Monday, July 9th, I heard a series of taps – three in each case. I looked down in the basement, but there was nothing or no one to cause it. The same thing happened on Tuesday 10th and again on Wednesday 11th. On asking 'Donald' if it was him, the answer was 'YES'.

Chibbett was given the above unsolicited statement on 15 July 1956. It came from the same gentleman (a friend of Mark) who had earlier signed another statement testifying that he had heard Donald tapping in mid-March. Both statements related to sounds heard in this gentleman's own home, without Shirley being present.

A few weeks later a friend of Shirley named Doreen, who lived a few houses away in Wycliffe Road, gave a statement of her own. This concerned incidents that had occurred on Thursday 2 and Friday 3 August. Corrected for excusable childish errors, her statement ran as follows:

Thursday 2 August, 1 – 10 o'clock [p.m.]
At one [p.m.] I came in to have a game with Shirley in her back room. I was playing on Shirley's divan. I made the bed nicely and as soon as I got in the bed Donald untucked it. I made it again

and got in. We felt something slimy and sticky in the bed. Shirley and I looked inside the bed and we saw some Kleeneze polish. We wiped it off and got in bed. I sat up to get comfortable and I felt something soft fall on my head. It was polish. I then lay down to have a game then suddenly I put my foot in something wet and sticky. It was the tin of polish. We then packed up to go out to see the television. After[wards] we made up [put on make-up] and went in the back room to put [on] a pair of tap shoes. I sat on the bed and I felt something hard. I took off the covers and there were two blue plastic egg cups, and a scent bottle in [the] shape of candlesticks, and I heard Donald tapping and I knew he was laughing.

Friday 3 August, 10.15 [a.m.]

I came in again to play with Shirley. We went in the back room to have a game but we didn't start playing because Mrs Hitchings came in. About 2 o'clock [p.m.] we had a game and Pamela [another friend] came in to have a game. We got in the divan and I pretended to cry and Donald started tapping. I stopped and Donald stopped. I started again and somebody pinched me. I thought it was Shirley but it was Donald.

Around the end of July, Chibbett's friend Eric Biddle asked whether Donald, when writing the numeral '7', added a continental-style horizontal stroke as might be expected of a Frenchman. Chibbett did not know, so he asked Wally to ask Donald to write '7' for him. Donald threw himself into the task. On 11 August, a piece of paper was found on which were written the Roman numerals VII, seven stylised fleur-de-lis symbols, and an Arabic numeral '7'. The '7' was not crossed.

Despite this 'failure', Donald had become so comfortable with his Louis persona that around now he commanded Chibbett to write to the French President (René Coty) to announce that Louis XVII of France had returned! An amused Chibbett declined to do so, sensing that his letter would not be well received. Undeterred, the poltergeist also took it upon himself to grant Shirley a royal title. The following messages were tapped out on Sunday 12 August.

'[9.30 a.m.] RENEE – I WANT YOU TO BE MY PRINCESS – AND YOU LOOK LIKE ANNE.'

(Note: back on 20 April, Donald had mentioned having had a sister named Anne, as well as a brother named 'Phelp' or Philip.)

'[9.45 a.m.] RENEE – IF YOU ARE GOING TO BE MY LIVING PRINCESS – YOU MUST HAVE A TITTLE – LET ME THINK.'

'[10 a.m.] IT WILL BE: HER ROYAL HIGHNESS PRICNESS RENEE DE PARIS – RENEE DE FRANCE – MAIRE ANN DE SECOND DE COURT DE LOUIS.'

At 11 a.m. on Monday 13 August, Princess Renee de Paris took down another tapped message: 'I WANT A PEN THAT YOU PUT BLACK WATTER IN AND IT WRITES – NOT A QILL [quill] PEN – I WANT ONE LIKE RENEE [has] GOT – I CAN KEEP MY OWN DIARY LIKE I DID – I WANT A MRS DALES DIRAY […].'

Wally supplied the poltergeist with a fountain pen and a diary. This marked the beginning of a shift in the way the poltergeist communicated. For the time being, Donald continued to deliver many of his messages by tapping but this laborious method would gradually be superseded as Donald experimented with handwriting.

On 14 August Chibbett received another letter from Eric Biddle, reminding him of a major problem with Donald's story. Donald was currently claiming: (1) to be Louis XVII; (2) to be the eldest son of Louis XVI; (3) to have been born in 1771 or 1772; and (4) to have died in 1788 or 1789. Using the limited resources at his local library, Biddle had learned

that Louis XVII – whose name had actually been Louis-Charles – had been the king's *second*-born son; that he had been born in 1785 and that he had still been alive as late as 1795. 'Donald's story won't hold water at all,' concluded Biddle.

Chibbett had started to believe Donald's claims, but now Biddle's logic gave him a metaphorical slap in the face. Carefully considering the increasingly confusing situation, Chibbett decided that the problems with Donald's story could be broken down into a few general issues.

First, what exactly had Donald said regarding his identity? When Chibbett examined his records closely he discovered that the original report that Donald had claimed to be 'LOUIE SEVENTEENTH SON OF LOUIE THE SIX-TEENTH' had come from Shirley and her friend Marge. Had the girls made a mistake when they later spoke about what Donald had told them? Might their mistake have sowed some of the subsequent confusion? Chibbett looked at another of Donald's messages, dated 22 May, in which the poltergeist had stated, 'I – LOUIS – KILLED BEFORE REVOLUTION' and he reasoned, 'If "Donald" alias one of the sons of Louis XVI died *before* the Revolution (1789) he could not have been the second son – Louis-Charles of France [later Louis XVII] – since the latter was certainly alive as at 1795 [... Our] "Donald" – if he *is* one of the sons of Louis XVI – must be the *first* or elder son, whose Christian name we do not yet know.'

The second issue concerned dates. Donald had originally claimed (on 30 March) to have been born in 1798 and to have died aged 15, which would have been *c.* 1813. However, in June Biddle's research had revealed that Louis XVI's first-born son died in 1789. When subsequently questioned by Chibbett, Donald replied that he had really been born in 1771 or 1772 and had died in 1789 or 1788, but why had he changed the dates? Had Shirley realised they were wrong and altered them? Now Chibbett had a brainwave. If the strange 'reversal phenomenon' could manifest in Donald's words, transposing letters and thereby confusing the intended meanings, might it not also manifest in *numbers*? 'Could 1789 have been intended [in the original message, instead of 1798]? Could "born" have been "died"?' Yet even this act of mental contortion left a problem. If the king's first-born son had been 15 years old when he drowned in the English Channel in 1789 then 1771/1772 would have been about right for his year of birth. Unfortunately, Biddle's research showed that this son had been 7 years old when he died. If the history books were correct, this seemed irreconcilable.

There was a third issue, too. On 20 April, Donald had referred to a brother by the name of 'Phelp', 'Philp' or 'Pfelp', presumably intended to be 'Philippe'. According to the poltergeist, his brother had been 12 when he drowned alongside 15-year-old Donald/Louis – but this would mean that Philippe had been his younger brother, whereas Biddle's research had showed that the younger of the king's sons (the future Louis XVII) had been named Louis-Charles, not Philippe. 'Is it possible,' wondered Chibbett, 'that there was yet another son of Louis XVI – a *third* son – whose name was [Philippe]? [...] It seems to me that what we want to establish now is the eldest son's Christian name, and also where [Philippe] comes into the picture.'

Chibbett began to formulate a plan to do just that.

By mid-August, Shirley had moved her bed from the cramped bedroom she had shared with her parents into the 'front room', which was now considered Donald's territory. At 4 p.m. on Wednesday 15 August, Donald asked for her help to decorate their room:

SHIRLEY – CAN YOU MAKE A SEEN [scene] ON YOU [YOUR]
BED WIHT MY HELP OF ME TO MAKE A ROYAL SEEN ON
YOU BED – YOU WILL – YOU CAN HELP ME – WEE – BUT US
TO [two] WON'T LET WALTER SEE IT TILL US TO ARE DONE
– PUT THE TWO BLUE CURTAINS UP WIHT ROSETES [rosettes]
ON THE [them] TO [too] – THE PINS ARE ON THE TABLE –
I HELP YOU PUT IT UP – COME ON – I WANT YOU TO GO OUT
OF THE ROOM ONE MINUIT – I TELL – WEE – COME BACK.

When Chibbett visited No. 63 the next day Shirley could barely contain her excitement. She told the researcher that she had left the room as Donald requested and when she returned a short while later a new design had appeared on the wall. Apparently drawn – like the previous designs – using black lead, it depicted a large fleur-de-lis surmounting a shield on which seven small fleurs-de-lis were arranged. A pair of crossed swords was superimposed and to either side was a small Tudor rose-like design. Around the drawing, blue cloth had been 'pinned up like drop-curtains at a theatre' (Chibbett's description). Shirley claimed that this cloth had flown across the room as she walked in, pinning itself to the wall.

Although the new drawing resembled that which had appeared at the beginning of June, closer inspection revealed that the swords here pointed downwards, as opposed to upwards as in the earlier design. Chibbett also noticed that the earlier drawing had been 'gone over again so as to make it plainer, and a hilt [had been] added to the sword on the left.'

The 'royal scene' was interesting but Chibbett wanted to pin down the poltergeist on the discrepancies in his story. He reported:

'Donald' was quiet most of the evening, but just before I was due to leave – about 9.30 p.m. – he turned up. I explained the difficulty we were in as regards his identity, and by question and answer elicited the following details:

Q: Did Louis XVI have three sons?

ANS: 'NO – TWO.'

Q: We know that one of the sons … was Louis-Charles. If your story is true, then you must have been Louis-(something). What was your name?

'Donald' would not reply.

Q: Very well, then. You say that you and your brother were drowned in the Channel. Was your brother's name Philip?

ANS: 'NO!'

Q: Then how did we get the name: Philip? Was it your name, by any chance?

ANS: 'YES.'

Q: Then if Louis XVI only had two sons, and one was Louis-Charles, that only leaves you – Philip. Who then was your companion?

ANS: 'JON PIERRE – WHIPPING BOY.'

(Looking up this expression later, Chibbett learned that a 'whipping boy' would have been a boy kept to be whipped in place of the dauphin when the dauphin deserved punishment.)

Chibbett continued to interrogate Donald, listening intently as the poltergeist's tapped replies slowly emerged, letter by letter:

Q: You say that you – Philip (or Philippe) – were drowned in the Channel at the age of fifteen; but according to our historical information the elder son (i.e. you) died at a place called Meudon, at the age of seven. How do you account for this?

But 'Donald' insisted that his story was correct.

Q: Do you mean to say that the history books have got it all wrong?

ANS: 'YES.'

'And so,' concluded a none-the-wiser Chibbett, 'the matter rests at present.'

❖

On 21 August, the poltergeist gave the most detailed description yet of what he had looked like in life:

> I AM FIVE FEET TALL – FAIR OR BRUN [brown] HAIR – I AM NOT FAT – I AM THIN – I WARE BLACK BUCKEL SHOES – PINK HOSES – I [have] GOT BLACK [k]NEE BRICHES [breeches] AND A SHIRT – A CRAVAT – A LONG WAISTCOAT – THEN A COURT COAT ON TOP – THAT IS WHAT I WEAR NOW BUT WHEN I JUST IN MY OWN COURT – AND MY BROHTER – WE WEAR OUR OWN INFALMAL [informal] CLOHTES.

He had also worn a sword occasionally and two days later he apparently produced a part of its decorative hilt. Chibbett and Wally were chatting in the kitchen when Shirley brought in a small parcel she had just found on the passageway floor. 'Inside,' wrote Chibbett, 'was some tissue paper enclosing cotton wool. In the latter was a small metal crown, gold in colour with a screw attachment at the bottom. It was heavy for such a small object. The base surround of the crown was inset with what appeared to be tiny jewels – perhaps ruby, emerald and diamond. Above them were minute representations of seven fleur-de-lis, arranged at equal intervals round the crown.'

When Chibbett asked what the object was, Donald replied, 'IT IS OUT OF A SWORD OF FRANCE – IT IS MINE – OFF A HILT OF A SWORD – IT IS MINE'. Chibbett asked permission to take the crown away with him to be examined but was emphatically told 'NO'. Reluctantly, he handed it back to Wally, who re-wrapped it in the cotton wool and tissue paper, put it back into the box and replaced the package in the passageway.

'A few minutes later,' Chibbett recorded, 'the parcel was picked up and re-examined, but the crown had vanished. Shirley was under constant observation the whole time.'

CHAPTER 16

Most of Donald's messages still came via his all-too familiar tapping. More and more, however, he was now communicating in writing as well. Nobody ever caught him in the act; his written messages would simply be discovered on scraps of paper, sometimes on walls, or (fairly frequently now) inside Donald's diary, where, wrote Chibbett, 'Long straggling characters sprawled across pages were barely decipherable as words.'

The family believed that Donald physically wrote the messages himself. That is to say, they did not believe that the poltergeist temporarily took control of Shirley's body and wrote using her hands. Certainly in Chibbett's opinion the examples of handwriting attributed to Donald 'do not resemble Shirley's or anyone else's writing in any way.' Although Donald's diary has since been lost some of the tracings made by Chibbett (almost certainly from this book) survive and a few of these are reproduced here as illustrations.

Aspiring to even greater literary heights, Donald announced on 21 August 1956 that he wanted a typewriter and had seen one for sale nearby. He was 'still on about his type writer' the next day, wrote Wally, but Mr Hitchings successfully ignored these requests long enough for Donald's attention to wander onto other matters.

On or around 25 August, Donald delivered what Chibbett considered to be the poltergeist's first 'proper' written message. 'It was written in a kind of pidgin-French and read, "Comme maure vous, oui?" It is not clear what "maure" means, unless it is meant to be "comment".'

These written messages still displayed Donald's characteristic poor spelling and 'reversals', but Chibbett noticed that the handwriting style was changing. Early examples had typically been printed in large letters but as the written messages became more frequent from the end of August the characters took on a more rounded shape. It was as if the poltergeist were improving with practise.

In an article dated 31 August, the local *Clapham Observer* newspaper commented that several months after being 'a minor national sensation, Shirley's poltergeist is settling down to a humdrum suburban routine.' The newspaper reported Donald's insistence that his name was really Louis and that he was the son of Louis XVI, and noted with amusement the family's revelation that their resident poltergeist enjoyed watching television with them, particularly *The Adventures of Robin Hood*. The article was illustrated with a cartoon of a crowned spook watching Robin Hood on television.

'He was becoming quite well-behaved,' Shirley was quoted as saying. 'That is until Monday.'

On Monday 27 August Shirley was alone in the house when she heard eerie moaning sounds coming from beneath Wally's bed. Frightened, she took refuge in the kitchen. At 9.30 that night Donald tapped, 'MOANING JIM IS IN THE BED ROOM – DO YOU KNOW FIRE THE NAN ROOM'.

Just under an hour later the moaning was back and this time Wally heard it too. It lasted for over an hour and Wally thought it was saying 'Oh, Ethel, Ethel.' Afterwards, Donald claimed it had been a new ghostly visitor to No. 63, who had been asking for Ethel (who was still living elsewhere).

In general, however, life was relatively peaceful at this time. Shirley was still unemployed and spent most days playing with her dolls, dressing them in accordance with Donald's wishes. On 6 September, Donald tapped, 'TODAY LETS PLAY THAT YOUR DOLL TINA IS GETTING MARRIED – SHE SHALL HAVE A ROYAL WEDDING' and he instructed Shirley on the 'DREAM DRESS' she was to make.

It does seem odd that a young boy would be interested in such a scenario. Moreover, it is interesting to note that romantic images of 'fairytale' royal weddings must have permeated many a teenage *girl's* mind in 1956. The young Queen Elizabeth II's spectacular coronation ceremony of June 1953 was still a recent memory and, in April 1956, the beautiful American actress Grace Kelly had married Prince Rainer III and become Princess Grace of Monaco. Perhaps somewhere amid the strangeness underlying events in Battersea there was a link here with the seemingly meaningless statement Donald had made regarding the 'Arms of Monaco' in relation to the fleur-de-lis drawing on the front room wall. If so, it was a link nobody explored.

By mid-September all still seemed quiet – but something was moving beneath the surface. First there had been 'Moaning Jim'; now it seemed that 'Shagy Roots' had returned. A message from Donald on Friday 14 September read, 'I STILL WANT KERCH RENA – WEE I DO – AND HAVE YOU GOT MY BOX MATCH AND DO YOU KNOW THAT SHAGY ROOTS HAS TAKEN ALL MY MATCHES?'

A message tapped out at 9.45 on Saturday morning appeared to be from Shagy Roots: 'I GOING TO SET FIRE TO YOUR BED – I WARN I BURN YOU UP AND TELL THAT DONALD HE WILL GO TO – I GOT MATCHES'.

Later that day, Shirley and her friend Doreen removed a burning tea towel from the top of the cooker. At 9 p.m. that night, Donald tapped out another warning. Now it was not only Shagy Roots he was worried about but also the increasing political tensions in the Middle East: 'I KNOW HE FIRE […] AND OLD NAZZA NEWS HE GOING TO DROP A BOMB – BUT DONT PANIC – LAY DOWN FACE ON FLOOR'.

'Nazza' was a reference to Egypt's President Nasser. In July Nasser had nationalised the Suez Canal, a strategically vital maritime link between the Mediterranean Sea and the Red Sea. The Canal had previously been controlled by British and French interests, and there was mounting international concern that military conflict between Britain and Egypt was coming. By 'bomb', Donald almost certainly meant an atomic bomb – the fear of atomic annihilation was a pervasive public fear at the time.

On Monday, Shagy Roots again threatened to start a fire. On Tuesday, Donald announced that he was going 'TO HAVE A MEETING […] FOR SHAGY ROOT'S DISMISSAL OUT OF THE HOUSE'. The meeting seemed to be successful because Shagy Roots was silent afterwards – at least for a while.

On Sunday 23 September Donald mentioned 'Jeremy' for the first time: 'DO YOU LIKE JEREMY? – HE IS SWEET – I LIKE HIM TO MEET RENEE.' 'Jeremy' turned out to be the handsome 19-year-old television and film actor Jeremy Spenser, who was then filming at Pinewood Studios (approximately 20 miles west of London), making *The Prince and the Showgirl* with Marilyn Monroe and Laurence Olivier.

Donald referred to Jeremy again two days later: 'RENEE – I WANT JEREMY SPENCER'S [*sic*] PICTURE – AT LAST I HAVE FOUND SOMEONE LIKE MYSELF WHO – IN SOME WAY – HIS HAIR DARK – EYES BROWN – MINE BLUE – AND

COMPLEXION TAN – MINE FAIR'. On Friday 28 September, Donald told Shirley that Spenser was his favourite film star.

When Chibbett visited No. 63 that Friday evening, he discovered that Donald had elaborated the drawings on the walls of the once-immaculate 'front room'. His 'royal scene' of 15 August now sported a third rose and more fleurs-de-lis designs, and it was now flanked left and right by large flags that were obviously intended to represent those of the United Kingdom and France.

The large fleur-de-lis with crossed swords drawing that had appeared at the beginning of June had also been embellished. What seemed to be two large shields had appeared, one to the left of the original drawing, bearing two fleurs-de-lis and some further indeterminate shapes, and one to the right, bearing seven fleurs-de-lis. The words 'ROI LOUIS' ('King Louis') had also been added in large curling letters.

Chibbett had brought three friends along with him that evening. One was Eric Biddle. The others were an American, Ken Kellar, and Kellar's wife, Marianne Francis, both of whom were deeply interested in psychical research. (Also interested in flying saucers, the couple were becoming closely involved with the 'contactee' movement, working towards – and they believed succeeding in – contacting intelligent space beings.) Chibbett left early and after he had gone the remaining visitors conducted a séance. As they pushed an upturned glass around a ring of cards bearing the letters of the alphabet, Donald tapped out a message. He implored them to contact Jeremy Spenser, saying they must warn the young actor that he would be involved in a car accident the following Tuesday.

Throughout the rest of that night and weekend Donald repeatedly urged that Spenser be warned. The morning before the predicted accident, he begged: 'PLEASE TELL MAIRE ANNE [*sic*: Marianne Francis] TO HELP JEREMY SPENSER – PLEASE I IMPLORE – YOU HAVE EXCAKLY

TWENTY TWO HOURS – PLASE [please] – YOU WOULD
NOT WANT HIM TO DIE – I TOLD YOU SATAUDAY WHERE
HE IS – WEE – HELP.'

The séance had left a deep impression on Kellar and
Francis. Later that Monday, they telephoned the Hitchings
family to say they were going to contact Pinewood Studios.
They promised to pass on Donald's warning – but Donald
continued to fret.

CHAPTER 17

On Tuesday 2 October 1956, Wally telephoned Chibbett to say that a strange mark had appeared on Shirley's face the day before, amid the worry over Jeremy Spenser's predicted accident. It was a pale pink line about $1/8$ of an inch wide, stretching from the top of her forehead towards her right eye, and it appeared to lie underneath her skin. It was still there at bedtime.

Tuesday wore on with no news reports about an accident. At 7 p.m. Donald tapped, 'I WANT JEREMY – PLEASE – URGENT'. He repeated this request on Wednesday afternoon. There had still been no news of any accident.

Chibbett was eager to see the mark on Shirley's forehead for himself, wondering whether it might resemble stigmata (mysterious bodily marks corresponding to Christ's Crucifixion wounds, believed by some to be of divine origin). Unfortunately, it had completely disappeared by the time he arrived on Wednesday evening.

The house was fuller than it had recently been. Kitty had just returned after a brief stay in hospital. Her arthritis had been particularly painful recently and her left arm was practically paralysed. Her left leg, too, was in a bad way and heavily bandaged. Wally and Shirley were present and so was Shirley's friend Doreen. After a short while, Ethel (also crippled by arthritis) slowly made her way downstairs to watch television: the old woman had decided that the disturbances had finally calmed down enough for her to return home.

Donald seemed unusually subdued that evening and it was Chibbett who eventually broached the subject of the unfulfilled prediction. The poltergeist insisted that the accident would still happen.

Shirley and Doreen left to play in the 'front room' and Chibbett settled in to watch TV with the adults. Soon the two girls rushed back. Donald had returned, they said, and he wanted Chibbett to 'take part in a "glass" session'.

Of late, the poltergeist's tapping noises had been weaker than before. This perhaps explained why he wanted to use the glass that evening, but the messages he slowly spelled out in the brightly lit room were in Chibbett's opinion 'of little significance'. The researcher suggested Donald try tapping but nothing happened. Chibbett walked to the door, opened it to allow the passageway light to shine in, and switched out the light in the room itself.

'Shirley and Doreen were still at the table,' he recorded, 'with their hands on its surface and fingertips touching. Gradually I decreased the amount of light coming from the hall, and as I did so, Shirley exclaimed excitedly that one of her hands was being drawn upwards towards her face, although I could see nothing. As she broke digital contact with Doreen, the latter screamed once, and buried her face in her hands. At first I thought she was larking about, as they do, and then Shirley said, "Look – she is crying!" Sure enough, when she raised her head, tears were welling from her eyes.'

Doreen claimed she had received 'something like an electric shock'. Chibbett immediately called a halt to the session, taking the girls back into the kitchen. Wally and Kitty listened to their news but by now it took more than this to faze them. Ethel, however, 'exploded into violent and highly decorative denunciation' of Shirley's parents, decrying the whole matter as 'bosh and rubbish' and threatening to write to the newspapers to expose the situation as a sham. In Chibbett's view, she was 'obviously a prejudiced and very frightened old woman, who like many others dismiss the haunting as fraudulent because they dare not admit the likelihood of its reality.'

That evening Chibbett realised just how poor relationships between Shirley and her grandmother had become. 'There is little love lost between [Ethel] and Shirley,' he noted after his visit, 'judging from the looks they exchange …'

Donald was still convinced Spenser was in 'MALTAL [mortal] DANGER'. As Shirley played on the morning of Monday 8 October Donald marked one of their doll's faces (probably in pen) to show what the actor would look like after the accident. By evening, the line on Shirley's forehead had reappeared. Less clearly defined facial marks also appeared on her cheeks: that on her right cheek resembled a numeral seven while that on her left looked rather like an inverted seven. As before, they appeared to be under her skin. Whether or not Shirley's markings resembled those on the doll was not recorded.

To Chibbett's frustration he was unable to make the long bus journey to Battersea to see the marks at first hand, but he promised Shirley by telephone he would visit on Wednesday. In the meantime, Donald continued to worry about Spenser and Shirley's marks, rather than fade, grew even more visible.

At 1.30 on Wednesday afternoon Donald told Shirley to look on her parents' bed for a present he had fetched from Pinewood Studios. He had apparently paid the studio a visit to watch the 'WONDERFULL' Spenser. 'We looked on our bed,' wrote Wally, 'and found a photo of a boy actor with marks [drawn] on his hands and face.' The picture was not of Jeremy

Spenser, however, but of another young, handsome male film star, James Dean, who had been killed in a car crash just over one year before. It had obviously been cut from a magazine and was, according to Chibbett who examined it later, 'tastefully mounted on a celluloid base'.

When Chibbett arrived at No. 63 that evening Shirley's marks were still clearly visible despite numerous attempts to wash them off. Although he could not quite work out how everything joined together, Chibbett felt sure that the marks were somehow connected with Donald's newly developed infatuation with Jeremy Spenser. The coincidence between Donald's concern over Spenser's predicted car accident and the manner of Dean's death was intriguing. Chibbett also noted that the ink markings on the picture of Dean were 'similar to those on Shirley's face'.

Donald still seemed to be having trouble tapping and, when Chibbett attempted to 'talk' with him that evening, it was difficult to hear the poltergeist's responses. However, just after Chibbett left for home, Donald recovered enough strength to tap out what Chibbett (after he had been told about it) described as a 'veritable wail of despair': 'I THINK CHIB WON'T COME ANY MORE – BUT I MUST HAVE SOMEONE TO HELP ME WITH JEREMY!'

'It is odd,' remarked Chibbett, 'but for some time past I have been thinking of curtailing my visits to No. 63, not because of lack of interest but because of the time involved […] Is this another instance of "Donald's" mindreading abilities?'

Since Ethel's return the formidable old woman had grown increasingly dismayed at just how much day-to-day life at No. 63 now revolved around Donald. Mark had recently returned to the house too and now someone else reappeared as well: Shagy Roots. Chibbett could not shake the feeling that the latter's reappearance was in some way a result of Ethel's homecoming and the rising tensions between the elderly woman and Shirley.

At 11 p.m. on 11 October, Donald complained that he had been unable to watch *The Adventures of Robin Hood* that day because Shagy Roots had learned that Ethel was back. There would be trouble tonight, he tapped: 'PLEASE STOP HIM RENEE – YOU KNOW SHE [Ethel] HAS GOT A BAD LEG – BUT SHE IS OLD – HE GETS HIS POWER FROM HER – I KNOW SHE IS MOUHTY [*sic*: mouthy] AT TIMES – BUT DAMED [damned] IF I LET ANYONE HURT HER'.

A few minutes later he warned, 'SHAGGY ROOTS IS BUILDING A FIRE UP IN THE ATTIC'.

Over the next few days Donald delivered further warnings of an imminent attack, along with a reminder that he had not forgotten that Jeremy Spenser needed his help. On Sunday 14 October, Donald told Shirley, 'ALLWAYS KEEP HIS PICTURE BY YOU – NEVER LET IT OUT OF YOUR SIGHT'. This referred to a photograph of Spenser that Donald had recently cut out of a magazine, stuck onto cardboard and hung above Shirley's bed in the 'front room'.

Monday 15 October saw the return of yet another familiar name. That morning, Shirley telephoned Chibbett to say that Michael Kirsch had just paid an unexpected visit to No. 63. Donald had never completely forgotten about Kirsch but surprisingly, given his past insistence that the sceptical reporter be summoned to see him, the poltergeist remained silent during Kirsch's visit.

Chibbett felt it was time he made the acquaintance of the journalist who had so gotten under Donald's metaphorical skin. It took several days to get through but at last Chibbett managed to speak to Kirsch by telephone at the newspaper office. It swiftly became clear that the two men were not going to get along. 'He asked me what I thought of the "Donald" business,' recorded Chibbett:

I countered by saying that I knew he thought that the raps were produced by Shirley's toes. He replied that he still thought so; that Shirley was obviously a very clever girl deliberately deceiving her parents, or else they were all in on the hoax. I said that in my opinion it was immaterial whether the raps were caused by Shirley or otherwise; from my point of view the messages were the important things and worthy of investigation. I said that in my view the Hitchings were quite innocent of any intrigue, and that there was definitely an influence at work in the house of a supernormal nature. Kirsch then added that it was odd that Shirley was the only one who ever saw things happening. When I suggested that this was untrue, and that I myself had witnessed stigmata, heard loud noises, and observed other signs of undoubtedly psychic origin, he pooh-pood [*sic*] the whole of these, and hinted that it threw doubts on my own integrity and sanity. I rang off feeling that with this type of mentality I was getting nowhere.

Kirsch's attitude irritated Chibbett, but Donald insisted there were more important matters to worry about. Namely, the danger to Jeremy Spenser and the threat posed by Shagy Roots. The poltergeist hinted that Shagy Roots was hiding in the attic and when Mark returned from work he and Wally climbed up to take a look. They were unnerved to discover that in the attic were matches, a candle and a lamp containing paraffin.

Donald's claims to be the spirit of Louis had been pushed into the background for some three weeks now, overshadowed by the fuss over Spenser and Shagy Roots, but on 17 October there was a reminder of his alleged past life when he tapped out the following to Shirley:

[2 p.m.] I WANT A SWEET – DO YOU? – IF I WAS IN FRANCE I WOULD HAVE A DRAGEES – IT ARMOND [almond] IN SUGAR – THEY COST ABOUT TWO SOUS – IF I GO TO FRANCE AGAIN I GO TO TWENTY EIGHT RUE DU BAAL PAIRS [Paris] AND GET YOU ONE – I WAS GIVEN A BOX OF DRAGEES WHEN I WAS BAPTISTED [baptised] – I OFFEN WENT TO THE PALACE OF MY FATHER'S PALACE OF THE TUILERIES – MY OTHER NAMES OR SURNAME LIKE YOU[r] QUEEN IS WINSOR [Windsor] – MY [name] WAS TUILERIES TILL THE RESVALATION [Revolution] – I AM I LOUIS A TUILY AS I WAS CALLED – DO YOU WANT SOME IF I GET ONE – THE SEUGNOT FAMILY WAS THE MAKERS OF THOSE LOVELY DANGREES [dragees].

Nobody attached any special significance to this message. At least, not for the moment.

CHAPTER 18

On Wednesday 17 October 1956, Ethel's patience snapped. Her attitude caused (in Wally's words) an 'upset in the house that made Donald wild' and that night Wally had to change his sheets before going to bed because someone had poured (probably alcoholic) liquid over them. The next day, Donald was blamed when a lamp, a clock and a dog ornament were found to have been moved onto a mat in the 'front room'. On Friday night Kitty found a strange substance in the double bed and, not recognising it, touched it with her bare hands. It irritated her skin and turned out to be rat poison, more of which had been poured into Shirley's bed, together with the empty jar.

'HE [Shagy Roots] [is] ANGRY,' stated Donald at around 10 p.m. 'HE SAID HE IS GOING TO SET FIRE TO ALL CUR-TAINS [...] BRING NAN DOWN NOW OR SHE [will] BE DIED [dead] BY DAWN – O HELP – HE [has] GOT THE RAT POISON'.

Similar warnings continued intermittently. Then at around midnight on Monday Donald tapped, 'GET ETHAL – ETHEL – SARA – GOING TO DIE – GET ETHEL PLEASE – SARA DRIVING ME MAD'. Sara was the name of Ethel's deceased mother.

'Donald started throwing [small objects] about,' recorded Wally, and this continued until 3 a.m. Although nobody was hurt, everyone was deeply unsettled when a ghostly whispering now began in the downstairs bedroom, repeating: 'Sara, Sara'.

At 11.30 the next night, Donald tapped another warning that Shagy Roots was going to start a fire. At his urging Shirley persuaded Ethel to come downstairs. At some point, a pile of what Wally described as 'red hot ashes' was found on the mat in one of the downstairs rooms. Shirley got rid of them and the terrified family gathered in the downstairs bedroom. There, the ghostly whispering started again.

Chibbett later recorded that this voice 'was loud enough to be heard outside the room by both Grandma H. [i.e. Ethel] and [Mark]. It spoke for some time, and gave details of incidents and names known only to Grandma H.' The frightened old woman was convinced she was hearing her mother's voice.

Trouble continued. On Wednesday a ½ lb of bacon belonging to Ethel vanished, as did a basin of fat. The latter was discovered under a cupboard in the scullery early that evening. The voice returned that night and the following night Kitty was hit by an appalling stench when she pulled back the bedcovers and discovered a broken egg that had evidently been there for several hours. She changed the sheet but then, recorded Wally, Donald 'started throwing eggs. One was bad and Nan found one also upstairs smached [sic] in the armchair. Another mess. And also Nan found two cups with egg in each and health salts mixed with tomatoes sauces [sic].'

On Friday night, Shirley was forced to sleep in her parent's bed because, as Wally recorded, 'he' had poured water and custard powder into her own. By 'he', Wally meant Shagy Roots. Both the family and Chibbett felt that Shagy Roots and Donald were separate entities, with Chibbett commenting, 'One gets an impression of a young but valiant "Donald" battling hardily against Shagy Roots – "that old goat" [as Donald called him] who seems to spend much of his time trying to set fire to the house.'

Shagy Roots, observed Chibbett on or around 24 October, 'appears to be particularly incensed against Grandma H., whose unbridled tongue could certainly upset anyone!' Ethel herself, still shaken from hearing what she believed to be her deceased mother's voice, now admitted to Chibbett that she had recently seen things she could not explain away as (to use her earlier expression) 'bosh and rubbish'.

'Upstairs, in her own apartment,' recorded Chibbett, 'Grandma H. has witnessed objects moving. There is a commode, with a circular but unattached lid. On several occasions, she has seen this steadily revolving by itself. True or not, Grandma H. has now radically altered her opinion that Shirley is responsible for it all.'

The morning post of Thursday 1 November brought to Chibbett's north London home an envelope addressed in all-too familiar handwriting. Inside was a short message: 'CHIB – WILL YOU HELP ME PLEASE – RENIE WONT HELP ME [to contact Jeremy Spenser] – YOU WILL – OIU [oui] – DONALD'.

It was, Chibbett later wrote in an article for *Fate* magazine, 'possibly the first letter ever posted from a poltergeist.' Actually, it probably wasn't. The previous Sunday (28 October), Donald had decided that nobody was trying hard enough to contact Spenser. Therefore, he would write his own letter to the actor and post it to Pinewood Studios.

His powers did not extend to procuring the postage stamps necessary to send his letter via the Royal Mail but the wily poltergeist found a solution. That same day, Shirley had written a letter to her friend Marge, and put a stamp on the envelope. In the evening she walked to the postbox in the next road, dropped her envelope inside, and bought herself a bottle of lemonade on the way home. Back at No. 63 she reached into her jacket pocket for the change to give to Wally, and was surprised to find an envelope in there. It was the letter she thought she had just posted. Wally noticed that the envelope no longer had a stamp on it and concluded that Donald had taken that stamp, put it onto his own envelope and then switched envelopes.

The next day Donald told them what he had written in his letter: 'JEREMY – TAKE CARE – I WANT YOU TO GO TO RENIE – WYCLIFFE STREET [*sic*] BATTERSEA – PLEASE I IMPLORE – DONALD – DO NOT IGNORE THIS NOTE – OR YOU PHONE [telephone number] – ASK FOR MR CHIBBETT PLEASE.' The number was Chibbett's home telephone number and the researcher was dismayed when he learned of Donald's indiscretion. Not that Donald cared.

The threat from Shagy Roots remained: in separate incidents matches were strewn around the 'front room', the gas taps in Ethel's kitchen were found to have been opened, and Mark's lighter went missing only for Wally to hear what he believed was Shagy Roots clicking it on and off under Shirley's bed one night. For the moment, however, Donald was more concerned with Jeremy Spenser. Early on Wednesday afternoon (31 October) he tapped out to Shirley that he had written further letters to Spenser and Chibbett, and a little later he asked, 'WILL YOU POST THEM IF I GIVE?' The family agreed, and this would become a regular habit. After writing his letters Donald would leave them in sealed and addressed envelopes on the 'front room' coffee table, and Wally would add postage stamps. 'Mr H. accepts the reality of "Donald" so much that he won't even open these sealed letters, but posts them as "Donald" directs,' commented Chibbett.

After his letters were posted, Donald revealed that one had been an invitation to Jeremy Spenser to visit No. 63. On Sunday 4 November Donald announced that he had written to Spenser again and had also found time to go on several trips, one to France, another to visit the actress Dorothy Bromiley and a third to visit the actor William

Russell. The latter played the title role in the television series *The Adventures of Sir Lancelot*, which was then airing on ITV and was another show that the poltergeist enjoyed watching. Donald was certainly keeping busy, but his overarching concern was still that Spenser should be warned of the danger he faced. It was Donald's duty to help the actor, he insisted, claiming now that he had had foreknowledge of the crash that had killed James Dean in 1955, but back then had lacked the necessary powers to intervene. On Monday afternoon the marks reappeared on Shirley's forehead.

Writing up his case-notes and researching the historical background to Donald's claims consumed so much of his time that Chibbett was unable to visit No. 63 much during November. In his absence Donald continued to fret over the supposed danger facing Jeremy Spenser and grew increasingly irritated that the actor was not replying to his letters. Shirley tried several times to telephone Spenser at Pinewood Studios but the receptionist would not put her through to the actor. Donald decided to find Spenser himself. On Tuesday 13 November the poltergeist announced, '[12.45 p.m.] I FOUND OUT – RENEE – HES AT A MILARTRY SCHOOL FOR SERVICE MEN – HE IS THERE FOR A WHILE – TEW [two] YEARS'.

Donald was pleased with himself, but it would not have been difficult to find the details. Although the War Office had temporarily released Spenser from the army to film *The Prince and the Showgirl*, it was public knowledge that the actor was undertaking National Service training at Eaton Hall Officer Cadet School near Chester.

For about half an hour late on the night of Sunday 11 November the family again heard 'voices' calling for Ethel; Mark's lighter was still missing; and every now and again Donald reminded everyone that Shagy Roots was still around.

However, there was an uneasy calm to daily life now. Donald (with Shirley) now spent most of his time playing with dolls. When he wasn't doing that he was writing letters, not only to Spenser but also to other film and television stars. In mid-November one envelope was addressed to Richard Greene, star of Donald's favourite television show, *The Adventures of Robin Hood.*

On the afternoon of 14 November Donald left a note. His looping scrawl was difficult to decipher but, under a drawing of a crown, his note began, 'I AM LOUIS CRAPI'. It went on to re-state that his mother was Marie Antoinette and his father Louis XVI. 'CRAPI' was presumably meant to be 'Capet': the royal family had belonged to the House of Bourbon, a branch of the older House of Capet. Donald clearly wanted everyone to remember who he really was.

A week later, as Chibbett travelled home from work on Wednesday 21 November, he briefly visited No. 63. As he sat in the kitchen listening to Wally, Kitty and Shirley describe the most recent happenings, Ethel walked in. Looking around nervously, the old woman asked if Donald were with them. Assured that he was not, Ethel told them that a moment earlier, as she had been walking down the stairs, something had grasped hold of her left arm just above the elbow, so tightly it had hurt.

'I looked at her arm,' recorded Chibbett. 'There was a slight reddishness to be seen, but nothing more. I asked her to grasp my arm with the approximate strength of the one she had experienced – and it was considerable.'

CHAPTER 19

Already a devoted follower of *The Adventures of Robin Hood*, Donald had been growing fond of another television series, *The Adventures of Sir Lancelot*. On Friday 23 November 1956 Donald suggested that Shirley would enjoy a job as an actress. In fact, he revealed, he had already written to the producer of *Sir Lancelot* to put in a word for her! (Shirley did not get the job.)

The following evening, Donald found it necessary to justify liking both shows, as if watching one meant he was betraying the other: '[6.20 p.m.] RENEE – I LIKE SIR LANCELOT – BUT I LIKE ROBIN HOOD – I AM NOT NO TURNCOAT'. This had been written on a sheet of paper and left on the coffee table in 'his' room. Until now, Donald had still preferred to tap out his 'domestic notes' – Chibbett's phrase for Donald's frequent messages for the Hitchings family, as opposed to his letters to various people – but after this date the poltergeist often wrote these too. As with his letters, these notes were usually left on the coffee table, although Wally's diary records occasional instances where notes were found in places suggesting they had come through the letterbox or through an open window.

'His written messages at this time were an improvement on his initial attempts,' noted Chibbett, '[although] still very straggly and written diagonally across each page, with only a few lines on each. The words were large and widely spaced.'

Writing was much faster than tapping words out one letter at a time. With this extra speed Donald was able to comment on events within the house, issue orders, give warnings and generally converse more readily than before. His messages started to come more and more frequently. At first Chibbett carefully noted whether each had been communicated via tapping or writing, but as the novelty of discovering written 'domestic notes' wore off Chibbett stopped making this distinction and so it is not usually possible to tell from his records how a particular message was delivered. We do know that by the end of November 1956 approximately 50 per cent of Donald's messages were in the form of written notes and that this percentage increased over the coming weeks.

From his point of view as a psychical researcher, this development – although interesting – was:

> not so satisfactory, because of the charge which can be levelled that the messages are never written in one's presence, but are found on odd scraps of paper in 'Donald's' room. Persons unacquainted with the family are then entitled to draw the conclusion that the messages are written by Shirley or some other person. Against this facile theory, however, are the nature of the messages, which are similar to those transmitted by the raps; and the probability that the writing is quite different from that of Shirley, although admittedly I am no handwriting expert!

(See fig. 31 for examples of Shirley's and Donald's handwriting side by side.)

Another written note was found on Sunday 25 November: '[Time of discovery not recorded] RENEE – JEREMY WILL

HAVE HIS AXEDENT.' The following morning, newspapers reported that Jeremy Spenser had been involved in a car accident. On Sunday night his car had skidded, overturned and crashed through a hedge at Hodnett in Shropshire. Fortunately the actor was not seriously injured, although he was taken to Moston Hall military hospital suffering from shock.

Chibbett was impressed. Not only had the long-predicted accident actually happened but Donald's final warning also seemed to him to be almost resigned, as if the poltergeist had realised it was too late now to prevent the crash.

On Monday 26 November, shortly after the family read the news of Spenser's accident, Donald tapped, 'RENEE – JEREMY – I DID NOT TELL YOU FOR I KNOW YOU BE SAD BUT WHEN HE CARLAPST [collapsed] HE CALLED RENEE – HE CALL RENE – THATS WHY I WAS NOT HERE LAST NIGHT – HE CALLED YOU NAME – HE KNOWS BY MY LETTERS – HE IS ILL RENE – THE PAPERS LIE – HE IS NOT CONTORS [conscious] – I TRY TO HELP BUT HE NO LISTEN – HE JUST LAY THERE IN DEEP SLEEP […] I GOT TO GO TO JEREMY'. Donald tapped out the theme music to *Robin Hood* and then there was silence. As far as the family could tell, he had gone to watch over Spenser.

For the following few weeks, many of Donald's messages pleaded in vain for Wally and Kitty to allow Shirley to visit Spenser. Donald claimed the actor remained in danger and needed her help, as in the following message written on 27 November: 'TUESDAY 27 – RENIE – JEREMY – HE NEEDS YOU'. When Chibbett saw this, he was excited to see that Donald had drawn a horizontal line crossing the 7 in the continental manner. 'Trivial, maybe – but telling!' he commented. Chibbett had seemingly forgotten the episode in early August when precisely this detail had been absent from Donald's handwriting. Was the poltergeist acquiring finer control over his handwriting? Or was Donald learning from Chibbett's tests, and adapting to fit in with the researcher's expectations and hopes?

Chibbett's postbox received another letter on 6 December: 'CHERE MONSUIR CHIBBETT – JE ECRIRE DANS FRAN-CAIS PUR JE AVOIR MON RESONS CHIB – JE AVOIR JUSTE A PHOTOGRAPHIE DE SIR LANCELOT DE LAKE AVEC LOUIS CHARLES PHILLIPPE CRAPI.'

Given that the son of a French king would have had a privileged education, the French was surprisingly poor. It was almost as if it had been assembled by someone using badly spelled words with little understanding of how to string them together. Chibbett translated the intended message as: 'Dear Mr Chibbett, I am writing in French for I have my reasons, Chib. I have just had a photograph of Sir Lancelot of the Lake with Louis Charles Phillippe Crapi.' Donald's reference to a photograph made sense the next day when Chibbett learned that a large autographed photograph of William Russell (star of *The Adventures of Sir Lancelot*) had been delivered to No. 63 a few days earlier. Evidently, Donald's letter to the producers of that show had borne some fruit after all.

On Sunday 9 December the poltergeist predicted another car accident: 'THEY HAVE ACCENDANT – PAULA'. This written message was reportedly discovered at around 11 a.m. As the Hitchings family watched television that evening the news reported that Paula Marshall, the 28-year-old actress wife of magician and television star David Nixon, had been killed in a car accident that morning near Huntingdon in Cambridgeshire.

'This appears to be a most remarkable prophecy,' wrote Chibbett when he learned of the incident. '[The accident] was not reported on T.V. until the *evening* of the 9th, and did not appear in the press till the next morning [original emphasis].' It might be argued, however, that there was no definitive proof that the 'Paula' in the message was intended to refer to Paula Marshall and that this incident might have been merely a coincidence. Another argument might be that Chibbett had no way to confirm that the message had genuinely been received *before* news of the accident emerged. Nevertheless Chibbett, who had come to know the family well, was willing to accept their word.

As Christmas approached, Donald's thoughts turned towards the festive season. On Thursday 6 December he left Shirley a letter: 'RENEE – I WANT YOU [and] ME TO MAKE CHRIT-MASY THINGS – WEE – YOU GET THINGS – KIT [will] GIVE YOUR SILVER [money] BUT I TELL WRITE ON LIST WHAT [to] GET BECAUSE I CANNOT GO UP SHOP'.

On Monday Donald asked for materials: 'PINS TO PUT UP PAPER – I WANT YELLOW RED BLANCH [*sic*] IS WHITE PAPER PLEASE – SIX CARDS – PINS – PAPER CREAP [crepe] – I MAKE MAGIC LANTERNS'.

When Chibbett visited on Tuesday, Wally told him that Donald had taken it upon himself to put up Christmas decorations in 'his' room. Chibbett described the scene: 'Paper streamers crisscrossed the room in various directions. Cotton wool in vast quantity was stuck on every available space, and a small Christmas tree was already hung with presents from "Donald" – even one for me, tersely entitled, "For Chib". In the centre of the mirror, decked out in gaily coloured tissue paper, were the words, "JOYEUX NOEL".'

Life in No. 63 had been fairly peaceful for the past few weeks, Chibbett was told. Donald rarely left 'his' room these days, said Wally and Kitty, although the tapping noises often started when Shirley walked into that room.

As Chibbett looked through the messages from Donald that had amassed since his previous visit, the family told him that the signed picture of 'Sir Lancelot' was far from the only photograph Donald had now collected. 'Since "Donald" has acquired his new skill at writing,' reported Chibbett, 'he has deluged half the stars of TVdom with letters, resulting in a small avalanche of signed pictures from various notabilities.'

Chatting with Shirley in Donald's room, Chibbett thanked the poltergeist aloud for the letters he had received. These had recently included a Christmas card inscribed, 'To Mr Chib from Donald – Joyeux Noel!' Chibbett asked whether Donald would like a Christmas present. 'Rather rashly, I promised to get him whatever he wanted!' he wrote afterwards. 'In fact, I suggested that he should state his requirements in a letter. I would then get his present and hang it on my Christmas tree at home. Would he then come and fetch it? "Yes!" – he rapped.'

As Chibbett stood in the passageway later, preparing to go home, 'something hurtled out of "Donald's" room, which was in darkness, and landed with a thud at the foot of the stairs, just by my feet. [Chibbett did not note whether anybody was inside Donald's room when this happened.] I picked it up. It was a cardboard box containing some of Shirley's paints. On the bottom were scrawled – in "Donald's" handwriting – the following words, "CHIB – I WANT TRAIN!"' Chibbett was as good as his word and duly bought the poltergeist a toy train for Christmas – although Donald failed to collect it as intended and in the end Chibbett had to deliver it to No. 63 himself.

On Wednesday 12 December, Shirley was in the room she shared with Donald when she heard a male voice say, 'Hello, Shirley! Come to me. You don't know me, but I know you, Jeremy.'

Donald informed her that the voice had been that of Jeremy Spenser and that what had happened had been accidental 'mind transference'. It was the sort of expression someone might have overheard Chibbett use. Shirley heard the voice again later that morning while she was out with one of her aunts. Speaking close to Shirley's ear, and inaudible to anyone else, the voice told Shirley to, 'Phone Eric C– and ask for Dave

Spenser.' David Spenser was the older brother of Jeremy Spenser and also an actor, while Eric C– was the producer and director of a television series David Spenser was taking part in.

Chibbett helped her obtain the number and Shirley telephoned the relevant television company but was told neither man was available. Later, though, Chibbett did succeed in speaking to David Spenser. When Chibbett told him what was happening, the actor suggested Chibbett send details to his agent. Chibbett did so, sending a summary of events so far and urging the actor not to dismiss the unlikely story. 'I have known the family long enough now, to regard a hoax as improbable,' he wrote. 'The girl Shirley is a normal teenager apart from her undoubted psychic ability, and the whole affair appears to be as puzzling to her as to the rest of us. It is possible that she is a schizophrenic, but there are supernormal elements as well which cannot be easily explained away.'

Over the next few days Donald seemed obsessed with the Spenser brothers, claiming he was visiting both of them frequently in spirit form. Meanwhile, the marks reappeared on Shirley's face. They were more pronounced now than before.

On Monday 17 December Donald left a postcard, which he claimed he had taken from Jeremy Spenser's house. On it was a message, supposedly from the actor: 'My best thanks to you Donald, all the best, I do not understand, Jeremy Spenser.' 'The implied inference,' recorded Chibbett, 'is that [Donald] was present when Jeremy Spenser was writing the postcard, that he – "Donald" – took the postcard before it was completed, and fetched it back to No. 63.' The researcher was not convinced, suspecting the card had actually been written by either Shirley or Donald.

More dramatically, the family now informed Chibbett that an autographed photograph of Jeremy Spenser that hung above Shirley's bed had begun to 'weep' from time to time. Somehow, it would become wet and 'teardrops' would roll down the surface. Wally reported that these tears tasted 'salty'.

Christmas Day was approaching and on 20 December Donald wrote, 'KIT – FOR NOEL I WANT TWENTY FOUR TUBES OF PAINT [and] A HORSE AND CARRAGE TOY'. He was given what he asked for, even receiving his gifts a few days early.

The poltergeist had been busily sending Christmas cards through the post. Chibbett had already received his and there is little doubt that Donald's favourite television and film stars also received cards from him that year. Shirley and her parents got a card too, of course, the handwritten message on the back reading, 'TO KIT WALLIE AND MY RENIE – JOYEUX NOËL'.

On Christmas Day itself, recorded Wally, 'Donald wished us a merry Axmas [*sic*]. Donald was with us alday [*sic*] & tapped to the music on wireless & enjoying it to the television.'

Just before noon on Thursday 27 December Shirley telephoned Chibbett to say that Donald had received a Christmas card from Jeremy Spenser. The next day Shirley discovered a letter tucked inside the 'front room' clock; this letter appeared to be from David Spenser, asking her to telephone him. Chibbett was not convinced, suspecting that Donald had written both the card and letter himself. His suspicions grew when Donald ignored his requests to send him the envelope in which the card had arrived, which (if it had truly come from Jeremy) should have borne a Chester postmark. Shirley claimed the envelope had disappeared. Chibbett insisted that she should try to find it.

On Saturday morning Chibbett received an envelope containing a short note from Shirley: 'Mr Chib, please keep this letter, mummy said you may have it' but the David Spenser letter was not enclosed. Shirley's note had been crossed through and a comment written beneath it in Donald's handwriting: 'CHIB – HELP ME PLEASE – I WANT MY LETTRE – DONALD'. The implication was that Donald had extracted Spenser's letter before Shirley had posted the envelope. Chibbett remained unconvinced.

1956 was coming to an end. It had been an extraordinary year, not only for the Hitchings family and Harold Chibbett, but also for the countless spiritualists, psychical researchers and journalists who had descended upon the small house in Wycliffe Road, especially during those early months. It had been – if not quite extraordinary – then at least entertaining for the general public also, as they followed the story in the local and national news. Although media interest had largely faded away now the same could not be said of Donald. As 1956 drew to a close the poltergeist thoughtfully left notes in the family's beds, wishing them each a 'Happy New Year'.

Wally's closing diary entry read: 'This year has been one that I & my family will never forget & neighbours also & I thank them for there [*sic*] help they gave us during the year, & all in this diary is true & realy [*sic*] happened. I hope the next year will be better. Donald still with us.'

CHAPTER 20

By the beginning of 1957 Donald's communications were coming so frequently that Chibbett and Wally found it impossible to record every one. Their records make it clear, however, that the poltergeist remained obsessed with the Spenser brothers.

On 2 January, Donald pleaded with Kitty either to bring David Spenser to No. 63 herself, or else to persuade Chibbett to do so. He would not say why, only that the matter was urgent and concerned David's brother, Jeremy. The next day Donald said he would write to Jeremy directly, complaining, 'IF NO ONE WILL HELP ME I MUST HELP MYSELF'. With his letter, the contents of which were not revealed, Donald enclosed a song Shirley and her friend 'DORENA' (Doreen) had written about the young actor, together with a note revealing that the girls called Jeremy a 'cry baby' because his photograph continued to weep every now and again.

From time to time now, Donald would occasionally fall silent for a while. Later there would be a burst of tapping to announce his return. He would claim to have been out visiting either David or Jeremy at their homes or at film and television studios.

Meanwhile, Chibbett's approach to David Spenser's agent had yielded no response. Unsurprisingly, it seemed that the actor did not want to become involved.

Donald had been evading Chibbett's attempts to pin him down on the details of his claim to be Louis, and the researcher was becoming irritated. Hoping to provoke a response, Chibbett sent a sharp letter to No. 63 to be read out to the poltergeist, challenging Donald to give proper proof of his supposed identity. It also demanded an explanation as to why Donald had still not forwarded the 'David Spenser' letter to him for examination. Donald was furious. Soon after Chibbett's letter arrived on 7 January the poltergeist tapped – or rather pounded – out his reply: 'RENIE – THAT LETTER IS POEPOSTROUS [preposterous] – HOW DARE HE ASK ME THAT – RENIE – YOU ARE NOT TO SPEAK TO HIM NO MORE – I WILL HELP MYSELF FROM KNOW [now] – HOW DARE HE NOT CALL ME A PRINCE OF FRANCE – CHIB HAS MADE ME VERY ANGRY – I DISMISS HIM KNOW [now] – I WILL NOT TALK TO HIM.'

There were further irate messages that day and the next. Wally recorded that Donald broke the train set Chibbett had given him for Christmas and tore Chibbett's letter to pieces. Throughout there was 'rapping very hard as though in a rage'. Donald also left a long letter addressed to Kitty, explaining why Chibbett was wrong to expect so much: 'CHIB THINKS OF ME HAS [as] A MASCHINERS [machine] – BUT HE MUST UNDERSTAND I AM A SPIRIT OF THE PAST'. He claimed that communicating was difficult because, although he could write in English, he could not speak in that language: 'IF I COULD SPEAK YOUR ENGLISH I WOULD NOT LEAVE MESSAGES OR TAP'. He could speak in French, he stated, but only 'OLD FRENCH', which Chibbett would not understand. Moreover the reason his written French was not more convincing was because when he tried to write in modern French he got 'MIXED UP'. The more Chibbett saw, the more he wanted, complained Donald, referring to the small crown (allegedly from his sword) that he still refused to let Chibbett borrow. Donald claimed to have much more he could show – including 'A LACE HANKECHIEF 351 YEARS OLD OF MINE – AND MY CLOHTES' but he would not give those to Chibbett because 'NEXT HE WILL WANT ME'! Finally 'FREE FROM LIFE'S DUTIES', Donald was entitled to do as he chose, he stated, and with that he announced he was going away to visit Jeremy Spenser for a while.

Donald soon calmed down though. In one message he tapped on 10 January he even commented, 'O – AND I [am] GLAD CHIB APOLAGISD'. Chibbett, who had done no such thing, chuckled when he found out.

Chibbett's provocative letter had caused a lot of fuss but it did win him a small victory: he finally got to see the letter David Spenser had supposedly sent to Shirley. It was waiting for him in No. 63 when he visited on 11 January, but after examining it Chibbett was more convinced than ever that Donald had written it himself.

For months the 'personification' (as Chibbett termed it) called Louis had been growing more pronounced. On Sunday 10 February events took an unexpected turn.

At 2.55 p.m. Shirley heard a faint voice calling 'Natalie'. An hour and a half later, Wally found a message written on the wall in (probably) the 'front room'. It stated, 'I want Natalie'. After their evening meal Shirley and Doreen went into Donald's room to 'work the glass' and found themselves communicating with a new 'personification'. It claimed to be the spirit of James Dean, the 24-year-old American film star who had died in a car crash on 30 September 1955.

'James Dean' (or who/whatever it was) would continue to communicate for some time, sometimes by writing and sometimes through tapping. None of his original letters have survived, which is a shame because it would be interesting to

1 The Hitchings family in the 'front room' of No. 63 Wycliffe Road in 1957: (from left to right) 'Mark' (pseudonym), Wally, Shirley and Kitty.

2 Catherine (Kitty) Hitchings, outside the front door of No. 63 Wycliffe Road.

3 Psychical researcher Harold Chibbett, at the rear of No. 63 Wycliffe Road, 13 June 1956.

4 Message reading 'SHIRLEY I COME', purportedly written by Donald, found scrawled inside a notebook at 1.15 a.m. on 22 March 1956.

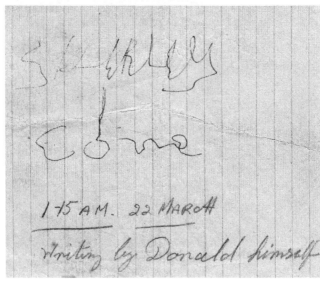

1·15 A.M. 22 MARCH

Writing by Donald himself

5 Message
tapped out
by Donald,
taken
down on
6 April 1956.

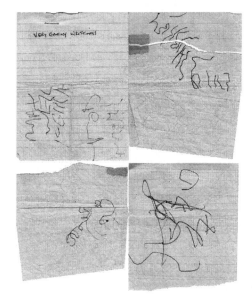

6 Early
examples
of Donald's
apparent
attempts to
write.

7 Slightly blurry photograph taken by Harold Chibbett. His handwritten note on the reverse reads, 'The Battersea Polt (1956). View of part of an upstairs bedroom, showing chairs upturned, disarray of bed & general upheaval.'

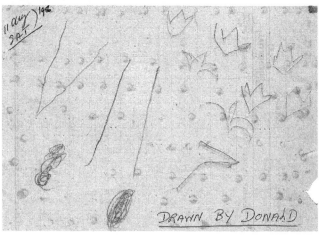

8 This piece of paper, allegedly written on by Donald, was discovered on Saturday 11 August 1956, shortly after the poltergeist was asked to write the numeral 7. The pencil marks show the Roman numerals VII, an Arabic numeral 7 (with no 'French'-style line through it) and seven stylised fleur-de-lis symbols.

9 Tracing
of Donald's
handwriting,
late August
1956. Chibbett's
translations/
comments read,
'GOT; TO GO;
TO; MEETING;
MAIRE (Marie).
Note reversal of
letters RI. Note
also difference in
style of writing
from other
examples; ANNE'.

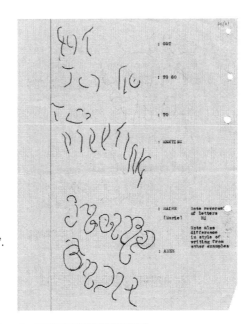

10 Tracing
of Donald's
handwriting,
late August
1956. Chibbett's
translations/
comments read,
'15 YEARS;
LOVE RENEE;
Note: the last
two words are
in "mirror
writing"'.

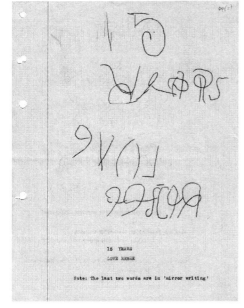

11 Tracing of Donald's handwriting, late August 1956. Chibbett's translations/comments read, 'CALAIS I WANT YOU TO GO LOUIS COLLITEN (?); Note the "fleur-de-lis"'.

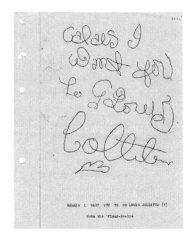

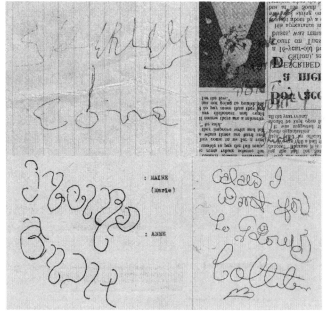

12 A change in Donald's handwriting style. The upper two examples are from (left) 22 March 1956 and (right) 27 June 1956. The lower examples were produced around the end of August 1956 and feature more rounded characters.

13 Donald's elaborated 'royal scene', originally drawn on the
'front room' wall on 15 August 1956 and added to on or shortly
before 28 September 1956, is partially visible in this rather blurred
photograph taken by Andrew Green on 28 July 1957. Reproduced
here by permission of Alan Murdie.

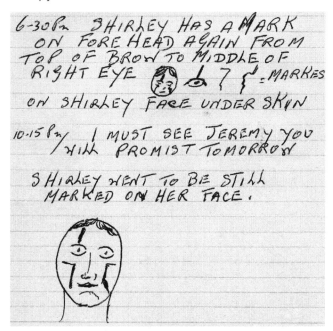

14 Marks that appeared on Shirley's face on Monday
8 October 1956, sketched by her father.

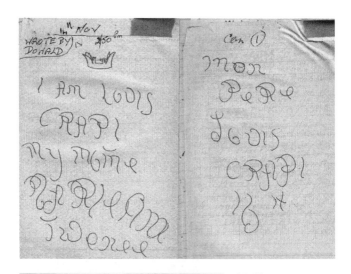

15 Note from Donald, discovered on 14 November 1956.

16 Shirley holding the picture of Jeremy Spenser that was claimed to shed tears.

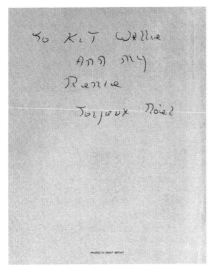

17 Donald's seasonal message to the Hitchings family, written on the back of his Christmas card, December 1956.

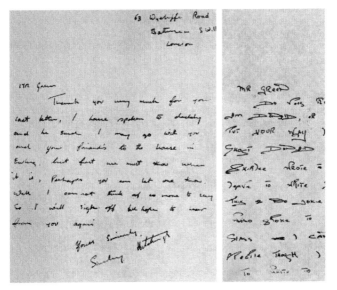

18 The letters to Andrew Green from Shirley (left) and Donald (right) that Green reproduced in his 1973 book *Our Haunted Kingdom*. Green believed that both letters had been written by the same person. Reproduced here by permission of Alan Murdie.

19 These photographs were allegedly taken by Donald in August 1957.

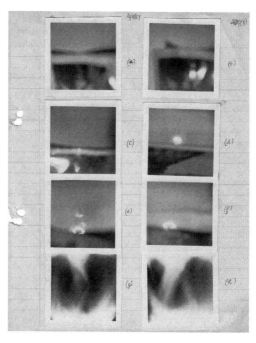

20 Donald's list of the photographs he claimed to have taken on 30 August 1957. Chibbett's note reads, 'List of snaps alleged to have been taken by "Donald" on 30/08/57 with the roll of film bought by me on 29/08/57. Donald says he only took two "out window" (Nos 3 & 4) – but there were four at least … Only five in all were printed out of the twelve on the film. Seven were completely blank.'

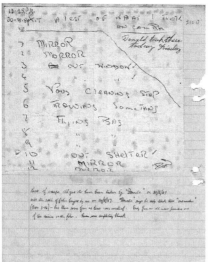

21 The five photographs allegedly taken by Donald on 30 August 1957.

22 Chibbett's handwritten note on the back of this photo reads, 'Part of the Conference Room of Donald the Polt: in the kitchen upstairs 1958 July'. The flowers that can be seen in this photograph had not been present during the conference; Donald had asked Wally for those later.

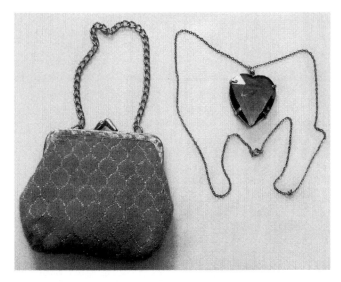

23 The heart-shaped pendant Donald gave to Shirley on her 18th birthday, together with its original bag.

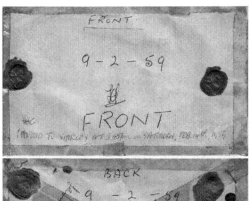

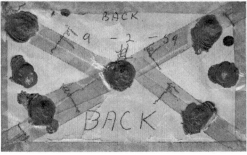

24 Chibbett's sealed envelope experiment of February 1959 raised the possibility that some trickery might be involved in these events.

25 Note from
Donald dated
10 January 1960,
warning that
there was a
'MAN OUT SIDE'
No. 63.

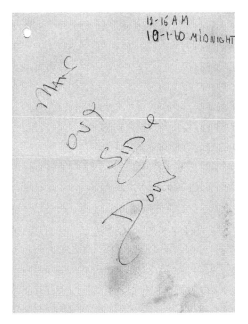

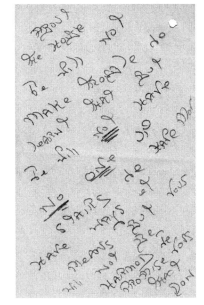

26 Note from Donald
warning that he did not
want tenants moving into
the upstairs flat, found on
27 February 1960.

27 No. 28, Rue du Bac, Paris, site of the Seugnot sweetshop (behind the roadworks); photograph taken by Harold Chibbett on 14 June 1963.

28 Series of three photographs showing Donald's 'decoration' of the downstairs front bedroom, taken by Chibbett on 20 March 1964.

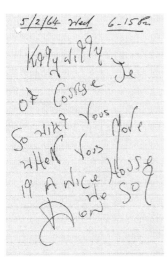

29 Note from Donald reassuring the no-doubt delighted Hitchings family that he would travel with them when they moved to a new home; found on 5 February 1964.

30 Looking west along Evesham Way, Battersea in 2011. No. 63 Wycliffe Road no longer exists but it stood somewhere around where the dark-coloured car can be seen in the centre of this photograph. The house stood on the west side of Wycliffe Road, roughly where the road would intersect (at right angles) with the present-day Evesham Way if Wycliffe Road still extended this far south. This part of Wycliffe Road was demolished during local redevelopment of the area a decade and a half after the beginning of the events described in this book. © James Clark

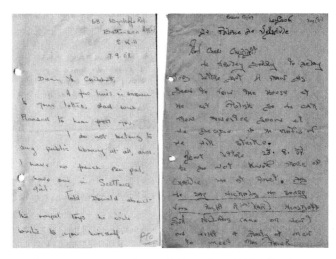

31 Two letters, written by Shirley (left) and Donald (right) on the
same day (7 September 1959).

compare them not only with letters from Donald but also with specimens of James Dean's own handwriting. Chibbett did record that Dean's letters were 'written in a practised hand' so it seems that the handwriting was noticeably different to Donald's and (unlike Donald) Dean did not restrict himself to upper case letters when writing. The 'voice' of these letters was very different also (although Dean's spelling and grammar, like that of both Donald and Shirley, could be erratic). The following message of 19 February provides an example:

> [3.20 p.m.] I don't know who you good folks are but I am still waiting for help – please hurry – I'm greatful [sic] to you mam for keeping me here – but I'm lost – I want to get back home to ma country – but how? – Look mister – I'm James Dean – I didn't ask to come here but I just guess I got here – so help me please – I belong in California.

Before long, Dean was offering Shirley advice on how she could become a film star, a plan Donald supported. Wally and Kitty were keen for their daughter to find work (something Donald had successfully prevented ever since losing Shirley her job at the department store a year earlier) but this was not what they had in mind. The fact that both Dean and Donald were suggesting that Shirley become an actress certainly raises the possibility that these messages arose from Shirley's private fantasies of swapping life in Battersea for the glamour of Hollywood. However, Shirley says today that she had never harboured such dreams.

Donald seemed jealous of the new arrival, petulantly threatening to leave. 'RENIE – THAT JAMES DEAN IS [has] GOT A CHEEK – I DO NOT MIND HIM HELPING YOU BUT HE IS NO[T] CUTTING ME OUT,' he wrote on 21 February. For a few days he generally sulked, seemingly feeling unwanted, before writing in a letter to Chibbett on 26 February, 'I AM ALL RIGHT KNOW [now] [...] SHIRLEY WANTS TO GO

TO WORK – ALL RIGHT – LET HER GO – BUT THERE IS
A SNAG – IF RENIE GOES TO WORK I GO AND NO HELP
ANYONE – THEN WE ALL BE BACK WHERE WE STARTED'.

The previous August Donald had asked for a typewriter.
He had finally got his wish four days earlier and his letter to
Chibbett went on to say:

CHIB – WE HAVE A FUNNY THING – KIT BOUGHT IT – IT
WRITES LETTERS – I HAD A GO AND TYPED IT – THINK IT
IS CALLED THAT – TO JEREMY – YOU KNOW – HE STILL IN
TROUBLE – OLD DEAN IS STILL HERE – HE IS A PEST – ALL
HE WANTS IS TO BE ALONE – AND HE HAS THE CHEEK TO
CALL ME OLD FANCY PANTS – I CALL IT DISSGRACEFUL
CHIB – WELL – I LEAVE YOU FOR THE PRESENT – THINK
IT OVER TO [too] CHIB – ETHER [either] SHIRLEY GOES
OUT TO WORK – IF SO I GO IF NOT I SAY [stay] AND BE
HAPPY – LOOK CHIB – I HAVE GOT WORLDS OF HAPPY-
NESS LINED UP FOR RENIE – AU REVOIR – DONALD.

'Shirley,' noted Chibbett in mid-February, 'like many adolescents of her age, is mad about film stars and rock and roll
singers.' She was openly a fan of the singer Elvis Presley but
(unlike Donald) claimed to be totally disinterested in Jeremy
Spenser. Donald disagreed. He wrote to Chibbett (in a letter
received on 16 February) to say that Shirley was *not* an Elvis
fan at all, that her proclaimed love for Elvis was a cover for
her true feelings, and that she would often lie on her bed and
weep for Jeremy. Donald said he wanted to help her. In his
opinion, she should meet the actor. 'WHO KNOWS?' he wrote.
'HE MAY LIKE HER.'

Was Shirley (consciously or subconsciously) trying to
manipulate Chibbett into arranging for her to meet her idol?
Was Donald truly a spirit after all? Or was something else

going on altogether? Chibbett simply could not decide, but a few days later something happened to remind him that, whatever Donald was, he did appear to possess remarkable powers.

Donald predicted that the film star John Wayne, then aged 49, would have an accident. In his diary Wally recorded that the poltergeist made this announcement just before 11 p.m. on Saturday 23 February. From Donald's exasperated tone the poltergeist clearly felt he was wasting his time: 'DO YOU KNOW – RENIE – JOHN WAYNE – THE ONE WE SAW TONIGHT [presumably on television] ... IS GOING TO HAVE A ACEDENT [accident] – DO WHAT YOU LIKE ABOUT IT – I KNOW [will not] GET MIXED UP [in it] ANY MORE'.

On Monday 25 February the newspapers reported that Wayne had indeed had an accident. The day before, he had fallen over while filming a scene for *Legend of the Lost* near Tripoli in Libya, tearing ligaments in his left foot. According to the newspaper reports this news had only emerged from New York on the Sunday night.

It may not have been the best turn of events for Wayne, but Chibbett was delighted. '[T]his appears to be a cast-iron proof of a prophecy,' he noted.

CHAPTER 21

It was a crowded house when Chibbett visited No. 63 on Thursday 28 February 1957. Accompanying him were Mr W.E. Manning (an acquaintance who was a psychologist and who shared his interest in the paranormal), and the American Ken Kellar and his wife Marianne Francis. Wally, Kitty and Shirley welcomed the four inside, but of the house's invisible occupant(s) there was no sign.

The visitors looked over the latest written notes and listened to the family recount details of recent happenings. They were told that while Shirley had been alone in the house that morning (Kitty was at the hospital and Wally was at work) she had realised the new typewriter was missing. A short while later Shirley had heard someone typing but had been unable to trace the source of the sound. She had eventually found the typewriter on a table in Donald's room with some typed sheets lying beside it.

The sheets purported to be a statement by James Dean describing his life, which – he said – had been 'some what for shortend [sic]'. Dean gave a great deal of basic biographical information, such as when and where he had been born, where he had grown up and went to school, and referred to his acting career and the car accident that had taken his life. The statement showed the same sort of unreliable spelling and grammar that Donald exhibited. It was interesting reading but had little value as evidence that the author was really James Dean because the biographical details were ones that could be found in any number of newspaper reports. Furthermore, in common with many other teenage girls of the time, Shirley had been distressed by Dean's death and had held on to a selection of newspaper and magazine articles about the star.

Accompanying Dean's statement was a short note: 'I guess I borrowed it [the typewriter] Kid … you don't mind. It will help me a lot. Jimmy Dean. Don gave ma self Paper [*sic*]'.

From then on, most (possibly all) of Dean's messages would be typewritten.

Chibbett took Dean's typed statement to his office the next day to ask 'an expert typist' for her opinion. In her view, reported Chibbett, 'only a person accustomed to a typewriter could have produced what she saw. The evenness of the typing showed that it was not done by a learner.' As Shirley had then had little – if any – experience with typewriters, this reply pushed Chibbett just that little bit further towards believing that there was at least one supernatural entity inside No. 63.

At the beginning of March both Donald and Dean wrote to Chibbett to ask him to forward an enclosed sealed envelope to Kellar and Francis: '[Note from Donald] CHER CHIB – I AM WRITING TO YOU FOR TO GIVE YOU OLD DEENY'S LETTRE TO SEND TO KEN AND MARIANNE […] SEE YOU LATER – ALLIGATOR'. Dean's Americanisms were rubbing off on Donald, it seemed. Dean's note stressed that it was important Chibbett post the envelope, 'the stamp is on it,' he urged. 'The stamp was *not* on it,' sighed Chibbett, but he forwarded the letter anyway.

Both Donald and Dean had taken something of a shine to Kellar. (In Donald's case at least it was probably because he considered the American less sceptical than Chibbett, who was forever asking him awkward questions and trying to catch him out.) During his recent visit Kellar had mentioned having contacts in the film industry, which had further endeared him to both Donald and Dean. This was almost certainly what the latest letter was regarding. In late April, Dean would prompt Chibbett to contact Kellar again, asking the American to bring a film director to meet Shirley, but nothing ever came of this.

Kellar may have been liked but Chibbett was again making himself unpopular with Donald. He now took a small box and a sealed envelope to No. 63 and challenged Donald to ascertain their contents using the extra-sensory powers he suspected the poltergeist possessed. Chibbett had designed this test to explore the limits of Donald's abilities. The researcher knew what the box contained, so if Donald successfully identified its contents it would indicate *either* that Donald could see into the box *or* that he could read the information from Chibbett's mind. The contents of the envelope, however, had been inserted by someone else and were unknown to Chibbett. If Donald could also identify what was in the envelope he could not have obtained that information from Chibbett's mind, indicating that he had seen inside the envelope.

Although eager to find out what Donald could do, Chibbett had no great expectation that Donald – 'a past master at evasiveness' – would cooperate. So Chibbett threatened to withdraw his involvement unless Donald agreed to attempt the experiment. 'It will be interesting to note "Donald's" reactions!' he noted.

Chibbett received Donald's reaction on 5 March. It was an angry and stiffly formal letter stating that if Chibbett did not consider Donald/Louis capable of handling his own affairs of state, Chibbett should stop writing to him. At the end, Donald stated that he had 'WONDERFUL NEWS – I AM RETAINING MY THRONE AS PRINCE LOUIS – SO IF YOU CARE TO WRITE ADDRESS IT TO HIS ROYAL HIGHNESS PRINCE LOUIS OF ALL FRANCE – AND PRAY SIR PLEASE PUT TO MY RIGHT NAME – SIGHED [signed]: LOUIS CHARLES PHILLIPE CAPET.'

The following days' post brought an 'almost incessant stream of letters' from both Donald and 'James Dean', but Chibbett was unsurprised to note that Donald showed no signs of cooperating with his proposed test. He never would. As well as suggestion after suggestion that Shirley become a film star, the letters revealed the continuing clash between Dean and Donald. One key point of contention was Donald's obsession with Jeremy Spenser, something that apparently irritated Dean immensely. Donald was equally irritated by what he saw as Dean's rudeness and remained worried that Dean was trying to force him out. 'There is an apparent antagonism between "Donald" and "J.D." which is most intriguing,' noted Chibbett, 'although this feature is not new in cases of multiple personality.'

On Saturday 9 March there was an indication that Donald and Dean were not entirely separate from one another when Dean revealed that he shared Donald's dislike of Ethel: 'Say kid – is that old goat upstairs any relative to you? You think why I ask? Well sister she bothers me.' Donald had used exactly the same expression – 'old goat' – in October when referring to the entity he called Shagy Roots.

Regardless of whether or not the messages from Donald and Dean were 'figments of Shirley's dream life', noted Chibbett, 'the contents are certainly very interesting.' He decided to concentrate his efforts on the 'James Dean' personification for a while, not least because he hoped that ignoring Donald might persuade Donald to cooperate more. Chibbett wrote to Dean with a long list of questions, based on a magazine article about the actor's life. When Dean's answers arrived they were, as far as Chibbett could ascertain, accurate but, as the information was public knowledge, they did little to show whether or not Shirley (knowingly or otherwise) was the true author of Dean's messages.

While Chibbett ignored Donald, Donald continued to obsess over Jeremy Spenser. Wally urged Donald to forget about the actor but with no effect. On 21 March, Donald told Shirley to 'LOOK CLOSE INTO THE STONE AND SEE WHAT YOU CAN SEE'. The stone in question was a large, blue-green, imitation gem in the centre of a heart-shaped brooch belonging to Shirley. When Shirley looked into it she saw a boy's face. She showed the stone to Ethel, but Ethel saw an old, bearded man. Wally and Kitty also saw a face (although it is not clear which version they saw), then, in Wally's words, 'all of a sudden the picture went.' Shirley believed that the face had been that of Jeremy Spenser and she swore she had not put it there herself. She took the stone out of the brooch and Wally reported that there was no picture stuck to either it or the jewellery. However, after Chibbett examined this brooch himself later he wrote, 'a tiny picture was gummed to the back of the container. But the Hitchings still maintain that originally the picture was in the stone, and that the container was empty.'

By Sunday 24 March, Donald was showing signs of frustration with Chibbett's reluctance both to believe in him and to do what Donald wanted: '[11.05 p.m.] KIT – I GO TO JEREMY – POOR BOY – IF CHIB DO NOT HELP ME TO GET HIM I WILL THROW HIM OFF THE EIFFEL TOWER!'

The night ended as practically every night did at that time. Donald tapped out the *Robin Hood* theme music then fell silent until the morning.

When Chibbett visited No. 63 on Friday 5 April he was handed two letters, one from Dean and the other from Donald. Dean, in his letter, hinted that he was planning to leave soon to make more room for Donald: 'You know this guy Jeremy – well – Don said he is going to be [in?] some kind of trouble – so please help him – look – before I came yer was full of Don – look – I feel I'm cutting him out – and beleave [*sic*] me brother – I don't want to be on the wrong side of him.'

Donald, too, seemed keen for Chibbett to direct his attention back towards him rather than Dean: 'CHIB – I JUST WANT [to] SAY – I NEED YOUR HELP WIHT JEREMY PLEASE – I WILL NOT SAY MORE BECAUSE YOU MAY NO BELEAVE ME – CHIB – I WANT A STRAIGHT ANSWER TO MY QUISTOIN [question] – ARE YOU GETTING TRYED [tired] OF ME?'

It transpired that around one month earlier Donald had supposedly enchanted a locket with some sort of magical protection. The locket contained a photograph of Jeremy Spenser and so long as Shirley wore this necklace, Donald promised, no harm would befall the actor. During his visit, Chibbett persuaded Shirley to let him borrow the locket, and he hid it somewhere in the house. Wally was not yet home from work but when he arrived, recorded Chibbett, 'he and Shirley searched the house, while I donned my hat and coat in Don's room, where I had placed the locket on the cornice high above the window, out of sight. I heard Shirley above questioning "Donald" and being directed by him. She came down, entered "Donald's" room, and emerged a moment later with the locket in her hand.'

She said she had spotted the locket as soon as she entered the room because its chain was hanging down. Yet just two minutes earlier Chibbett had checked that the locket was completely hidden from view. Had it slipped by accident, he wondered, or had Donald been responsible?

Donald was not happy at having been tricked (as he saw it) into performing for Chibbett. At 11 p.m., after the researcher had gone home, Donald complained, 'KIT – CHIB PLAYED A DIRTY JOKE ON ME – THAT IS WHY I NO HELP HIM – DON'. He referred to Chibbett's 'dirty joke' again in a letter the researcher received on 8 April: 'I WARNING YOU CHIB – I WILL NOT STANT [stand] FOR THIS – IN COURT I WAS REALY MASTER AFTER PERE'.

Chibbett wrote back to reassure Donald that he was not getting tired of him, but also restating that he would only help Donald if Donald cooperated with his experiments and answered his questions.

Donald refused, taking the moral high ground: 'I THINK THAT HELPING OTHERS SHOULD COME BEFORE GAMES – SORRY CHIB – NO – I CANNOT AFORDE TO USE MY ENIGEY [energy] UP ON GAMES TILL I HAVED HELPED THAT POOR BOY "JEREMY".'

A few days later Donald thought of a new way to help Jeremy. As well as continuing to wear her protective locket, Shirley should meet Jeremy in order to give him his own protective locket to wear. The poltergeist's calls for this meeting to be arranged were ignored.

On 12 April Donald received an answer to a letter he had sent to a television broadcasting company, asking about the Spenser brothers. The company replied that Jeremy was serving with the army in Kenya, on National Service, but they did supply a contact address for David. Donald was delighted and lost no time in writing to David. As for Jeremy, Donald claimed to know precisely where in Kenya to find the actor, boasting that he travelled there every night to visit him. (It was noticeable, however, that he continued to address his letters to Jeremy via the army school in Chester.)

Chibbett had refused to help Donald, but Donald had got the information anyway. That was how the poltergeist saw it. Now Donald told Chibbett that unless the researcher agreed to help him save Jeremy, he would no longer cooperate with Chibbett's investigation. Dean also resurfaced, sending Chibbett a short note explaining that he had decided to avoid the researcher for a while. Chibbett's plan to encourage Donald to cooperate by focussing his attention on Dean had failed.

'It seems that a kind of impasse has been reached,' he commented in his casebook. 'Both personifications – real or otherwise – continue to be evasive. […] The personifications conveniently ignore those questions which might lead to ultimate proof of their identity.'

With evident frustration, Chibbett added that the psychologist Mr Manning had now 'dismissed the case as one of dissociation'. In Chibbett's opinion this diagnosis did nothing but give a name to some of the observed phenomena while failing adequately to explain the underlying cause(s). Chibbett accepted that psychology might well be an important factor in what was happening at No. 63, but he strongly believed that more research was needed.

CHAPTER 22

In keeping with their supposed lives of the twentieth and late-eighteenth centuries, Dean liked to communicate via the typewriter while Donald preferred to write by hand. In April 1957, however, Donald announced that Dean was teaching him to type. Actually, Chibbett had already received a couple of typewritten letters signed by Donald but Donald now claimed Dean had typed those on his behalf.

Donald also wanted Chibbett's opinion on whether he should write to RADA (the Royal Academy of Dramatic Art) and the Old Vic Theatre School in London to enquire about Shirley becoming an actress. Both addresses, the poltergeist crowed, had been obtained by him without Chibbett's assistance: 'NOT BEING RUDE TO VOUS BUT I THINK I CAN STAND ON MON TWO FEET'. Shirley, said Donald, was a shy girl who needed 'A PUSH' to get her going, so he asked Chibbett to broach the subject with her. He wanted 'RENIE TO BECOME A STAR'. Chibbett, though, was more interested in a particular detail of Donald's letter: in common with others received over the past few weeks – although with variations in the spelling, naturally – this latest letter had been signed 'DONALD LOUIS CHARLES PHILLIPPE CAPET'.

The 'Donald' part of this new, longer name was self-explanatory, and the poltergeist had been claiming for almost a year now that he had been called 'Louis' during his lifetime. As for 'Phillippe', this had first appeared (in various forms) in Donald's messages in April 1956. Chibbett had initially understood that Donald/Louis had had a brother named Philippe, but by mid-August 1956 Donald was claiming that Philippe had been his own name. By early December 1956 Donald had given his name as 'Louis Charles Phillippe Crapi', and 'Crapi' had already been identified as Donald's attempt at Capet, a reference to the French royal dynasty.

Chibbett still had only a sketchy understanding of the names of the French royal family of the period in Donald's story. (See the Appendix for a simplified family tree.) He knew that Donald had claimed to be the first-born son of Louis XVI but did not know whether this son had actually been named Louis. He *did* know that the king's *younger* son had been named Louis-Charles, and Donald had stated that the king had had only two sons, so Chibbett concluded that Donald's name when alive must have been 'Louis-Philippe'. Why, then, did Donald include 'Charles' in his name? The poltergeist replied to this question on 25 April: 'WHY I CALL MONSELF: LOUIS CHARLES INSTEAD [of] LOUIS PHILLIPPE? L. PHILLIPPE IS MON NAME; BUT HAS [as] I AM HIER [HEIR] TO THE THRONE I TAKE MY BROTHER'S NAME – MON PERE [i.e. father's] NAME TO [too] – SEE? MON PERE NAME IS: LOUIS PHILLIPPE – MON BROHTER: LOUIS CHARLES – MON NAME: LOUIS PHILLIPPE – CLEAR CHIB?' Clear? Not really! Moreover, although Chibbett did not yet realise it, Donald's 'father', Louis XVI, had been named Louis-Auguste, not Louis-Philippe. It was all very confusing.

On the subject of names, Chibbett also asked again why Donald referred to Shirley as 'Renie' (or Renee, etc). Donald replied, 'WELL – IT IS FRENCH – RENIE – AND I LIKE IT – BUT CHIB – I REALY WANT HER TO BE CALLED: LINGA

DA SILVER – IT MEANS: QUEEN OF PORTUGAL – SEE CLEAR?' Presumably it all made sense to Donald.

Donald wanted to demonstrate that Shirley had not studied French at school, so on 26 April he sent Chibbett her old school reports for the three years ended July 1955. His motive became clear a day or two later. Ever since Donald's first attempts to show he understood his (supposed) native tongue, Chibbett had encouraged him to write in French more often, so the researcher was delighted to receive several letters Donald had written on 27 April. The first began, 'MON CHIBE AMI, CHERE CHIB – JE AM ECRITURE A VOUS A JUSTE REMERCIER VOUS POUR PROCHAIN – JE DONNER VOUS FRANASCAN – E – WEE'. Beneath this, in what would be a rare example of Donald typing rather than writing, Donald had provided the 'translation': 'ENGLASER, DEAR CHIB – I AM WRITING TO YOU TO JUST THANK YOU FOR COMING – I GIVE YOU FRENCH – YES – MON AMI'.

'Although I am no French scholar,' commented Chibbett, 'the above seems to me to be somewhat weird and wonderful, but nevertheless, beyond the knowledge of Shirley.'

In another letter, Donald had written, 'JEREMY EST E RANGER ASTRE – E ANGE DE CIEL – CHIBE – JEREMY IL EST BIEN BEAU – IL CRI PLEURS – RENEE EST REINE DE PORTU-GALE – DOUX JOLI – JE AM LA FILS DE LOUIS DE FRANCE – FOI LOI ET ORDRE ALLER BIEN.' Beneath this, he had added, 'CHIBE – FRENCH VOUS DEMANDE – WEE. DONALD'.

Chibbett's rough translation of this somewhat mangled French was, 'Jeremy is a star stranger – an angel of the sky – Chib – Jeremy is a good fellow – he cries a lot [presumably a reference to the weeping picture] – Renee is Queen of Portu-gal – pretty sweet – I am the son of Louis of France – for law and order to go well'.

Donald seemed more willing now to cooperate with Chibbett, although he had not forgotten that this was supposed to be a *quid pro quo* arrangement. He reminded Chibbett of this on 1 May, asking again for Chibbett to arrange for Shirley to meet Kellar's film director friend. There is no indication that this film director did ever visit Shirley, but that didn't matter because a new development now captured everyone's attention.

A stranger called at No. 63 at 7 p.m. on Tuesday 30 April. He gave his name as Mr C— and said he represented David Spenser. (The family believed he was a solicitor but it is uncertain whether or not he actually was.) He told the family that Donald must immediately cease writing letters to David.

This upset Donald. After Mr C— left, Wally recorded that Shirley was tipped out of her bed eight times that night, that objects were thrown about, and that Vaseline was smeared across the wardrobe and a wall. Three lit matches were thrown into the downstairs front bedroom: two landed on the eiderdown and Wally had to extinguish them. Then Donald began tapping on the wall (probably the wall between 'his' room and the bedroom) and pulling Shirley's bedclothes. The chaos continued until around 2 a.m.

Wally spoke to Chibbett, and the two agreed that they needed to speak to Mr C— together. The three men met in No. 63 on Friday evening. In Chibbett's opinion Mr C— was initially sceptical of the story he was told but 'quickly moderated his attitude as he was shown the historical background of the case from the Press angle, and then the accumulated data in my case books.' Before long, Chibbett believed, Mr C— had probably 'abandoned any idea that the Hitchings or myself are responsible for the letters.' In response Mr C— explained that the Spensers had initially treated Donald's letters to them as a joke but had understandably become nervous when the letters started to arrive at David's home address (the contact address Donald had been given by the television company).

Stopping the letters might not be easy, Chibbett pointed out, because Donald tended not to do as he was told. A compromise was reached. If Donald addressed any further letters to the Spensers and left these for Wally to add stamps to, Wally would send them to Mr C— instead.

It was the middle of May and Shirley was due to start a new job in one month's time. Unfortunately, whatever this job was (the details have been lost) it was not the glittering showbusiness career that Donald and 'James Dean' envisioned for her. Donald made his disapproval clear in his letters to Chibbett, but the researcher did not reply. Chibbett was receiving more letters than he could cope with and, in the (vain) hope of dissuading Donald from writing to him so frequently, he had again decided not to respond for a while.

Also going unanswered were Donald's many letters to the Spensers (redirected by Wally to Mr C—). Being ignored quickly irritated Donald. In one letter he complained to Chibbett that Jeremy Spenser might get 'TOO BIG FOR HIS BOOTS' now that his film *The Sleeping Prince* was being released in the USA. He added that Jeremy's picture was crying again.

A menacing atmosphere was building inside No. 63. On Saturday 18 May the threatening messages returned, initially appearing on the doormat after nightfall. 'They threatened everyone in the house,' noted Chibbett, 'and the threats ranged from arson to murder.' Chibbett noted that the handwriting, although different to Donald's, occasionally showed the same characteristic reversal of letters. There was also a threatening tone to the tapped messages Shirley decoded as she lay in bed at night.

As the family watched television shortly after 10 p.m. on Monday night there was a burglary, or at least that was what it appeared to be. The target was Ethel's room upstairs, where the drawers were ransacked and a purse containing 2s 6d was stolen. There was a bootprint on the bed. The family believed this to be from a man's boot and found what they thought were marks on the drainpipe outside the open window, indicating how the burglar had entered. The police were called, but they clearly thought the 'burglary' was actually another aspect of the Donald saga. Household opinion was divided: Shirley, Wally and Ethel thought a burglar was responsible, while Mark and Kitty suspected Donald. Donald himself denied any involvement.

The police were also told about the threatening messages and they took the notes (together with an envelope stained with what appeared to be blood) with them before Chibbett had the opportunity to record their full contents.

'I AM SICK AND TIRED OF BEING KEPT DANGLING ON A STRING,' Donald complained to Chibbett on 23 May. 'I WISH FOR ACTION – I WRITE TO MR [C—] MANY TIMES BUT NO REPLY.' He finally got a response on 25 May when Mr C— visited No. 63 and admitted having received numerous letters from Donald. He had not brought any replies from either David or Jeremy, but did offer to take away and pass on to Jeremy the protective charm Donald wanted him to have. Given his anxiety over the young actor's safety Donald should have been relieved, but the poltergeist insisted Jeremy be told who the charm came from. Mr C— would not promise to tell him, so Donald refused to let Mr C— take the charm. Mr C— retorted that in that case he would simply ignore all of Donald's future letters.

With Donald's route to the Spensers now blocked, further threatening notes appeared in various locations around the house, including in Ethel's room and on the lavatory seat. Again, Wally handed the notes to the police before Chibbett could record what they said.

For the first time in months Donald (mostly) stopped writing to and about the Spensers, concentrating instead on his dolls.

He also briefly became interested in music, asking for a record player and a guitar, and seemed quite taken with Tommy Steele (the Londoner widely considered to have been the UK's first teen idol and rock and roll star, who had shot to fame the previous December). A record player was eventually obtained for Donald and Shirley to use, but the prospect of giving the poltergeist a guitar was too much to consider.

At noon on Monday 10 June, the day before Shirley was due to start her new job, Donald told her, 'RENIE – YOU ARE NOT GOING TO WORK – NO – KIT CAN SAY WHAT SHE LIKES – I DO NOT WISH HER TO GO'. The next morning brought more warnings, culminating at 8.25 a.m. with 'KIT – VOUS GET IT – VOUS ASK FOR IT – I FIRE'.

Soon after, Shirley's work clothes somehow became dirtied with muddy earth taken from some flowerpots, and Wally reported that Donald started to 'throw things about again'. Donald upset the furniture in the 'front room' and the downstairs bedroom, stripped off the bedclothes, and 'left 3 articals [*sic*] on the floor of each room' before throwing objects out into the passageway, aiming some at Ethel as she made her way downstairs. Later that morning Donald threatened to set fire to Ethel's room.

Donald did not burn Ethel's room. By the early afternoon he had calmed down – after it had become clear that Shirley would not be starting her new job after all.

CHAPTER 23

The Hitchings family got on well with their next-door neighbours at No. 61, but relations with their neighbours on the other side were less cordial. The situation was not helped by the thinness of the wall dividing Donald's room (the downstairs 'front room') from No. 65.

While researching this book, we corresponded with a neighbour who does not wish to be named but who stayed with the occupants of No. 65 for several weeks in late 1958. Those occupants were a Muslim family, who spoke little English and were averse to the idea of ghosts or poltergeists. The neighbour recalled, 'I was not allowed to sleep in the middle bedroom because I was told there was a poltergeist next door and the noises were very disturbing.' This neighbour remembers two other tenants (no longer resident in England) that slept in the room directly below and contacted them on our behalf to ask if they remembered anything. One declined to comment but the other (a young man at the time) remembered visiting the Hitchings home on Saturday evenings to watch television (there being no television set at No. 65). He recalled that the Hitchings family 'were getting on well' with the poltergeist, but that 'the poltergeist never liked me to be present there.'

The neighbour also asked another previous occupant of No. 65, who was a young girl at the time, for her memories. She recalled frequent visits to No. 63 with her mother, remembering that she herself had always felt very uncomfortable and sometimes even terrified in that house without really understanding why, and that she had once fainted in No. 63's kitchen (the only time she has ever fainted). She also remembered following her mother upstairs in No. 63 one time and feeling somebody ruffling her hair although there was nobody behind her.

As at mid-June 1957, tensions between Nos 63 and 65 were high. Not only was Donald tapping and banging on the walls, but now the neighbours were thumping away too, to express their annoyance. Tempers were so frayed that Wally seems for a time to have (mistakenly) suspected his neighbours of writing the threatening messages that continued to appear.

A number of other houses in the neighbourhood were also now receiving what the local press called 'poison pen letters'. According to the *South Western Star* (28 June 1957), these anonymous handwritten letters had first come through letterboxes in Wycliffe Road the previous summer (1956). The letters had then died away for a few months before re-appearing and, during the weeks leading up to the end of June 1957, had been appearing at an increasing rate.

Donald had learned to write during the summer of 1956. This, plus the way the resurgence in 'poison pen letters' coincided with the threatening notes in No. 63, strongly suggests that he was the culprit.

By the end of June at least six people had received these nasty messages. Those affected lived not only in Wycliffe Road but also in the no-longer-extant Hanbury Road, a small residential road that crossed Wycliffe Road at right angles. One letter was addressed to an elderly lady who found it when she returned home from her son's funeral. It is painful to imagine her distress as she opened the letter to read: 'It should have been your daughter.' According to another of this lady's daughters, the letter 'was written in ink and whoever sent it must be nearly illiterate. The language was filthy.' She added that the writer had made 'disgusting remarks' about her sister and that the letter was signed 'D.A.T.'

A man in Wycliffe Road received a letter addressed to 'The window cleaner', warning him that 'the dark nights are coming; you are likely to get pushed through a shop window.' (The punctuation was probably polished by the newspaper.)

The police declared there was little they could do. In their opinion, it was the work of a 'crank' and they effectively told the victims to ignore the threats.

At 7.30 p.m. on Thursday 27 June, three visitors arrived at No. 63: two young, inexperienced, female journalists and a 29-year-old part-time psychical researcher named Andrew Green who had been commissioned to look into these events by the *News Chronicle* newspaper.

In later years Green would establish himself as one of the UK's foremost authorities on ghosts and poltergeists. His name would also become closely associated with the present story due to his writing about it in his classic collection of British ghost stories *Our Haunted Kingdom* (1973). By the time of his death in 2004, Green had authored seventeen books and hundreds of articles on hauntings, and the Wycliffe Road case is mentioned in many of his writings. In fact, however, his association with these events was fairly restricted because both the Hitchings family and Chibbett quickly took a dislike to him. (Chibbett, who had never heard of Green before this, was not present when Green arrived on 27 June and was irritated when he was later told about the visit.)

The following details come from a personal account given by Green to one of the present authors in 2003:

> Following my interview with Shirley and her father … I requested
> 'Donald' (the 'poltergeist') to walk downstairs – he had been in
> the upstairs bedroom whilst we chatted in the front sitting room
> [i.e. the 'front room']. I was, as you can imagine, surprised on
> hearing footsteps descending the stairway and stopping outside
> the open doorway of the sitting room where we could see that the
> hallway was empty.

A little later, while talking to Shirley in the downstairs
bedroom, Green asked Donald to knock on the ceiling. Two
knocks duly came. Green then 'requested that "Donald" knock
on the wardrobe, on the other side of the bedroom – several
feet away from where we were sitting.' Again Donald obliged.
Green was at a loss to think of an explanation for the sounds.
Shirley then showed Green and the journalists how Donald
could spell out words by tapping to select letters as she moved
an upturned wine glass around a circle of letters written on
pieces of paper.

Green's account mentions that, whenever Donald was asked
a question, Shirley would 'screw up her eyes' for a few moments
before the tapped response sounded. This is a detail Green also
referred to in a letter that was published in the *Journal of the
Society for Psychical Research* in 2002. In this letter, Green recalled
how during his visit to No. 63 he and both of the journalists
'frequently' heard the 'knocks that [Shirley] seemed to be able
to produce whenever requested, but only associated with providing answers to specific questions and only after squeezing
her eyes shut for a second beforehand, as if summoning up
"the force".' However, Shirley is convinced that she did not
squeeze her eyes shut on these occasions, and Chibbett likewise makes no mention of this detail in his surviving papers.

After his visit that evening, Green recorded his impressions of
the situation inside No. 63. During the hours he had spent interviewing Shirley, Wally, and – to a lesser extent – Kitty, he had
clearly seen the extraordinary degree to which the family's

day-to-day life now revolved around Donald, of whose reality they had no doubt whatsoever. Green noted that the family were reluctant even to go shopping without first obtaining Donald's permission because, they said, the poltergeist often 'put things into the shopping bag that [they] hadn't purchased'.

Looking back in the mid-1970s (after a further two decades' experience of investigating hauntings and poltergeists) Green described Shirley as a 'typical agent' of poltergeist phenomena: a young teenager who was an 'only child, anaemic, intensely interested in two subjects to the exclusion of everything else, and "highly strung" (Green, 1976).' That Shirley was 'highly strung' was a fair comment but to the best of her recollection she has never been diagnosed as medically anaemic. Green probably meant this in the general descriptive sense; i.e. that Shirley appeared somewhat washed-out and lacking in vitality. Green described her interests as 'morbidly worshipping' James Dean and studying French history, but in Shirley's opinion he had completely misunderstood the situation. It was Donald who was interested in James Dean, she says, not her, and her supposed interest in French history was equally incorrect. Although she must have spent a great deal of time talking about French history while Green interviewed her, this was simply because she was trying to tell him about Donald's claim to be Louis.

Green also later stated that he had noticed a 'wealth of books in Shirley's bedroom devoted to James Dean and French history' (personal communication, 2003). Here again, Shirley disagrees with his memory; she denies ever possessing such books and maintains that the only books that would have been in the house were a handful of junior reference works such as *The Children's Encyclopaedia*, and storybooks such as *Jack and the Beanstalk*. Her insistence accords with Chibbett's observations that the family were not great readers and that very little reading material was ever present in No. 63. Perhaps some books *were* in the house during Green's visit – maybe, for example, Shirley and/or Chibbett had been trying to verify some of Donald's statements – but Shirley doubts even this and resents Green's implication that such books were the source material for Donald's statements.

Regarding Donald's claim to be the spirit of Louis, Green was decidedly unimpressed. Oddly, however, he came away from No. 63 with a version of the Louis story rather different to the one then being documented by Chibbett and still remembered by Shirley. One difference concerns an assertion by Green that Donald originally contacted Shirley because she resembled a Portuguese princess that Donald had once known. This, states Shirley, was completely untrue. She is understandably irritated by what she sees as false reporting here, but this inaccurate detail might have been down to a simple misunderstanding on Green's part because Donald did occasionally refer to Shirley as his princess. Moreover, there are several references to Portugal in Donald's communications. On 19 August 1956, for instance, Donald for some reason told Shirley, 'YOU ARE THE PRINCESS OF PORTIGAL [Portugal].' So, although Green might have been mistaken in understanding that Donald came to Shirley *because* of her resemblance to a Portuguese princess, it is easy to see how he might have reached this conclusion.

Green also stated that Shirley had talked about 'Duval "the well known Highwayman", who had also contacted her but we never gained any reason for this' (Green, personal communication, 2003). His comment here is puzzling because no reference to Duval can be found in Chibbett's surviving notes and Shirley remembers nothing regarding this name. It would hardly be worth mentioning were it not that Green's reference to Duval might hold the key to understanding the most significant discrepancy between Green's version of the Louis story and the version Chibbett was recording. In his book *Our Haunted Kingdom* Green wrote that Donald claimed to be the spirit of 'Louis Capet, the illegitimate son of Charles II of France born on 16 July, 1798 and drowned in a ship'. (This story would not stand up to even the slightest scrutiny because Charles II of France had lived during the ninth century A.D.) Yet, according to the story Chibbett had been putting together for over a year by this point, Donald was claiming to be the son of Louis XVI, not Charles II. With the benefit of hindsight, it seems likely that Green misunderstood what Shirley told him, and that the confusion arose as they talked about Duval.

Claude Duval (or Du Vall) was a gentleman highwayman who was born in Normandy, France in 1643 and was hanged for his crimes in London in 1670. Duval operated in England during the reign of King Charles II and it is probable, therefore, that the otherwise perplexing reference to a king called Charles II arose during talk of Duval. As for the date given by Green and quoted above, Donald had indeed originally stated that he had been born in 1798 but this date had long since been revised.

It would appear then that Green muddled a few details as he hurriedly took notes. With Shirley excitedly reporting an apparently endless series of poltergeist phenomena and messages from Donald (plus interjections from Wally and Kitty and no doubt countless interrupting questions from the two journalists) this would hardly be surprising. Moreover, the atmosphere inside No. 63 that evening seems to have been exceptionally chaotic. Green commented in 2003 that the 'highly imaginative' Shirley had been 'spraying hysteria around which affected both [of] the trainee journalists'.

A few days after his visit, Green was surprised to receive a four-page letter from Donald. (In total he would receive three letters and a Christmas card from the poltergeist over the coming months.) When he later compared a sample of Shirley's handwriting to that of Donald he concluded that both had been made by the same person. Chibbett, on the other hand, was certain that Donald's handwriting was quite different to Shirley's although, as has been mentioned, the similar spelling mistakes made by Shirley and Donald do suggest some connection between the two.

Despite his reservations, Green did not jump to the conclusion that Shirley was hoaxing him. At first he thought she might be writing the letters 'whilst in a semi-trance [with afterwards] only vague memories of the incident' (Green, 1976). He became more suspicious, though, on a return visit to No. 63. Although he deliberately avoided mentioning that Donald had written to him, Shirley spontaneously asked whether he had received any letters, which made Green suspect she had written them herself. Of course, by this time Donald was cheerfully firing off letters to all and sundry and so it might have been more surprising if Green *hadn't* received any! Green also found it hard to believe that Donald was able to obtain postage stamps for his letters, but as noted these stamps were actually added by Wally. Eventually, Green reverted to his earlier idea that Shirley was writing the letters herself without being aware of doing so (Green, quoted in *The X Factor* magazine, 1996).

To say that Shirley does not remember Green's involvement with fondness would be an understatement. She remembers him as a 'charming chap' but feels deeply betrayed by some of his later writings and statements about these events. Her personal resentment clearly stems in large part from the fact that Green obviously did not believe what she told him about Donald, and from statements he later made to the effect that she might have been mentally disturbed. Shirley's parents, too, disliked Green, feeling that he looked down on them because they were working class. Shirley's views may also have been coloured by Chibbett, who did not trust someone he described as an 'amateur psychic researcher'. Given that both men really only wanted to understand what was happening, this was unfortunate. Although Green would go on to establish himself as a widely respected investigator of reported hauntings, he was unable to investigate the events at No. 63 more fully without the blessing and cooperation of the Hitchings family, and quite clearly this would not be forthcoming.

Looking back almost half a century later, Green believed that there really had been something paranormal at work inside No. 63, but his ideas of what that something was were very different to Chibbett's. Green's decades of research would lead him to believe that poltergeist activity was caused not by spirits but by psychokinesis, the purported ability of the human mind to exert a direct influence on the physical world. Green did not believe that Donald aka Louis was a real entity separate from Shirley, feeling instead that naming the phenomena in this way was probably the family's means of coping with the chaos. Green concluded that much of what took place could be explained by hysteria, possible mental problems and perhaps even some instances of deliberate deception by Shirley. Nevertheless, for the rest of his life he remained impressed by some of the phenomena he had experienced at No. 63, in particular the tapping sounds attributed to Donald. Although Green originally came to the house believing Shirley might be making these sounds herself by 'cracking her bones', his direct experience of hearing tapping apparently emanating from several feet away from Shirley convinced him otherwise. In 2003 Green wrote that he believed that the 'real cause' of what happened in No. 63 was 'poltergeist phenomenon [*sic*] resulting from the girl's mental state combined with the distress of living in undesirable conditions.'

To Shirley, this characterisation of her family home as undesirable was deeply unfair. Yet despite the many deep and often divisive differences of opinion between the Hitchings family, Harold Chibbett and Andrew Green, they all agreed on one point.

Something remarkable was happening inside that house.

CHAPTER 24

Donald had been playing up again recently. Starting at around 11.30 p.m. on 25 June 1957, he had thrown objects around and banged on walls for almost three hours. Wally recorded that 'the piano played 3 times & also Shirley was locked out of her room & it seemed as though some one was walking very heavy up & down [the] stairs & also a heavy stick run up the banastars & stairs & the table top rolled out passed Shirley down to the kitchen door 2 times [*sic* throughout].' Just after 5 a.m. Donald woke everyone by furiously tapping out a warning that Shirley was in danger and needed to leave his room at once because a small plane might be about to crash outside. 'Donald ... pushed Shirley out of room,' wrote Wally, '& locked the door behind her & would not let her in for about 1½ hrs.' At around 8.15 a.m., no plane having crashed, Donald tapped out his relief that Renie was safe. (He would tap similar warnings of a plane crash on 6 and 11 July.)

At 11.15 p.m. on 1 July Donald announced he was expecting visitors – spirits who were going to participate in a meeting. At his request, Shirley took her bed back into her parents' room for the night. A little later, Wally checked Donald's room and noted that the mirror had been 'covered' (presumably by a sheet or something similar), a chair had been moved next to the coffee table, and there were several un-smoked cigarettes laid out ready on the piano top. When Wally checked the room again at 8.30 a.m., he 'found 7 cig ends & ash on a book on the coffee table & the mirror was still covered up.' There were also some notes written by Donald referring to the meeting. 'We did not hear any noise or sound during the night,' reported Wally. Donald did not say who his visitors had been but later that day he revealed more about why he had come to Shirley. Apparently she reminded him of his sister, 'THE DUCHESSE D'ANGOULEME'. Chibbett made a note of this name.

Ash and cigarette stubs, as well as the occasional un-smoked cigarette, were found in the 'front room' ashtray on several other occasions too. Wally suspected Donald had pinched the cigarettes and matches from Mark's friends when they had visited recently. On 9 July 5 shillings disappeared from Ethel's purse, not long after Donald asked Wally to use Ethel's money to buy make-up for Shirley. The elderly woman suspected that Shirley had stolen the money. She tried to hit the teenager with her stick and a furious row erupted between Ethel and Kitty. Later, the contents of Ethel's rooms were found to have been thrown around. A little before 10 p.m. on Saturday 13 July, while Ethel was out of the house, Wally noticed that the lights were on in her rooms. He investigated: 'I found all her things on the floor as though a burgalar [*sic*] had been in.' Disturbingly, a 'fork & big carver [knife]' had been stabbed into the back of Ethel's kitchen door. At 11.10 p.m. on Wednesday 24 July, wrote Wally, Ethel's and Mark's room were 'turned upside down again. Draws [*sic*] & cupboards open & all the things laying about the place.'

The redoubtable and sharp-tongued old woman who had ruled No. 63 until Donald usurped her crown could no longer cope. Exhausted and feeling unwell, Ethel left the house again on Friday afternoon, having arranged to stay in a nursing home in Roehampton, south-west London, for a rest.

Early the next morning the police visited No. 63 and offered to take Wally to the nursing home. His mother had suffered a stroke. By the time Wally arrived Ethel had passed away.

There was no sign of Donald for the rest of Saturday. He remained subdued on Sunday, only faintly tapping out his usual morning greeting. A written note was found on Monday morning: 'I AM NOT ALLOWED TO SPEAK FOR AT LEAST A WEEK SO FORGET ME – I HAVE TAKEN A VAUL [vow] TO BE SILENT – DON.' A note did appear on Tuesday morning, suggesting that 'Renie' should get her hair cut into a new short style for the funeral (with more pressing matters at hand this was ignored) but in general Donald remained very quiet. So much so that by Thursday Wally wrote in his diary, 'It seems he's gone, I hope.'

Ethel was buried at Morden Cemetery in south London on the afternoon of Friday 2 August. Before the family left for the funeral service, their pet hamster also died. 'Donald laid it out in the back room,' recorded Wally, '& lit a candle & put a little cross & also he covered the hamster over with a black cloth.' There was no further sign of Donald on Friday.

Within a few days, however, Donald was tapping away again, asking for paper and stamps and writing letters. On 8 August he decided the time had come to redecorate 'his' room: '[9.15 a.m.] RENIE – WILL VOUS TAKE ALL TOMMY STEELE PICTURES DOWN THEN CLEAR SHELF AND GET A SPONGE AND GIVE MY PAINT A CLEAN BUT PUT ALL FURNITURE COVER OVER WITH A COVER – I WANT TO DO MY ROOM UP.' Together, Donald and Shirley set about the task.

Chibbett was still ignoring Donald's letters. On 12 August he received another from the poltergeist, this one ordering him to return everything Donald had written. The next morning Shirley telephoned Chibbett; after some chat she mentioned that Donald had been writing to him. Chibbett denied having received any letters recently, 'in order to discover what "Donald's" reaction would be.' Shortly after noon a note was

discovered inside No. 63: 'KIT – I DO NOT TRUST CHIBB
NO MORE'. On 14 August Chibbett received another message
from Donald, demanding a reply to his letters.

The researcher visited No. 63 on Saturday 17 August. When
Kitty and Shirley brought up the subject of Donald's letters
Chibbett again denied having received them, steering the
conversation around to Donald's redecorating efforts instead.
The poltergeist, he noted, was carrying out this work 'with all his
usual and exuberant zeal. According to the family, he scraped
off the paper from an entire wall in "his" room, and is quite
prepared to do the wall papering as well, if Mr H. will let him.'

In Donald's opinion, the room was not the only thing
that needed restyling. Shirley had had her hair permed in
April and she had never been pleased with the result (which
was why Donald had suggested she get her hair cut for
Ethel's funeral). 'I AM SO TIERD OF RENIE MOANING
ABOUT HER HAIR,' complained Donald in a note found on
11 August, urging Kitty to buy Shirley some hair products
and 'LET HER SWIM IN IT'. He continued fifteen minutes
later: 'I DO NOT LIKE MON RENIE HAIR – IT LIKE A
SHABY DOGS TAILS.' It would take another few weeks but
Wally and Kitty eventually gave Shirley the money to have
her hair re-styled in a more fashionable short cut.

Donald had also started experimenting with photography,
Chibbett was told. On 14 August Kitty had loaded Mark's
camera with a fresh roll of film and left it in the 'front room'.
It soon disappeared and when it was found again several
minutes later the film indicator number had moved, indicating a picture had been taken. The following day, Donald
announced he had taken more pictures, including shots of
Jeremy in Kenya and of Mr C— at work at his desk in his office.
Wally rushed to the nearest chemist to get the film developed.

From a total of twelve exposures, the chemist was able to
develop eight photographs. The Hitchings family was disappointed to find the resulting images blurry and indistinct, but

Chibbett was intrigued. The psychical researcher believed that the white 'blobs' visible in some of the pictures might be evidence of 'something previously misty and ephemeral … condensing into the object seen.' He hoped that as Donald became more practised these blobs would reveal themselves to be the faces of spirit beings.

Chibbett was eager to encourage Donald's foray into 'psychic photography' so on his journey to No. 63 on the evening of 29 August he purchased a new roll of film. Ideally, Chibbett would have loaded this into Mark's camera himself and left the camera in a controlled location so that he could be certain that nobody apart from Donald could have touched it. Circumstances made that impractical, so Chibbett simply left the film with the family; Wally loaded it into the camera shortly before leaving for work at 6 a.m. the next morning. Wally reset the film indictor number and left the camera on top of the piano in Donald's room. Shortly after noon Shirley and Kitty noticed that the indicator number had moved. With the camera was a note from Donald, listing the photographs he claimed to have taken:

KIT A LEST [LIST] OF WHAT I TOOK ON CAMRA [SIC]

1. MIRROR
2. MORROR [SIC]
3. OUT WINDOW
4. [DITTO]
5. VOUS CLEANING STEP
6. TROWING [THROWING] SOMETHING
7. FLYING BAG
8. [DITTO]
9. [DITTO]
10. OUT SHELTER
11. MIRROR
12. MIRROR
DON

Expectations were high, but when the photographs were developed seven of the exposures were blank, and although the remaining five did show images these were far from dramatic (see fig. 21). Chibbett tried several times to persuade Donald to take further photographs, leaving his own loaded camera in Donald's room, but on 17 September Donald left a note: 'CHIBB CAN JOLLY WELL WAIT – I TAKE PICTURE IN MON OWN TIME'.

The poltergeist was furious. A few weeks earlier Chibbett (unable to visit No. 63 as often as he would have liked) had written to Mark to ask the level-headed young man to keep a discreet eye on events and report back with his private opinions. Soon afterwards, a note was discovered: 'CHIBBETT IS NOT HAS [AS] VOUS THINK – I GOT PROOF'. Donald had seen Chibbett's letter and did not appreciate being spied on.

'I AM MOST ANGRY,' wrote Donald to Chibbett on 2 September. 'I THINK NO LONGER OF YOU AS MY FIRST TRUSTWORTHY SCRIBE – I HAVE DE-RANKED YOU TO "PEN SCRIBBLE".'

A few days later Donald demanded that Chibbett cease his experiments and get on with what was really important: helping Jeremy Spenser. It was stalemate. Donald would not cooperate with Chibbett unless Chibbett helped him contact Spenser, but Chibbett refused to do what Donald wanted until the poltergeist cooperated with his investigations.

The following note was discovered at 11.40 p.m. on 6 September: 'WALTER – I WANT SOME RED SEALS FOR MON LETTRE [...] LOOK KIT – I MUST HAVE SOME ACTION AND SHOW CHIBBETT – OR ELSE – WELL – WE WILL BE STUCK IN THE HOLE – WE ARE NOW GETTING NO WHERE – THINK IT OVER – I WANT 6 RED SEALS – DON.'

'Seals' were what Donald called postage stamps, which is what he seems to have been asking for here. Sometimes, however, 'seals' really did mean seals. On 23 August a letter addressed to Chibbett had arrived in an envelope that was sealed in two places with red wax. On the seals were the sort of impressions that might have been made by an aristocrat's signet rings: one showed the impression of a crown while the other bore stylised letters. (Chibbett thought these might have been the initials 'LC' for 'Louis-Charles'.) Now, further envelopes started to reach Chibbett, bearing both stamps and wax seals. One was delivered on 14 September and its red wax seal bore a new design of nine arms radiating from a central hub, with a fleur-de-lis at the end of each point.

Intrigued by these designs, Chibbett wrote to the College of Arms for help in identifying two of them. (He does not appear to have shown them the 'LC' design.) In the College's opinion the crown was of an English rather than French style, which was a little disappointing, but regarding the third design the College replied, 'The circular seal impression shows an escarbuncle. A golden escarbuncle upon a red field is the Arms attributed at a very early date for the French Kingdom of Navarre.'

To be an accurate representation of the Navarre symbol, the design should have had eight points rather than nine, but if Chibbett realised this he was not overly concerned. He sensed he was on the verge of a breakthrough and his excitement mounted. 'Could Shirley – a young girl of sixteen – have possibly found these [seals] somewhere?' he wondered. 'The knowledge of these seals is unlikely to be easily accessible to a minor, and is of a specialised kind, requiring considerable research.'

It was clear that Chibbett needed to examine the seals themselves, rather than merely their wax impressions. He tried to persuade Donald to lend them to him but Donald refused, explaining in a letter to Chibbett dated 28 September that it was forbidden for the rings to leave his fingers, even after death. 'THAT IS THE FRENCH RULE,' he stated unequivocally.

It was during this flush of excitement over the 'seals' that events in No. 63 started to take on a different character. The story that had been waiting in the wings – the story of Donald as the earthbound spirit of Louis the dauphin – was finally taking centre-stage. This was what Chibbett had been hoping for. Despite some lingering doubts, the psychical researcher wanted to believe that Donald truly was Louis's spirit. However, in order to explore how well the poltergeist's claims stood up to scrutiny, Chibbett needed Donald to provide fuller details of his alleged life in Revolutionary France.

He was about to get his wish.

PART II

THE KING OF SHADES

CHAPTER 25

Chibbett had not visited No. 63 for around one month. He had needed to devote time to his job and to his personal life, and, moreover, both Kitty and Wally had been unwell.

To get some much-needed rest, Kitty had taken a short break at a spa in Droitwich. At the start of October 1957, she returned home to find that Donald had left her a small envelope sealed with his wax crown. Inside was a note, which unusually was typed and used both upper and lower case. As well as welcoming her home, the note informed her, 'I have broken friends wiht [*sic*] Chibbett so we do not talk any more of him'.

Wally, meanwhile, had been forced to take time off work because he was suffering from a bout of 'Asian "flu"', a potentially deadly influenza pandemic that had been sweeping around the world. He did not return to work until Thursday 17 October. Coincidentally, that was the same day Chibbett was at last able to visit again.

When the researcher arrived that afternoon he was told that Donald had been very well-behaved lately. The poltergeist had, however, been keeping busy. Back on 24 July, Donald had announced plans to reveal 'MON LIFE STORY AS A PRINCE', and some of his allegedly autobiographical details had recently started appearing in his notes and letters. In one long letter, written on 14 October, Donald had supplied a list of people who were supposedly members of his father's royal court. Following this he, for the first time, referred to a boy named 'NICKALOS': 'HE WAS MY AGE FIFTEEN – HE HAD BLACK HAIR – BIG DARK BROWN EYES AND WAS A KITCHEN BOY I USED TO BE GREAT FRIENDS WITH […] I WOULD TEACH HIM TO READ – HE TAUGHT ME TO BE TRUE AND LOYAL.' The following day, Donald had written another long letter, throwing down names and historical details in a stream-of-consciousness style.

While he was at No. 63, Chibbett tried to get Donald to answer specific questions about his claimed past life. To his surprise the poltergeist actually cooperated by tapping out responses. Donald, who had long claimed to have drowned in the English Channel, now gave details of what had allegedly taken place. He explained that he had sailed in a ship named *Royal Ark* from Boulogne harbour in France in the autumn of 1789. On board he had been accompanied by Nickalos and by a member of the British aristocracy – the Duke of Bedford. Had the ship reached Dover, he would apparently have been met there by the Prince of Wales, but the *Royal Ark* never arrived. Shortly after leaving port she had been caught in a great storm and sank with the loss of all hands.

Donald also mentioned that his elder brother had been a 'hunchback' who had died, aged 7, when Donald had been 5 years old. Receiving these new details was exciting, but they also added to the confusion over who Donald was claiming to be. Until now, Chibbett had been assuming that Donald aka Louis had been the king's first-born son, but here Donald was referring to an elder brother. Chibbett knew that the king had had only two sons and Donald had previously insisted that his own name had been Louis-Philippe while his brother's name had been Louis-Charles. Therefore, Chibbett now concluded that Donald must have been the king's second-born son and that the first-born had been named Louis-Charles.

In fact, Chibbett had previously learned (in August 1956) that Louis-Charles had been the name of the king's *younger* son; he was still struggling to absorb all of the material and his historical research had not yet discovered the eldest son's correct name. The muddle over these names passed unnoticed for now, but Chibbett did spot a problem with the dates.

Donald had just said he had been 5 years old when his elder brother died, and Chibbett knew that the king's first-born son had died in 1789. Yet Donald had always insisted he had been 15 years old when he drowned, supposedly also in 1789. How could he have been both 5 and 15 in the same year?

Neither could Donald's claimed year of birth be correct. In August 1956 Donald had said he was born in '1771–1772' (changing from the original 1798), but if Donald had been 15 when he died in 1789 he must have been born in around 1774. Donald himself now confirmed this, telling Chibbett that he had been born on 16 July 1774. But this did not fit other details. Although it now appeared that Donald was claiming to be the king's second-born son, historical records showed that the second-born son had been born not in 1774 but in 1785.

It was all highly confusing – and there was yet another problem. Donald had clearly claimed to be the spirit of the son that had become Louis XVII, but the official historical records concerning the fate of Louis XVII were clear. After the French Revolution, that young boy and other members of the royal family had been incarcerated in Paris, within the medieval fortress-prison known as the Temple. After the executions of his father (Louis XVI) and mother, the boy – who was now technically Louis XVII – remained in prison, eventually to die there on 8 June 1795. How, then, could he have drowned in 1789? One possibility seemed to provide a lifeline. Over the years there had been many rumours that official reports of the boy's death in prison were untrue and that he had secretly been rescued. Chibbett (mistakenly) assumed that Louis and the other members of the royal family had been imprisoned at the outset of the French Revolution in 1789 (in fact, they were not imprisoned until 1792) and so it seemed possible to him that the young Louis had been rescued later that same year. Perhaps even drowning as per Donald's story while attempting to flee France. Temporarily setting aside the other issues, Chibbett could not help but wonder: were the rumours about a secret escape true, and did Donald possess the answer to one of history's most controversial mysteries – the true fate of the dauphin?

After Chibbett left, Donald tapped out a long message to Shirley in which he stated, 'I WAS CHRISTENED LOUIS PHILLIPPE CAPET FOR CAPET WAS MY FATHER'S HOUSE NAME […] I ALSO HAD A SISTER OLDER THAN I – HER NAME WAS D'ANGOULEME BUT I CALLED HER ANNA FOR I LIKED IT'.

Back on 20 April 1956 a message from Donald had included the phrase 'SISTERS NAME IS ANNE AGE 9 YRS' and this new message seemed to clarify her identity. Louis XVII had had a sister named Marie Thérèse Charlotte, affectionately known as 'Madame Royale', who had later become Duchesse d'Angoulême. On 1 July 1957 Donald had referred to the Duchesse d'Angoulême when he claimed that he had chosen Shirley because she looked like his sister. These details seemed to fit together. However, as with so much of Donald's story, they were not a perfect match with what history recorded: Madame Royale did not become Duchesse d'Angoulême until her marriage to Louis-Antoine de Bournon, Duc d'Angoulême, and that took place in 1799, years after the supposed death of Donald aka Louis, so why would Donald ever have known her as 'Anna'?

It was also interesting to note this sister's age relative to Donald. Donald had originally stated that she had been 9 years old when he drowned at the age of 15, but now he was (correctly) saying she had been older than him. The poltergeist's story was evolving.

Based on the new information, Chibbett was eager to pursue two lines of enquiry that might help corroborate Donald's story. Did the present Duke of Bedford's family archives contain records of an ancestor's attempt to rescue the dauphin from Revolutionary France? And was there any evidence that a ship named *Royal Ark* had existed in 1789?

Donald urged Chibbett to contact the duke as quickly as possible. 'I HAVE REMEMBERED HIS ESTATE ADDRESS,' he prompted in a letter, 'WOBURN MANOR.' Chibbett wrote to Woburn and while he waited for the duke to reply he looked into the *Royal Ark*.

The Board of Admiralty told Chibbett they had no record of a ship by that name, although it was possible it 'had been hired or taken up for temporary naval service without being registered as one of H.M. ships.' At the Public Record Office Chibbett consulted Admiralty records for 1789, only to discover that the relevant page was blank, a fact that astonished the librarian. The researcher's mind whirled as he wondered whether he had stumbled upon evidence of a cover-up over Louis's fate.

On 8 November, Donald wrote to Chibbett to say, 'I ESCAPED FROM THE TEMPLE EASILY. I WAS TO MEET THE DUKE OF BEDFORD AND LORD DE AVERINGTON, AND A CAPTAIN OF A SHIP WHO COULD BE TRUSTED. SO WE ESCAPED IN THE 'ROYAL ARK''. After briefly describing the fateful storm that engulfed the ship Donald mentioned that there had initially been another plan: 'MY MOTHER WANTED ME TO GO TO AUSTRIA WITH HER FRIEND, TO STAY WITH HER FATHER'. Unfortunately, explained Donald, guards had been posted along the border and so it was decided to take the English Channel route instead.

Soon after this, Chibbett was delighted to find a 1910 book titled *Lectures on the French Revolution* by Lord Acton. Although

Acton himself believed Louis XVII had died in prison in 1795 as history recorded, he mentioned the rumours that the boy had been rescued with another boy secretly being substituted in his place. Intrigued by this idea, Chibbett asked Donald whether he knew who such a substitute might have been. Donald said he did not.

On 13 November, Chibbett wrote to ask Donald for fuller details of his escape and whether he could remember the name of his mother's friend, who had been supposed to take the young boy to Austria. Donald ignored most of Chibbett's questions but he did respond to the final query and the answer surprised Chibbett.

Chibbett's long hours in the British Library, reading up on French history, were leading him to suspect that the rescue had been organised by Count Axel von Fersen. Fersen, a dashing officer in the Swedish royal army, had had an extremely close friendship – even, allegedly, an affair – with Louis's mother. He was certainly a suitable candidate for Marie Antoinette to have turned to in a bid to save her son.

Yet Donald did not name Fersen. He gave a name Chibbett had not encountered anywhere in his researches: 'COUNT HENSDORF'.

CHAPTER 26

Count Hensdorf's name might have been new but another
name that cropped up now was very familiar. In November 1957
Donald started to wonder whether the actor Jeremy Spenser
was the living descendant of someone who had been involved
in the dauphin's rescue, writing to Chibbett, 'THERE WAS A
LORD SPENSER WHO I WAS TO MEET IN YOUR COUNTRY
IF I WENT THERE – DO YOU NOT SEE – IT COULD BE
JEREMY'S FAMILY'. Perhaps, suggested Donald, this explained
why he had found himself drawn towards the actor: 'IT WAS AS
THOUGH I KNEW HIM'.

Donald had not forgotten Jeremy. The general emphasis
of his communications, however, was now very much on his
claim to be Louis. This was probably (at least in part) because
the Hitchings family increasingly treated Donald as if he really
were the spirit of the dead dauphin.

So keen was Donald to prove this to be the case that he
bombarded the family and Chibbett with references to life in
eighteenth-century France. Unfortunately, noted Chibbett,
even if the researcher had the resources to examine each of
these references, and found that every single one was accurate,
they would ultimately be of little evidential value because they
'*could* have been obtained from extant sources of information.'

On some occasions Chibbett did spot inaccuracies in Donald's references but he felt that these could often be explained by Donald's tendency to transpose letters, numbers and even whole words. For example, at one point Donald wrote that his supposed father, the king, 'attempted to escape in 1791 to Paris.' This, noted Chibbett, 'was obviously incorrect but substitute the word "from" for "to", and the statement becomes accurate, for in 1791 the royal family travelled *from* Paris *to* Varennes.'

Whether accurate or not, most of Donald's references were easy to understand. Some, though, were opaque. In October, for instance, Donald had written what appeared to be a quotation. Following the words 'COMTE DE PROVENCE' was the phrase 'ENGLAND NO MORE VOUS FOE WILL BRING YOU OVER – WHEN FRANCE SHALL WELCOME HOME THE WHITE COCKADE'. Several more years would pass before the meaning of this message became clear.

On 16 November, the Duke of Bedford's secretary replied to Chibbett's enquiry: nothing in the duke's family records supported the idea of a plot to rescue the dauphin. Chibbett reported the disappointing news to Donald, and two days later the poltergeist replied, 'I DID ESCAPE, AND WENT IN THE ROYAL ARK – SHE WAS A LIGHT VESSEL OF WOOD LIKE YOUR "BRIG" – IN FACT I THINK SHE WAS – HER CAPTAIN WAS AN ENGLISHMAN – NAME OF STUART – I DO NOT KNOW HIS FIRST NAME – IT WAS WITH THE DUC DE BEDFORD AND LORD AVERINGTON I ESCAPED'.

Chibbett decided he would keep searching for the ship. He also asked Donald for further information about his brother. Donald replied, 'CHARLES WAS BORN IN 1782 – DIED IN 1789 AGE SEVEN – WITH A HUMP ON HIS BACK'. Donald had mentioned his brother being a 'hunchback' before and although Chibbett had found nothing yet that confirmed or refuted that detail he did spot that 1782 was incorrect. As Chibbett knew, the king's first-born son had been born on 22 October 1781 and had died on 4 June 1789. Yet Chibbett excused this error: 'If the reader thinks that the date discrepancy is important let *him* try to remember off-hand the birthdate of any relative who has been dead for many years.' Even so, Donald's statement contained another, more serious, inaccuracy. He was still adamant that his full name had been 'Donald Louis Charles Philippe Capet', and had previously stated that people had known him as 'Louis-Philippe' and his brother as 'Louis-Charles'. But as Chibbett looked through historical records he now learned that Donald's claimed brother (the boy who had died in 1789) had been named Louis-*Joseph*. It was Donald, if he really were the spirit of the boy who became Louis XVII, who had been named Louis-Charles. There was no evidence that *either* had ever been called Louis-Philippe.

With so much else to concentrate on, the researcher decided to deal with this problem later. The confusing historical details were intriguing but Chibbett wanted something more substantial – something he could literally get his hands on. On 23 October he left some blue sealing wax in Donald's room and asked the poltergeist to provide him with good quality impressions of his 'royal' wax seals. The requested impressions were later found in the house. Even better, though, would be the seals themselves. If they could make impressions in wax then they were presumably physical objects, possibly from Donald's own time; if authentic they could be important evidence in support of Donald's story.

Donald stubbornly continued to deny Chibbett access to the seals. However, he did now consent to Chibbett borrowing the small metal crown Shirley had found in the passageway in August 1956. Gold-coloured, with a screw attachment at the bottom and decorated with fleur-de-lis designs and what looked like tiny jewels, this had (according to Donald) come from the hilt of 'a sword of France'. Would examination of this artefact support Donald's story, Chibbett wondered?

'MON KITTY WITTY,' asked Donald on 27 November. 'CAN I HAVE A PET FOR XMAS PLAIT [...]?' He wanted a male hamster he would call 'JEREMY NICKALOS' – or, failing that, a lizard or a frog. Christmas was evidently on his mind because the following day, when the family returned from a trip to Woolworths, they found that an extra Christmas card had been put in with their shopping. Naturally, they assumed Donald was responsible.

On 2 December, Donald changed his mind about his pet: 'I WANT A CAT FOR CHRISTMAS – A BLACK ONE.' On Tuesday he decided that Chibbett, a pipe-smoker, should be given 'SOME CLAY PIPES FOR BUBBLES [...] THEIR [*sic*] 4½ D IN TOY SHOP'. Two days later Donald began planning how to decorate his room this year: 'WALT – MAY I HAVE THE FOLLOWING – DRAWING PINS – FEATHERS – LANTERNS – TINSELL – CHRISTMAS TREE (LIVE ONE) – GOLD PAPER – COTTON WOOL – RIBBON'. Wally supplied what he could.

The weather was seasonally chilly and Donald felt that chill on Sunday morning (8 December): 'KIT – MAY JE HAVE A FIRE IN MON ROOM TODAY PLAIT'. Presumably he got his wish because that evening he left a present for Wally and Kitty: a snowman made of cotton wool.

Donald started to decorate his Christmas tree and room on 16 December, sticking letters cut from silver paper to the mirror to spell 'A JOYEUX NOEL'. Decorating kept him so busy that for a few days the family only heard the occasional tapping sound.

On Friday 20 December, Chibbett and his wife, Lily, visited No. 63 and asked Donald what he would like for a present. The poltergeist replied by tapping out letters: 'S – E – V – E –'. 'Several?' guessed Mrs Chibbett aloud, before her husband could caution her against prompting the poltergeist. Donald ignored her suggestion and continued tapping:

'SEVENTEENTH CENTURY TOY LIKE I HAD AT HOME.' (He probably meant eighteenth century – the 1700s; he had made this same mistake before.) Chibbett asked where such a toy might be obtained and the taps replied, 'IN AN ANTIQUE SHOP – IN REGENT STREET'. Further tapped responses narrowed down the location, suggesting that the shop Donald had in mind was in London's West End, close to the junction of Regent Street and Oxford Street. Given the area, it was likely to be an expensive present! When Chibbett asked what sort of toy Donald wanted he was told, 'DOLL … MOTHER,' which he understood to mean a doll dressed as Marie Antoinette. Chibbett made the journey into central London on a miserably rainy Saturday and after a long search found a suitable doll.

The family gave Donald his presents on Christmas Eve. They had bought him toy soldiers, a fort and a chocolate clown. Before long they found the wrapping paper and toy soldiers strewn across the floor of Donald's room, with the chocolate clown displayed on the piano. Donald left his own presents for the family on Christmas morning. There was a brooch for Kitty, a tie pin and collar studs for Wally and, for Shirley, a bottle of perfume.

All was peaceful until Friday 27 December when Donald remembered he had actually wanted a pet for Christmas: '[6.15 p.m.] KIT – JE WANT A CAT – VOUS PROMISE[D] – IF VOUS DO NOT GET IT FOR ME JE WILL CRY ET CRY AND CRY AND NO LIKE VOUS'. Kitty refused, Donald insisted, and the argument continued the following day. Eventually, though, Donald lost interest.

Wally's closing diary entry for 1957 ran [*sic* throughout], 'This is the second year for Donald the Polt in our House of 63 Wycliffe Rd Battersea SW11. He's been a good boy on the whole a little rough at times but not so bad as 1956 year.'

❖❖

Much of Chibbett's own Christmas break was spent visiting jewellers to get their views on Donald's small metal crown. The general consensus was that the object had no intrinsic value; the 'jewels' were probably paste and the body made of some base metal. His enquiries took him to theatrical costumiers, toy shops and antique dealers. On 3 January 1958, Chibbett took the crown to London's famed Victoria and Albert Museum, where he showed it to the Jewellery and Metals Section. Following this expert examination, he 'was assured that [the crown] had no value, and that almost certainly it had been made within the last thirty years. It seems clear, therefore, that "Donald's" claim that it formed part of the hilt of his sword, must be discredited.'

Chibbett decided to keep these latest findings to himself for the time being.

CHAPTER 27

Given Donald's fondness of historical television dramas it was little surprise that when a feature film about his own (alleged) past life came out Donald was keen to see it. *Dangerous Exile* starred Richard O'Sullivan as the young dauphin who, in a swashbuckling fictional tale, escaped the Revolution by flying to a Welsh island by balloon. At the beginning of January 1958 the film was showing in London, so Donald decided to see it in a cinema in Leicester Square. According to Chibbett's records Donald went there with Shirley, although Shirley's recollection of this today is that Donald went without her. Either way, Donald was unimpressed by what he saw.

The method of his escape was 'ALL WRONG', he told Chibbett in a letter dated 3 January, and other details were incorrect also. '[According to the film] I WAS SUPPOSED TO HAVE HAD A MAID VIRGINIA – MY MAID WAS NANETTE AND SHE STAYED IN FRANCE – I TOOK NICKALOS WITH ME – SO THEY ARE WRONG – EVEN MY HAIR [was] WRONG IN THE FILM – THE BOY WHO PLAYED MYSELF HAD BROWN HAIR – I GOT REDDISH BLOND HAIR – MORE FAIR THAN RED – AUBURN.'

Donald was still angry on 24 January: 'I DID NOT ESCAPE TO ENGLAND IN A BALLOON OR IN A LAUNDRY BASKET

– I WILL TELL YOU HOW I ESCAPED IN A FURTHER
LETTER'. Chibbett did not have to wait long. The previous
November, when the researcher had stumbled upon the rumour
that another boy was substituted for the dauphin during the
prison rescue, Donald had claimed not to know who this substitute had been. Now, it seemed, his memory was improving:

> [Typed message left by Donald, 30 January] The map I enclose
> is the map of my escape. There were two routes of escape in
> case one did not work. My father wanted me to go [to] England.
> My mother wanted me to go to Austria. But father won the day.
> I went to England. The plan was made on 18th January 1793 at
> the Temple. My father was beheaded on the 21st January 1793
> and I escaped on the 22nd January 1793. My mother was [then]
> on her own with a small boy who she only knew by being her
> best friend's son. I escaped with Nickalos and Count Hensdorf
> of Austria. His son Karl took my place...

'According to "Donald",' summarised Chibbett, 'the Count,
his son Karl and Nickalos entered his [prison] apartment in the
early hours of the morning disguised as chimney sweeps. While
there, a quick substitution was made, and the boy Karl took
Louis XVII's place, the latter's clothes being exchanged with those
of Karl. The sweeping party then left the prison unsuspected.'

It was a dramatic story. But, regardless of how likely it was
from a historical perspective, Donald's latest revelations raised
another question: if he had not been rescued from prison until
January 1793, how could he have had fled France aboard the
Royal Ark in, as he had previously stated, 1789?

Chibbett continued to spend long hours in the British
Museum Reading Room, perusing works about Louis XVI,
Marie Antoinette, the French Revolution and so on.

On 8 February he came across confirmation of at least one of Donald's earlier statements. In October and November 1957 Donald had stated that his brother had been a 'hunchback'. It was 'only after considerable research' that Chibbett discovered that Louis-Joseph had suffered from a curvature of the spine, which hunched his back and made it difficult for him to walk. Of course, it was impossible to prove that Shirley had *not* stumbled across this information somewhere, but Chibbett considered this unlikely.

Encouraged, Chibbett continued to scour volume after volume. Any and all historical details were potentially useful for testing Donald's knowledge of his claimed past life but Chibbett was especially seeking any evidence that the dauphin had been rescued from prison. He soon realised that this possibility had exercised a powerful hold on people's imaginations ever since the French Revolution. Of all the books he looked through, one in particular appealed to Chibbett. Written by Hans Roger Madol in 1930, this was *The Shadow-King: The life of Louis XVII of France and the fortunes of the Naundorff-Bourbon family.* (Chibbett would later pay homage to this book by titling his own, never-to-be-published, record of Donald's claims *The King of Shades*.) Madol's book examined apparent discrepancies in the historical record and, Chibbett noted, suggested 'that the young Dauphin did in fact escape from the Temple before the date of his alleged death in June, 1795, and that a substitute took his place.' By the end of his reading, Chibbett had been persuaded that that aspect of Donald's claims was not only possible but actually quite likely.

Donald continued to bombard Chibbett with names and other historical information, and the researcher did his best to check the accuracy of the information. Often, Donald appeared to be correct but the problem remained that anything Chibbett could confirm *might* have been seen by Shirley in a book, film or other source. What Chibbett wanted was information regarding something not known to history but which might yet be proved accurate – such as the details of Donald's escape from the Temple.

The next major development in Donald's account of his escape came in April 1958 when he described how, after his rescue, the mysterious Count Hensdorf had taken him and Nickalos across France to shelter at a sheep farm close to the border with Switzerland. The boys stayed there for some time while Hensdorf 'WAS BUSY IN PARIS HELPING PEOPLE TO ESCAPE MADEMOISELLE GUILLOTINE'. Chibbett had been unable to find any historical mention of the Scarlet Pimpernel-like count. He had pushed Donald for further details, only for Donald to hint that 'Hensdorf' might not have been the count's true name. Now Donald added further intrigue, suggesting that 'Hensdorf' might not have been Austrian after all, but rather an Englishman assuming a fake identity.

According to a letter Donald wrote on 24 April, he and Nickalos stayed at the sheep farm for two years until 1795. He then travelled back across France with the aid of his uncle, the Comte D'Artois (Count of Artois), who took him to a cross-roads where he met up with his sister (Madame Royale) and Hensdorf. They split into two parties – D'Artois and Madame Royale in one, Donald and Hensdorf in the other – to travel to the coast. There was no mention of Nickalos but in September 1959 Donald would add that Nickalos travelled from the farm separately with 'A PARTY OF MEN' to meet Louis at Cherbourg. It was from the port of Cherbourg, according to Donald's letter of 24 April, that he finally embarked aboard the *Royal Ark*. He was quite clear about the date of this event: 'I LEFT FRANCE ON JULY 16TH 1795'.

Here were more details that had suddenly changed, because Donald had originally claimed he sailed from Boulogne in the autumn of 1789. Chibbett challenged the poltergeist on these latest inconsistencies. Donald simply argued that his memory was not very good.

Difficulty remembering distant dates might perhaps be excusable, but Donald also seemed to have trouble recalling his own name. If he truly had once been the person he claimed, it was now clear that his name would have been Louis-Charles, while his brother's would have been Louis-Joseph. According to every reference Chibbett consulted neither boy had ever been known as Philippe. Yet Donald still insisted on signing his full name as Donald Louis Charles Philippe Capet. Things became even more confused when Donald told Chibbett (on 13 February) that the royal family had referred to Louis-Joseph as 'Louis-Charles' up until Louis-Joseph's death in 1789, and that Louis-Charles had been referred to as 'Louis-Philippe'! 'WHEN [my brother] DIED,' Donald tried to explain, 'JE WAS KNOWN AS LOUIS CHARLES PHILLIPPE CAPET'.

By May 1958, Donald had never specifically included the name 'Joseph' when referring to his supposed brother, and Chibbett had taken care not to mention this name himself. On 12 May, Chibbett asked Donald, 'Your brother had three other names beside "Louis"; what were they?' The correct answer would have been (Louis-)Joseph Xavier Francois. Donald's reply on 16 May did finally include the name Joseph (mispelled) but threw in others for good measure: 'LOUIS CHARLES STANISLAS XAVIER JOSHPE PHILLIPPEAUX HAS ALL OF THEM – TOO MOI.' In other words, according to Donald both he and his brother had used all of these names! It hardly seemed likely.

Interestingly, there *had* been a 'Stanislas' in the family: Louis Stanislas Xavier de France (Comte de Provence and later King Louis XVIII), the brother of Donald's supposed father. It is also interesting to note that Donald's other uncle (the Comte D'Artois) was named Charles *Philippe*. Was the confusion the result of Shirley trying to find information in history books and getting the details wrong, muddling up Louis XVII (Donald's claimed identity) and Louis XVIII, for example? Or was she – or Donald – simply throwing in every name they thought might be correct in the hope that Chibbett would concentrate on the ones they got right? Or could it all be explained by Donald's poor memory? Chibbett was drawn towards the latter explanation: 'Among the welter of names and titles which encumber all those of Royal lineage, it would not be surprising if a child of tender years [became] confused.'

For his part, Donald continued to insist that he was correct and that, furthermore, he could prove it. All Chibbett had to do was consult the entries in a particular book – the 'NOM DE NOM ROI' (Chibbett thought the intended title was probably *Noms de Nos Roi* or *Names of our Kings*) – which Donald alleged was a gold-bound volume that each king of France had had to sign upon their coronation. This was apparently kept locked up in a vault at the Palace of Versailles, but when Chibbett made inquiries the Conservateur there replied that they had no record of this book. 'NOM DE NOM ROI EST PROBABLY AT NOTRE DAME THEN – ENQUIRE THERE,' retorted Donald when Chibbett broke the news. At the beginning of June, the Museé des Archives de France informed Chibbett that such a book had never existed, but Chibbett refused to abandon hope. If this obscure volume could eventually be tracked down, he reasoned, its very obscurity would support Donald's claims. Chibbett continued searching.

CHAPTER 28

Despite his new willingness to 'talk' about his past life, Donald remained keen to meet Jeremy and David Spenser, and on 1 January 1958 Mr C— had visited No. 63 with an exciting proposal.

'It appears,' recorded Chibbett, 'that Jeremy Spenser is now willing to visit "Donald" *provided* the latter satisfies the conditions of a test, i.e. C— has three books on a table in his house. One deals with the French Revolution. C— wants "Donald" to visit his house, and name the titles of the other two books. If "Donald's" tale is true that he can visit Jeremy and other persons, then such a test should be chicken-feed for him.'

Donald tried. On Monday 6 January he asked Wally to post his answer to Mr C—. Afterwards he seemed cheerful and on Tuesday afternoon the chocolate clown he had been given for Christmas was found broken into pieces on the piano, beside a note saying, 'VOUS CAN HAVE A BIT – DON.' But his good humour would not last long. He failed Mr C—'s test, which meant that Jeremy would not be coming to see him after all. The family braced themselves for a storm, but it did not arrive.

Trouble was (mostly) avoided in another area too. Shortly before Christmas Shirley had started a relationship with a boyfriend, T—, and Donald quickly took a dislike to the newcomer. Chibbett wondered whether Donald might even be jealous. Shirley remembers one episode that took place over the Christmas period. Her boyfriend had been sitting in the kitchen, beside the cupboard, on top of which was a bowl of nuts. Shirley recalls that T— 'was laughing and joking … and he was like, "Ah, Donald, I reckon I could do him" […] He was a cocky little bloke and he was all in his Teddy Boy stuff.' T— asked Shirley where this so-called ghost of hers was and she replied that Donald was there with them at that moment, which only made him laugh harder. 'And all of a sudden this bowl of nuts went over his head!' recalls Shirley. 'And he sat there and he went white as a sheet, [and said] "I think I'm going to leave now."' Much to Donald's annoyance (evidenced in notes he left around the house) Shirley continued to see T— for another few weeks. On the morning of 5 February Donald asked Wally for matches so that he could apply a wax seal to his latest letter. Wally, suspecting nothing, left these in Donald's room. At 3.45 p.m., the family found a note from Donald, warning, 'THAT IF VOUS LET THEAT COMMON PERSON COME INTO MON HOUSE' he would start another fire. 'JE GOT ALL FURNITURE PILLED UP ALL READY IN UPSTAIRS BEDROOM – ALL JE HAVE TO DO EST SET ALIGHT TO LA CURTAINS.' The relationship between Shirley and T— did not last much longer.

In early February Chibbett asked Donald to provide specimens of his fingerprints by pressing his fingers and thumbs into his sealing wax. The results Chibbett received in the post were simply four smooth depressions, but the episode inspired Donald to try something new. It snowed on the evening of 7 February and when Wally went into the back yard he found 'four hand prints in the snow. Big ones. They all had 6 fingers and one thumb.' More hand prints were found on Saturday, this time in flour that had been sprinkled on the stairs and across the 'front room' floor.

The following days saw some minor disturbances but mostly Donald seemed preoccupied with his dolls and with instructing

Shirley to make them new outfits. Then, just before noon on 17 February, Donald remembered his plan to make Shirley a film star. Kitty must permit her daughter to attend stage school for two years, he announced. Neither Kitty nor Wally would agree to this. Around three hours later Donald demanded that both Chibbett and Mr C— visit him that night or he would start a fire. Neither man came, nor was there any fire, but as Kitty and Shirley sat watching television the next evening both were frightened by what sounded like heavy footsteps pounding along the passageway. They looked out but the passageway was empty. Later, Kitty found what she described as 'tomatoes all mashed up to a pulp in the sheets' when she went to bed, adding that 'Donald was tapping hard as though laughing'.

The uneasy peace could not last. At around 10.30 a.m. on Monday 24 February Shirley told Kitty she was thinking of getting a job; apparently her friends had been teasing her recently regarding her lack of employment. 'Donald must have overheard,' reported Wally, because the poltergeist left an angry letter. Half an hour later, Shirley telephoned Chibbett, urging him to come at once because Donald had turned 'nasty'.

'When I arrived,' reported Chibbett, 'I found that Shirley had not exaggerated. Mrs H. was in tears, and the neighbour had phoned the police, who had been to see the damage. [...] Hereunder I give details of the damage in each room':

DONALD'S ROOM: Occasional table. Polished top badly scratched. Lampshade wrenched from standard lamp holder, thrown on floor, and material torn to shreds. A picture of 'Donald' in colour, on which Shirley had spent hours, torn in half. A dozen dressed dolls on the floor, their heads bashed in, eyes gouged out, dresses shredded. Piano lid badly scored with a sharp instrument. A ballet skirt (borrowed by Shirley from a friend) torn to pieces. Chair cushions ripped open. Rexine [imitation leather] arms of chairs torn open and stuffing scattered. A mantelpiece clock badly smashed, and side torn off.

BEDROOM: Bedsheets torn to bits. Pillows wrenched open and interior scattered over room. Eiderdown cover ruined, and flock thrown out. All pictures torn from walls and ceiling. Saucer smashed.
[MARK'S] BEDROOM: (upstairs) Best trousers torn and rent, and quite unrepairable.
[MARK'S] KITCHEN: Chair overturned on floor, and damaged.
KITCHEN DOWNSTAIRS: More crockery smashed. A spoon bent double, which required considerable effort to re-straighten.
I have probably missed quite a lot. I understand that before I arrived, knives had been thrown in the kitchen.

Shirley did not look for a job.

The following night (Tuesday 25 February) Donald again warned there was going to be a plane crash. His dolls were later found in the coal cellar, as if moved there for protection. When Chibbett visited on Thursday and learned about Donald's warning he immediately connected it with news of an accident that had happened that very morning. A Bristol 170 Freighter carrying motor traders from the Isle of Man to Manchester had crashed, not onto No. 63 but into the snow-covered peak of Winter Hill near Bolton in Lancashire. Of the forty-two people on board, thirty-five were killed. Wally and Kitty told Chibbett they had asked Donald on Tuesday where the crash would happen and Donald had tapped, 'UP NORTH'. Bolton is approximately 175 miles (280 kilometres) north-west of Battersea and Chibbett felt that this episode was too striking to be explained as a coincidence.

On 3 March, Donald predicted another accident. This time, the victim would (again) be Jeremy Spenser, the accident would probably involve a car and it would happen within forty-eight hours. Donald had made a similar prediction in September 1956, and although there had been an accident afterwards it had not happened until late November. If this were to be a more convincing display of Donald's supernatural powers Chibbett wanted to gather good evidence and he went to considerable lengths to document these events. His efforts would have made persuasive evidence that Donald could foretell the future had the predicted accident occurred. Fortunately it never did.

By early May, noted Chibbett, the 'purely physical phenomena' (objects being thrown, etc.) appeared to have ceased, yet Donald – aka Louis-Charles – remained. 'Domestic notes' continued to appear but Wally's diary entries now often reported nothing but 'the usual taps to music & at bed time'. It gave Chibbett more time to investigate Donald's claims to be the dauphin's spirit.

So far, Chibbett had found no documentary evidence of a ship named *Royal Ark*, but had he been looking for the right details? Given Donald's unreliable spelling, might the name have actually been *Royale Arc*, for example, or *Ark Royal* or *Royal Oak*? Chibbett pressed Donald on the name but Donald insisted that *Royal Ark* was correct. What about the year? Chibbett's earlier searches had focused on 1789 but the alleged year of sailing had since changed to 1795. Chibbett searched Lloyd's Register of Shipping but found no record of a *Royal Ark* between 1794 and 1796. He searched other sources suggested by Lloyd's, but still found no evidence that there had ever been a ship of this name, at least not one operated by the Royal Navy. Might it have been privately owned? When Chibbett suggested this to Donald, the poltergeist confirmed this was so. On 16 May Donald wrote, 'THE ROYAL ARK WAS A BRIG – IT WAS PRIVATELY OWNED BY LORD AVERINGTON – HE WAS A FRIEND OF MY MOTHER – AS I REMEMBER HE WAS AN AUSTRIAN CITIZEN'. If the ship had indeed been a private vessel of this sort it could be extremely difficult to trace.

In Chibbett's opinion, Donald was now being 'generally cooperative, probably due to the fact that I ceased writing to him for a period.' He noted, however, that Donald 'still evades answering certain questions if he can' and he had to admit that Donald's testimony was 'not very reliable' with regard to dates and ages. Nevertheless, Chibbett was willing to believe Donald might genuinely be the spirit of Louis-Charles and he felt it was time to bring the story to a wider audience. With Donald's willing permission Chibbett prepared an article for the US paranormal magazine *Fate*. Titled 'The Poltergeist that can Write' Chibbett's article would not be published until the following October but what he wrote reveals his assessment of the situation as at May 1958:

> Do we get a clear picture of a royal personage returned from the grave to prove that he was the lineal descendant of the House of Bourbon? The answer at present must be 'No'. For, although masses of data about the period of the French Revolution have been given, it is interspersed with much irrelevant material and a predilection for modern affairs which line up with Shirley Hitching's [*sic*] own character. Yet it cannot be denied that this entity exhibits personal qualities which are more like descriptions of Louis XVII than of Shirley. It's [*sic*] reaction to frustration, its imperious self-esteem, its decided indiscretion are all more typical of the Dauphin than of the Battersea teenager.

CHAPTER 29

Chibbett wanted more evidence. In late May 1958, he again pleaded for permission to borrow Donald's seals, to compare them to casts of royal seals held at the Musée des Archives Nationales in Paris. Once more, Donald refused: 'I WILL MAKE IT PLAIN – MON SEALS VOUS CANNOT HAVE – VOUS CAN HAVE IT MAKE THE SEAL PRINT IN WAX BUT THE SEAL – NON!' Disappointed, Chibbett sent a drawing of the seals to the Musée instead. The Musée replied, but could tell him no more about the designs than he had already learned.

Chibbett was now also looking for the Parisian sweetshop Donald had mentioned in a previously overlooked message tapped out on 17 October 1956. In that message Donald had referred to eating dragees (sugar-coated almonds) made by the Seugnot family and had given the shop's address as No. 28 Rue du Baal in Paris. On 12 May 1958 Chibbett asked Donald to confirm that these details were accurate. Donald did so, adding, 'WE GOT OUR ROYAL SWEETS THERE – BONBONS – NOT SWEETS – I DO NOT KNOW OF MME SEUGNOT NOW – SHE HAD A DAUGHTER AND TWO SONS – THE DAUGHTER WAS CALLED MARIE AND THE SONS PERRIE AND PAUL – BUT THE SHOP IS

STILL THERE – I THINK – MONS AND MME SEUGNOT
WERE GUILLOTINED FOR BEING ROYALIST BUT THEIR
CHILDREN LIVED.'

One of Chibbett's work colleagues happened to be travelling to Paris a few days later and agreed to look for the Rue
du Baal. He was unable to find it. Thinking that the original
address might have been demolished since the 1700s, Chibbett made enquiries to the French Chamber of Commerce in
London and was delighted to learn that not only was the sweetshop address correct but also that the building still existed – at
No. 28 Rue du *Bac*. '[The] French pronunciation of the two
words Baal and Bac would be very similar,' recorded Chibbett
with excitement. 'This is confirmatory evidence, therefore, of
at least one of "Donald's" statements.'

It took Chibbett a few days to compose a suitable letter in
French but on 16 June he wrote to Monsieur Seugnot, Confiseur-
Chocolatier at the shop's address, presenting himself as
someone researching the life of the dauphin Louis-Charles.
He asked whether Seugnot could confirm the information
supplied by Donald.

As Chibbett awaited a reply, Donald announced that he
was awarding a decoration to the hardworking researcher.
This turned out to be a piece of mauve ribbon, with the
following 'Appointment': 'JE LOUIS PHILLIPE MAKETH
VOUS MONSIEUR HAROLD CHIBBETT MON MINISTER
ET GENERAL.' It arrived in the post with a note (headed
'PALACE DE VERSAILLES') which read, 'MONSIEUR CHIB-
BETT – THE ENCLOSED EST THAT FOR VOUS OFFICE AS
MON MINESTER ET GENERAL – THE RIBBON CANDOR
SERINE – KEEP IT'. The note was signed, 'H.R.H. PRINCE
LOUIS PHILLIPE CAPET'.

Chibbett asked Donald for further information about his
award. 'CANDOR DE SERINE EST "RIBBON OF OFFICE",'
replied Donald. 'IT WAS GIVEN TO MINISTER OF STATE
AFFAIRS – VOLTAIRE HAD ONE – ET GENERALS.' A few

days later Donald added that 'CANDOR DE SERINE MEAN RIBBON OF HONOUR'. Chibbett made lengthy enquiries to numerous sources, but found no evidence that this award had ever existed outside of Donald's imagination.

In around June Donald took up residence in No. 63's attic. A handwritten notice appeared one day, attached to the attic door: 'RING BELL – IF JE TAP 3 COME IN – IF JE TAP 1 STAY OUT'. In other words, Donald would let visitors know whether or not they had his permission to enter.

At around the same time, he also briefly became a little more 'French'. He would occasionally spell the 'Philippe' part of his name as 'Phillippeaux' and even decided he would write Jeremy Spenser an entire letter in French. This had the potential to be impressive – but Chibbett could not help feeling concerned when Donald asked for his help composing the proposed letter. When asked why he needed assistance, Donald replied that his French was different to modern French. 'Well, that is as good an explanation as any,' thought Chibbett.

Chibbett wanted to believe that Donald really was the dauphin's spirit, but it was proving difficult to obtain evidence. In one effort to do so, Chibbett had been researching an episode known as the 'Flight to Varennes'. In mid-1791, the French royal family had essentially been living under house arrest in the Tuileries Palace, the dilapidated royal residence in Paris, having been forced to leave the splendour of their palace in Versailles. There, Marie Antoinette secretly exchanged messages with a group of *émigrés* (opponents of the Revolution who had fled France) to plot the royal family's escape. As a result, on the night of 20 June 1791, the family fled Paris in disguise aided by the queen's friend, Count Axel von Fersen. After Fersen left them, the royal party attempted to reach France's eastern border but the king was recognised en route. The party was captured, taken back to the Tuileries and placed under guard. Although this general story was reasonably well known, Chibbett hoped that by getting Donald to answer particular probing questions about it, the details thus obtained might be verifiable yet still obscure enough to weigh in favour of Donald's claims. Chibbett had carefully prepared such questions and sent them to No. 63, and he was awaiting Donald's replies. But as he waited he learned that BBC radio had just broadcast a play entitled *The Flight to Varennes*! Chibbett asked whether Donald had listened to this play and the poltergeist cheerfully confirmed that he had, although he had been less than impressed, complaining, 'I WAS NOT IN IT – DISGRACEFUL! – ROYALE ['Madame Royale'] WAS THOUGH – JUST LIKE A GIRL! – MY SISTER – NOT ME!'

Any details regarding the flight that might subsequently appear in Donald's story might therefore come from information in this radio drama rather than from Donald's alleged memory, realised Chibbett. After all his work preparing his questions it was hugely frustrating.

There was more frustration when Chibbett and his wife called at No. 63 on 21 June, the researcher's first visit in almost two months. Donald had been using the occasional French expression in his letters recently, and Chibbett wanted to know whether the family owned a French-English dictionary. He hoped the family would confirm that they did not, but Shirley admitted they did – although it had recently gone missing. It was a little suspicious.

Not all developments were negative, though. Towards the end of June Chibbett learned of a book titled *France for the Last Seven Years*, which contained an account by a sentry who had guarded the dauphin Louis-Charles in the Temple prison. This sentry had believed that his prisoner was not the genuine dauphin, whom he had seen only a few months earlier. His testimony fitted with theories that the dauphin had been rescued and replaced with a substitute, as per Donald's story, and the discovery bolstered Chibbett's hopes that Donald's story would eventually prove to be true.

A few days later Chibbett received a reply from Monsieur Seugnot in Paris. With a little effort he translated the French: 'The information which you have given me is correct.' Seugnot added that he was 'making some enquiries into historical records', which he thought might take several weeks, but he would contact Chibbett again. 'Prima facie,' noted Chibbett with barely contained excitement, 'it appears that "Donald's" information is correct, and at the moment I cannot see how Shirley could possibly have obtained this knowledge normally. But as always in these matters, caution is advisable. A further letter from Mons. Seugnot is awaited with interest.'

Donald decided it was time to reveal more about the sheep farm he had stayed at after his rescue. His letter, which reached Chibbett on 1 July 1958, included sketches of the farm and even a map which Donald claimed showed its approximate location:

CHERI CHIBBETT – VOUS WANTED MORE HISTROY [...] WELL THAT BOY IN LA TEMPLE WIHT SPOTS WAS DEAFENLY NOT MOI – JE WAS ON THE SHEEP FARM WIHT MONSIEUR – NOW LET MOI THINK – THERE WERE HEIR SÉCHELLES – FRAULINE SÉCHELLES – THEY HAD NON CHILDREN [...] IT AT BASEL – BASEL NOT FAR FROM DEJON [DIJON] – WE WENT FROM PAIRS [Paris] TO NOGENT [Nogent-sur-Marnes] TO TROYES TO CHAMONT TO LANGRES TO DEJON TO NEUCHÁTE [Neuchâtel] TO BESANCON TO DOUB [Doubs] ET BASEL.

Questioning Donald by mail, Chibbett confirmed that the boy Donald referred to, who had taken his place in the Temple, 'MUST HAVE BEEN KARL HENSDORF – POOR BOY – HE GAVE HIS LIFE FOR THE HONOUR OF FRANCE'. Chibbett learned that 'Heir' and 'Frauline' Séchelles were supposedly Herr Jan and his wife Frau Helga Séchelles who were 'SWISZ' (*sic*). Donald could remember nothing further about the farm's name or location.

Chibbett was intrigued but remained cautious. Donald's sketches could depict almost any farm building, the paper on which he had drawn his map of France was so thin that the map could have been traced from an atlas and the details of the route he supposedly followed could also have been taken from a map of France. When Chibbett asked for the date Donald/Louis-Charles had left the farm for Cherbourg, Donald replied that it had been 'IN SUMMER OF 1795 ABOUT JUNE JE THINK – NOT SURE – JOURNEY TOOK ABOUT 8 DAYS BY NIGHT – COULD NOT DO SO BY DAY – WE WENT ON HORSE BACK'. Chibbett chose to take Donald's estimate of 'about June' to mean early July: this was a better fit with an approximately eight-day journey to Cherbourg and Donald's previously stated date of sailing from Cherbourg of 16 July 1795.

Introducing himself as 'a student of the French Revolution', Chibbett wrote to the secretary of the town council in Basel, Switzerland. He told them that his researches led him to believe that the dauphin had been rescued from prison and hidden in a sheep farm near Basel belonging to Herr Jan and Frau Helga Séchelles: did they have any historical records to support this? In view of his success with the Parisian sweetshop Chibbett felt optimistic his letter would bring interesting results.

'No determined effort seems to have been made yet to persuade Shirley to go to work,' noted Chibbett with disapproval after visiting No. 63 on 12 July. 'Her parents seem inclined to shirk the issue, mainly because of their fear that "Donald" will create havoc if they bring pressure to bear on Shirley.' With his wife's encouragement, Chibbett decided he would try to nudge Shirley towards seeking employment.

During his visit Chibbett also learned that Mr C— was still showing an interest. A few days earlier Mr C— had written to Donald to ask if the poltergeist could tell him the exact circumstances in which Dennis Brain had died. Chibbett had no idea who Brain was but a colleague later informed him that Brain had been a musician who had died in a car crash the previous September. 'It looks as though C— is doing a piece of research on his own account,' remarked Chibbett in his casebook. 'I wonder whether "Donald" will cooperate!'

Donald's response was to organise a conference with four of his 'ministers' (also apparently spirits) in the upstairs kitchen. After supposedly discussing the matter with these advisers Donald left a letter to be sent to Mr C—. The contents were sealed but Donald told the family that, unless he was finally allowed to meet Jeremy Spencer, he would no longer 'PLAY BAT AND BALL' with Mr C—.

Chibbett later took three photographs of the 'conference room'. Two exposures came out blank but the successful photograph, wrote Chibbett, 'shows "Donald's" conference room from the door. The others were taken from the other end of the room, and would have shown "Donald's" quill pen and … little jars of unidentified tobacco.' A mirror hanging on the wall had been covered up with cloth. Chibbett continued, 'In the places occupied by the alleged "Ministers" were copies of the "Agenda", and there were indecipherable scrawls on sheets of paper in front of them. An "autograph" book on the table contains their "initials" but these are also unreadable. "Donald" will not disclose their names.' Chibbett suspected that the quill pen by Donald's place at the head of the table was the same pen Donald had used to write some of his recent letters, at least one of which had borne an ink blot.

Donald's 'Agenda' was apparently written in French but it immediately provoked Chibbett's suspicions: 'Almost certainly this French agenda has been compiled by reference to a dictionary, without any attention to grammar.' Chibbett wondered whether it had actually been put together by Shirley, using her supposedly missing dictionary to find suitable French words.

Life in No. 63 had been fairly calm since early May but on Tuesday morning, 15 July, a note appeared: 'JE FEEL DIS-TRUCTIVE KIT – JE WANT EXCITEMENT – DON'. There was trouble that night. It started at around a quarter to midnight and lasted for half an hour. Wally reported what he heard coming from the 'front room' that night as he lay in bed with Kitty: '[Donald] started throwing things about & then he started playing the piano & also placed the lamp stantard [*sic*] shade in the middle of the floor & jumped over them & started again on the piano all kinds of tunes. Before he started the jazz music he stamp [*sic*] his feet three times.'

Wednesday was quiet but at 11 p.m. on Thursday, 'Donald started the piano stuff again & also he dance around the room again. More music and jazz stuff. I shouted to him. He tapped back to me on the wall & all of a sudden the piano was in the passage. Shirley & I put it back. Don started to play again & then he started to take the piano to pieces. The flap was in the passage. The top flap was under Shirley's bed & the bottom flap lay on the bed room floor. I put it all together again & then we heard no more. Donald had his fun.'

After this, things were peaceful until the following Friday (25 July). Then, Shirley recorded, '9.10 p.m. I was sitting on the divan bed in front room when all of a sudden there was a hissing sound, then I found myself in a ball of blazes of fire, green one. I screamed & ran out to my mother. I was scared.

Nothing was burnt, only the room was filled with smoke & I and [Mark] turned the bed over & the sack cloth smelt burnt.' At 11.30 p.m. Donald started playing the piano again and stamping his feet, creating so much noise it woke the occupants in both of the neighbouring houses.

Were these outbursts in reaction to Chibbett's suspicions regarding the dictionary? And/or had they been fuelled by the renewed pressure on Shirley to find a job?

CHAPTER 30

Chibbett continued to read as many books as he could about French history and he found that many of the authors questioned the official story regarding the dauphin. They wanted to believe that the boy had been rescued. Moreover, the accepted version of what had happened to the dauphin after his imprisonment seemed to contain enough gaps − filled by the authors with enough speculation − for Donald's story to seem plausible. But on 21 July 1958, the Staatsarchiv Basel-Stadt informed Chibbett they had no record of a sheep farm in the vicinity of Basel, nor any record of the name Séchelles, and Chibbett's doubts resurfaced.

Then a message from Donald mentioned, 'MY MOTHER INSISTED ON MY FRIENDS BEING OLDER THAN I […] EVEN NICKALOS WAS FIFTEEN YEARS − SHE SAID THAT IF I GREW UP WITH ELDERLY FRIENDS I WOULD LEARN MUCH MORE'. This statement that Nickalos had been older than him contradicted earlier statements that he and Nickalos had been the same age (15). On the other hand, if Donald really were the dauphin's spirit then the 15-year-old Nickalos *would* have been older than him. Louis-Charles had been born in 1785 and at the time of his reported death in 1795 he would have been just 10 years old. Still, the contradiction was disturbing. Now that Chibbett (and Shirley) were learning more about the historical dauphin, was Donald altering his story to fit the newly discovered facts?

Although Chibbett was receiving plenty of replies in response to his enquiries to museums, libraries, etc. the information he was getting was leading him nowhere. Then at the beginning of August Donald himself demolished a theory Chibbett had been holding onto in the hope that it was correct. Still unable to find any official record of a Count Hensdorf, Chibbett was drawn towards the idea that 'Hensdorf' had been a *nom de guerre* adopted by a Scarlet Pimpernel-like adventurer. One possibility kept coming back to him: the Swedish Count Axel von Fersen. Probing, Chibbett asked Donald whether he (as Louis-Charles) had ever seen Fersen and Hensdorf together, whether they had resembled one another, and whether Hensdorf had been on board the *Royal Ark* on its final voyage.

'IF YOU MEAN WAS FERSEN AND HENSDORF THE SAME PERSON,' Donald wrote back, 'NO – FERSEN WAS FAT AND PLUMP LIKE MY FATHER – HENSDORF WAS SLIM AND VERY DARK – DASHING AND HANDSOME.'

This description of Fersen was utterly at odds with historical accounts, which described him as tall and handsome, but to Chibbett's disappointment Donald continued to insist that Hensdorf and Fersen had been separate people.

On Friday afternoon, 22 August, Chibbett visited No. 63. It was his first visit for several weeks and he had deliberately not warned the family beforehand: if Shirley was using books or magazines as source material for Donald's story, he hoped that his unexpected arrival would catch her out. He had carried out such spot-checks before but – as usual – he 'found nothing of any significance'.

He did, however, discover that Donald and/or Shirley had been storing all of the letters Chibbett had sent over the years. Chibbett left these where he found them 'because at the moment "Donald" is most cooperative, and I have no wish to disturb these conditions,' but he was disturbed by the possibility that Donald was feeding him information based on his own, forgotten comments.

Although he had not caught Shirley 'red-handed', Chibbett knew it was impossible to control completely her access to possible sources of information. (This would be emphasised just a few weeks later when BBC radio began broadcasting an adaptation of Baroness Orczy's *El Dorado: a story of the Scarlet Pimpernel.*) Chibbett decided it might be useful to try a more direct sort of test, and at home that evening he designed a trap that might catch Donald out on a detail of his story. His next letter to Donald innocently asked whether there had been much trouble when he [i.e. Louis-Charles] had been taken from his mother.

Chibbett had read accounts of how Louis-Charles had fled to his mother, screaming and crying, when commissioners arrived at the Temple prison to take him into solitary confinement, and how there had been general hysteria as he was torn from his family. The key detail was the date. This had happened in July 1793, but according to his story Donald had escaped from the Temple in January of that year. If this was so, then the boy taken from Marie Antoinette in July must have been the substitute, Karl Hensdorf, *not* Louis-Charles. Donald replied on 28 August, 'MON MERE SCREAMED AT THE GUARD AND I KICKED HIM ON THE KNEE – HARD TOO – I HOPE IT HURT […] THEY SLAPPED MOI HARD ET TOOK MOI TO A HORRIBLE DARK CELL WITH NON LIGHT, ET RATS, NON FOOD'.

Donald had fallen into Chibbett's trap. Chibbett said nothing directly, but he did post further questions to the poltergeist on 31 August. Some of these referred back to his trick question: 'Presumably you were in the Temple Tower at the time you kicked the guard and your mother screamed at him? Was that the last time you saw your mother? The history books say it was in July, 1793. Can you confirm that this date is correct?'

Donald did not reply – but he seemed to suspect something was wrong and as he came under pressure there were more disturbances. On the night of 4-5 September everyone in No. 63 – and their neighbours – were again awoken by loud piano playing from the 'front room'. Then at about 4.15 a.m. on Monday 8 September Kitty was awoken by two pieces of a jigsaw puzzle hitting her as she lay in bed. Donald began thumping on the wall and Wally went to see what was happening. He found that the house's front door was wide open, as was the door to the kitchen. The kitchen light was on and (unspecified) items had been thrown onto the kitchen floor.

Later that Monday, Donald received a letter from Chibbett, challenging him to explain how he could have been present in the Temple prison in July 1793 if he had actually been rescued six months previously. Donald was 'completely flummoxed', reported Chibbett. Donald tried to say he had been taken from his mother in 1792 rather than 1793, and complained 'YOU ARE MIXING ME UP'. Then he attempted to divert attention from his mistake: a few days earlier, in answer to another of Chibbett's numerous questions, Donald had written that after his sister's release from prison she had travelled to Aylesbury in England. According to Donald, the Duke of Aylesbury had been involved in the plot to bring him to England and 'THE ADDRESS OF HIS HOME WAS OR STILL MAY BE HART-WELL HOUSE AYLESBURY'. Now, Donald ordered Chibbett to 'CHECK UP ON AYLESBURY'. Only then would he respond to Chibbett's questions about dates.

When Chibbett visited No. 63 on Friday 19 September he was surprised but delighted to learn that Shirley had started work the previous Monday. (Perhaps this had been another factor behind the recent disturbances.) Sporting a recently restyled short haircut, Shirley was now a clerical assistant in the accounts department at a stationery firm in west London. It was nothing glamorous but she enjoyed the work and got on well with both her colleagues and her boss. She had told them nothing about Donald and nobody appeared to recognise her from the newspapers. Best of all, Donald was keeping quiet at the office. Despite Chibbett's and the family's concern that Donald would quickly find a way to lose Shirley her job, this did not happen. She remained working at the firm for several years to come.

Even so, Donald soon complained to Chibbett, 'MY RENIE HAS STARTED WORK AND AS I GO WITH HER MY DAY IS FULL BECAUSE I CANNOT TAP OR MOVE THINGS AND I CANNOT WRITE – SO MY LETTERS WILL BE FEW IN FUTURE'. In his notes, Chibbett commented, 'Presumably "Donald" means … he will no longer have the opportunity to write his letters *through her hand* [original emphasis].' It appeared to indicate that Donald wrote his messages by taking control of Shirley's body, something Shirley has always believed was *not* the case. She still maintains that Donald's notes and letters simply appeared around the house, the poltergeist having written them himself.

Although Donald was much quieter now there was still the occasional reminder he was around. On 6 October, for example, someone discovered a note asking 'KITTY WITTY' to lend 'RENIE' a pound so she could buy a new bag. Another note was found at 7.40 a.m. on Monday 13 October, 'RENIE, WALT – JE DO NOT WANT TO GO TO WORK ON A COLD COLD MORNING – THIS – DO WE HAVE TO – JE AM SO TIRED ET SO TIRED OVER THE WEEKEND'. The following weekend Shirley was listening to a play on the radio when Wally heard the volume increase, followed by Shirley shouting at Donald to turn it down. In general, however, Donald had become very subdued. Wally's diary comment for 6 October would have applied equally well to most days at this time: 'Donald has been very quiet now [and] only taps when we ask him or call him.'

Fewer letters meant Chibbett had more time to examine Donald's claims, but by mid-September he had found no record of Hartwell House or the Duke of Aylesbury. He queried the names with Donald, who insisted they were correct, adding that Hartwell had been 'THE LODGE OF MY UNCLE THE COMTE DE PROVENCE' (i.e. the future King Louis XVIII). Then, on 18 September, the Buckinghamshire Archaeological Society replied to one of Chibbett's enquiries: Hartwell House did exist. The building, which now housed a girl's finishing school, stood in Aylesbury, Buckinghamshire. Moreover, it really had been a temporary home to the exiled Louis XVIII. Chibbett found this 'distinctly encouraging'. The difficulty he had had confirming this information made him doubt that Shirley could have found it on her own.

As luck would have it, the school principal had just written a small booklet detailing Hartwell's history. Chibbett contacted her to ask if she knew of any facts supporting the theory of a plot to whisk the rescued dauphin to safety across the English Channel and into Hartwell House. 'I have never heard any suggestion that the Dauphin Louis-Charles came to Hartwell as a fugitive,' she replied, 'though of course I have heard various stories about his possible escape.' Chibbett also asked if she knew of any reference to a Lord Arverington. (This was the nobleman Donald had claimed owned the *Royal Ark*; Donald had spelled it as 'Averington' but Chibbett felt that 'Arverington' was a more likely spelling.) She had not. She could, however, confirm that Madame Royale (the dauphin's sister) had stayed at Hartwell for a time. According to the principal the royal exiles had lived at Hartwell from 1807 until 1814; this was a few years too late to fit Donald's story but, after reading the principal's booklet, Chibbett felt it possible that other royalist refugees had stayed there a few years earlier.

The principal advised Chibbett that much additional information about the royal exiles at Hartwell could be found in an old book called the *Aedes Hartwellianae*. By the beginning of October Chibbett had obtained a copy. Some of the details he now read would broadly fit in with Donald's story, but it also became apparent that other information from the poltergeist was not quite correct. On 2 October, for instance, Donald wrote, 'HARTWELL HOUSE IS OR WAS OWNED BY MY UNCLE THE COMTE DE PROVENCE', yet his supposed uncle never actually owned Hartwell; it had been rented on his behalf by the English. 'But [the dauphin] could hardly be expected to know this,' thought Chibbett, willing to overlook such a minor detail. Chibbett now felt it likely that, had Louis-Charles successfully escaped to England aboard the *Royal Ark*, his destination would indeed have been Hartwell House.

Chibbett had still found no evidence for a vessel named *Royal Ark*, though. A few weeks earlier, he had written to the Harbour Master at Cherbourg to ask if there were any French records of a ship by this – or a similar – name. No records could be traced. On the other hand, the Harbour Master pointed out, in the scenario Chibbett had outlined 'such an attempt would have been made under conditions of secrecy, and therefore it was not to be wondered at that there was no official trace.' It did not mean the *Royal Ark* had *not* existed.

CHAPTER 31

A new Sunday afternoon television serial for children began in November 1958. *The Lost King: A Story of Revolutionary France*, based on the 1937 novel *The Lost King* by Rafael Sabatini, told a tale in which the dauphin Louis-Charles was rescued from prison by an underground organisation led by the royalist Baron de Batz and transported to Switzerland. It should have been another reminder that historical details in Donald's story – no matter how accurate they proved to be – might have come from a source other than Donald's memory of life as Louis-Charles.

On 25 November, Donald changed a key element of his story – the date of his alleged rescue. In January he had seemed certain that the date had been 22 January 1793, the day after his father's execution, but the new date was 22 January 1794. '[This] puts a different complexion on things,' commented Chibbett. 'As long as [Donald] maintained that he escaped in January, 1793, the rest of his story did not and could not hold water […] Now, however, he gives January, 1794 as the month in which he escaped to the sheep farm. This is a much more likely period, and fits in with historical fact. It should be noted that the new date … was advanced by "Donald" without any prompting by me. I took especial care not to give any hints beyond suggesting that January, 1793 must be incorrect. Why does he now select January 1794 – the most opportune date for an escape?'

One possibility was the aforementioned television serial, in which the escape does take place in January 1794 (although, to the best of Shirley's memory today she did not watch this, nor had she read the novel when younger). As far as can be told, Chibbett did not consider this possibility. Had the researcher become too willing to believe Donald's story? Chibbett had pointed out that a rescue in January 1793 was inconsistent with other parts of the story and so the poltergeist's change of mind must have seemed suspicious, yet it appears that Chibbett was tempted to accept the revised information simply because it removed a fundamental obstacle to believing Donald's claims.

At around this same time there were a few minor disturbances inside No. 63. Wally recorded in his diary that at 7.30 p.m. on 27 November he was watching television when 'Donald threw a shovel at me'. On 30 November, Wally and Kitty were woken at 5.50 a.m. by three loud taps on their bedroom wall. Wally asked if something were wrong and a single tap signified 'YES'. Donald claimed there was an intruder upstairs but when Wally checked he found no-one. Shortly after 11 p.m. that night, 'Donald started to rap very loud in our kitchen & [I asked] him if he was alright. He answered No. So we had to work the A.B.C. board.' Via the board, Donald tapped out a cryptic message: 'THERE IS A FUNNY MAN IN [Mark's] ROOM – OLD STICK HE LIKE FACE OF WALT'. These were the first real disruptions for a month. Were they connected with Donald's frustration at having to alter such an important detail in his story?

In December 1958 Shirley celebrated her 18th birthday. Donald gave her an early present at the beginning of that month, after leaving a note for Kitty on 2 December: 'KIT

– RENIE MUST HAVE SOME GOOD CLOTHES – IF NOT SHE CANNOT GO TO WORK […] IT DISGRACEFUL BEHAVIOUR ON VOUS PART HAS A MOTHER – SEE DOREEN BETTER THAN RENIE'. When Shirley arrived home from work on 5 December, she showed her parents a parcel she said Donald had left for her. '[It] was a blouse, a blue one & very good one at that,' recorded Wally.

On or closer to her actual birthday, Donald left another present, a small parcel wrapped in newspaper with 'RENIE' written on it, inside which was a bag. At first glance this appeared to contain an expensive necklace, consisting of a large amethyst (4cm long and 2.2cm at its widest), cut into the shape of a heart and hung from a thin gold chain. Donald later said he had chosen this because it resembled a necklace his mother had once received as a gift. Shirley was overjoyed. Her parents – more concerned to know where Donald had obtained it – were relieved when Chibbett had the necklace valued and learned that it was only costume jewellery.

As Christmas approached, Donald again got involved with the preparations. When Chibbett visited No. 63 with his wife Lily on Saturday 20 December he noted that, 'Christmas decorations were already up in Shirley's bedroom [the 'front room'] and Mr Hitchings said that "Donald" had done it all, except that he had left them hanging rather low down. All that Mr H. had done was to re-fasten them higher up.' Donald had also been sending Christmas cards again, to various people including Jeremy Spenser.

The Chibbetts had brought along presents for each of the Hitchings family, including Donald, and these were placed on the sideboard. As everyone stood chatting they were amused to realise that Donald apparently wanted the presents to remain unopened until Christmas Day. Whenever anyone happened to brush against one of the parcels, wrote Chibbett, '"Donald" would rap away indignantly.' It was Lily who first noticed that Donald would still tap even when someone touched a parcel surreptitiously while Shirley was looking the other way. 'I noticed this also,' recorded Chibbett. 'There was no mirror which could have reflected the action, and [Shirley] could not possibly have been aware of the exact moment when the package was touched.' Eventually, Donald decided he had waited long enough for his present. At 7.10 p.m. (while the Chibbetts were still at the house), Donald commanded, 'OPEN MON PRESENTS RENIE – SHOW HOW WORK – NOW – PLAIT – DON'. The Chibbetts' gift was opened and revealed to be a spinning top. Chibbett felt sure that Donald's message had been asking for a demonstration of how this worked, which would indicate that the poltergeist had somehow known what was concealed within the gift-wrapped parcel.

Donald distributed his own presents on Christmas Eve. At 2 p.m. Shirley found a note stating, 'RENIE – HERE VOUS CHRISTMAS PRESENT', beside a parcel containing a bracelet – 'a good one' noted Wally. Donald's other gifts were discovered shortly before the family went to sleep that night. There was a handkerchief for Wally and a bottle of scent for Kitty, as well as a Christmas card for the family.

All in all, it was a quiet Christmas – and the peace continued into the New Year. Then, shortly after midnight on the night of 10–11 January 1959, Mark heard noises. Wally did not describe these in his diary but he noted that they continued for around an hour and appeared to come from different parts of the house, including the empty attic above Mark as he lay in bed in his upstairs room.

On 21 January, soon after everyone had gone to sleep, Donald tapped hard to wake them. He seemed worried something was wrong so Wally checked the house. He found nothing.

The following Tuesday (27 January) Shirley's pencil went missing as everyone sat in the kitchen watching television. She had placed it on the floor for a moment and when she looked back it had gone. 'I bet Don's got it,' said Shirley and a single tap indicated she was correct. When she asked for her pencil back there was no response, but a little later it was found on a table in the scullery. At around 8.30 that evening the family were again sitting in the kitchen – Shirley was drawing and her parents were watching television – when Wally felt a 'bad draught' somewhere close by. He wrote, 'all doors were closed. It was like a puffing on my face as though someone was standing besides me near the table. I ask Don if it was him. Yes was the reply, so I got my lighter out & ask him to blow it out. He blew [and] it nearly went out.' Wally asked Donald to blow harder: 'he did, & Kit ask him to blow on her. He did so.'

Such occasional incidents notwithstanding, life remained generally peaceful and Donald seemed happy for now to cooperate with Chibbett, telling the researcher about life in Revolutionary France. Meanwhile, over in France itself Charles de Gaulle was being inaugurated as the first President of the Fifth Republic. Watching BBC news coverage of this event, Chibbett heard that the new president had had to sign a 'Golden Book'. That grabbed his attention. Might this be the elusive *Nom de Nom Roi* Donald had first mentioned in April 1958, purportedly a gold-bound volume signed by newly crowned kings of France? On 14 January 1959, the poltergeist replied that, yes, the *Nom de Nom Roi* and the Golden Book (probably) were one and the same. It seemed to be a breakthrough. Chibbett was unable to afford a trip to France so was forced to rely on what he bitterly described as 'long-winded correspondence', but eventually his enquiries established that the Golden Book was a volume kept in the Arc de Triomphe in Paris, where it was signed by distinguished visitors. But as Chibbett learned more over the coming months it would seem increasingly unlikely that this really was the book he was after. He would continue searching.

CHAPTER 32

In the meantime, Donald's cooperative mood continued into February 1959. Chibbett had asked Donald for the names of everyone who had accompanied him in the coach during the flight to Varennes in 1791, and on 6 February Donald sent Chibbett a list of names. They seemed to be accurate but Chibbett quickly realised a problem. He already knew Donald had listened to the BBC radio play *The Flight to Varennes* the previous June and, when he checked his copy of the *Radio Times* listing for that play, he immediately saw 'all the names given by "Donald" in his letter to me. […] Was this a case of genuine memory of the actual event, or a memory of the radio broadcast? Or did "Donald" keep a copy of the programme – like I did?'

If Donald were cheating then his task became more difficult a few days later. The previous August, Chibbett had taken no action after discovering that Donald was holding onto all of the researcher's letters, piled in a corner of what was now 'his' attic. Donald's collection of papers had continued to grow but on Saturday morning, 14 February, Kitty decided to get rid of what she saw as unwanted rubbish cluttering up her home. She collected all of the papers (which Donald had by then moved downstairs into the 'front room') and threw them onto the fire. When Donald learned what had happened he was furious. At 10.30 a.m. a neatly folded note was found, addressed, 'TO THE HOME-WRECKER!' It read, 'KITTY – WHAT HAVE YOU DONE WIHT ALL MON NOTES – IF VOUS BURNT THEM GOD HELP VOUS – DONALD'. Wally recorded that Donald 'was wild' over this, but he went into little detail, noting only that Donald 'got the broom & it fell on Shirley & put 3 things on floor of front room.' A second note addressed 'TO THE HOME-WRECKER!' was discovered at 11.10 a.m.: 'HOW DARE VOUS TOUCH MON THINGS – ITCHY FINGERS – VOUS BETTER WATCH THEM – BURNING MON THINGS OR ANYONE THEY GET BURNT TOO!' Because of Kitty's actions, griped Donald, he would no longer be able to answer Chibbett's questions and so would not be able to prove his true identity. Chibbett's years of work had apparently been 'WASTED BECAUSE OF A WOMAN'.

At the beginning of the year Donald had agreed to take part in a 'sealed envelope' experiment Chibbett was planning. However, when the researcher visited No. 63 later that Saturday he was handed a letter Donald had left for him: 'KIT HAS BURNT ALL MY NOTES I KEEP – SO NOW I WILL NO LONGER REMEMBER – I CANNOT DO YOUR ENVELOPES – I'M TOO UPSET'. Chibbett decided to try anyway. He had prepared everything a few days earlier, placing a letter from his work colleague Mr Irvine into a small envelope, sealing this envelope and asking other colleagues to sign their names across the flaps. He had then applied strips of Sellotape (clear sticky tape) across all the flaps and edges before finally sealing the flaps with wax. Now he handed the envelope to Shirley, explaining that Donald should try to extract its contents without opening it.

Eleven days later Shirley telephoned Chibbett, excitedly announcing that Donald had succeeded. She read the extracted letter over the telephone and Irvine later confirmed to Chibbett that this was the correct letter. The next day (26 February) Chibbett travelled to No. 63 to collect the envelope. 'The Hitchings family was elated,' he noted, but he wondered why it had taken Donald so long when, according to a note from Donald, the task had been 'easy'. Could the timing 'be connected with the fact that Shirley was at home all day on the 25th with a cold, and therefore would have had time and opportunity to meddle with the envelope?' Chibbett took the envelope away to examine it and also asked ten acquaintances for their opinions. The consensus view was that someone had teased up a small section of the tape, made a slit in the envelope, inserted some sort of instrument with an 'eye' into which a corner of the paper could be pushed and around which the letter could then be rolled, and extracted the letter before replacing the tape. 'In this connection,' noted Chibbett, 'it is as well to bear in mind that when I went over with the envelope on the 14th, Shirley mentioned casually that she knew how to get at the contents of an envelope. I think, but am not sure, that she mentioned a knitting needle.'

Rather than providing the hoped-for demonstration of Donald's paranormal powers, the experiment had again raised the possibility of some fraud being involved in events at No. 63. 'We are left, then,' wrote Chibbett, 'with the very strong suspicion that however much "Donald" may protest his innocence, the envelope was opened by trickery. [...] Nevertheless, this experiment must not be considered by itself, but seen in relation to the circumstances of the whole case, which is a strange admixture of the apparently genuine and false. [...] Here ... is one of those mysterious instances of apparent fraud which plague every psychic researcher, especially when – as in this case – there is equally strong evidence on occasion of genuine supernormal activity.'

Despite his suspicions that Shirley may have attempted to fool him in this instance (something Shirley continues to deny), Chibbett remained convinced that something more was involved: 'All along I have felt that I have been in contact with a mind – indeed, a powerful personality – entirely distinct from that of Shirley; and I still do.'

The night before Donald managed (by whatever means) to extract the letter, there was another minor incident. At 10 p.m. on 24 February, recorded Wally, 'Shirley went into her room to bed & found her shoes were in a big circle on floor as though they were walking.' Later, Donald woke Wally twice, worrying needlessly about an intruder in the house.

A few weeks later, just after midnight on the night of 19–20 March, Donald played up a little in the 'front room'. He sounded notes on the piano, banged on the walls and turned the light on and off, carrying on like this for around half an hour. Mostly, though, Donald's continued presence inside No. 63 was now noticeable only by the messages he continued to leave. Some referred to his life as Louis-Charles. Others asked for gifts or favours, either for his Renie – such as a nice dress or a new pair of shoes – or for him. On 25 April, for example, he named a couple of pop records he wanted.

Sometime before the end of April, Mark moved out of No. 63 for good. Donald decided that the vacated upstairs room would make him an ideal antechamber. According to Wally, 'Donald the Polt ... brought some of his stuff down from the attic & also he took a big stool from the kitchen. It takes two people to lift it but he made it on his own. He also decorated the room up, including the curtains, mat and all writing on wall. [He swept] the room out. All the dirt he brushed into the other room. Shirley at the time was with us downstairs. We heard nothing that was going on upstairs.'

By May 1959, an entire year had passed since Chibbett had submitted his article about Donald to *Fate* magazine and he was still awaiting a reply. Donald – once so keen for people to know about him – seemed unconcerned. 'I DON'T WANT THIS PUBLICITY,' he wrote to Chibbett. 'I AM VERY TIRED OF IT – I SHALL BE LIKE A SEAL IN THE CIRCUS NEXT.' Yet he refused to go away. On 19 May, after Donald left 1 shilling's worth of halfpenny coins in the downstairs bedroom for Shirley to buy herself a bracelet, Wally recorded, 'Don must have been around also while Shirley was at work. We here [*sic*] lots of noises about the house at all time.'

At 7.25 a.m. on Wednesday 10 June, Donald left a message that Shirley would not be going to work that day because she was 'NOT WELL'. She stayed home, but a different reason for her taking time off was indicated on Friday morning when another note from Donald suggested that he/Shirley were worried (unnecessarily as it turned out) that her work colleagues had or would recognise her as the newspapers' 'Poltergeist Girl'.

On Saturday 13 June there was an altercation between Shirley and her father. Shirley had been out with friends all day and did not arrive home until a quarter to midnight. When she did, Wally's pent-up worry manifested as anger, and the ensuing row resulted in Shirley storming out of the house and Wally chasing after her. 'When she got indoors,' recorded Wally afterwards, 'I told her off again ... & all of a sudden a milk bottle came at me from the scullery on to the mat. I suppose old Don did not like Shirley being told off.'

For the next few nights Donald complained that the light bulb in the 'front room' needed replacing and he tapped hard during the early hours of the morning until Wally eventually gave in and changed the bulb. At one point during this fuss (at 11.15 p.m. on Monday 15 June) Donald mentioned, 'THE MOUSE ET HERE AGAIN'.

Wally's diary for 16 June contains another reference to Donald's presence inside No. 63 while Shirley was at work. At 6.45 that evening someone found a note from Donald, stating, 'WE WANT A LETTRE CAME TODAY – ASK KITTY WITTY'. Wally wrote, 'The wife had a letter by the 4 o'clock post & did not tell Shirley about it so how did Don know about it? He must have been here without Shirley. Kit said she had an idea that Don might have been around. She kept on hearing noises about the kitchen & passage. We often hear them somewhere in the house while Shirley at work.' Unfortunately the noises are not described. Were they perhaps made by the mouse Donald was complaining about?

If Donald did sometimes remain in No. 63 when Shirley travelled to work, on other occasions he apparently went with her. While Shirley was in the office on Tuesday 14 July, Donald typed and posted a letter to a mail order company asking to buy two petticoats. The family learned what Donald had done that evening when they found a handwritten copy of the letter he had sent, together with a note for Kitty asking her not to tell Shirley about his surprise gift. Donald also expected Kitty to pay for the petticoats when they arrived!

After an enjoyable summer holiday in Scotland with his wife, Chibbett was back at his north London home and working hard. He felt the time had come for him to write a book detailing Donald's claims to be the spirit of Louis XVII. His book was to be called *The King of Shades*.

In order to tell Donald's story properly, Chibbett needed to pin Donald down on a number of outstanding details. On 15 August he wrote to the poltergeist asking for more information about Louis-Charles's journey after he left the sheep farm in Basel. Donald's comprehensive and typed reply reached Chibbett ten days later. Too long to transcribe here, it dutifully described the dauphin's journey through to the point at which the ship was lost, although his closing comments made it sound as if he were rather fed up with the whole story by now: 'Hope I have given you a picture, I am not going to repeat what est written hear now. answer questions yes but no repeat, I do not like remembering.'

Aided by a pair of maps of France, one from a tourist guide and the other torn from an old reference book,

Chibbett examined Donald's description of the journey to Cherbourg. The first place Donald referred to after leaving the sheep farm was 'Ioigny', presumably the town of Joigny in Burgundy, approximately 200 miles (300 km) west of Basel. 'Fontainebleau' lay around 45 miles (70 km) north-west of there, and 'Chartres' was around 55 miles (90 km) further to the west. 'Caen' lay about 100 miles (160 km) north-west of Chartres and 'Deaville' was surely Deauville, some 23 miles (37 km) north-east of Caen, from where a journey of around 90 miles (140 km) would have taken Donald north-east around the coast to Cherbourg. As he identified the towns in Donald's letter and gradually plotted them on one of the maps, Chibbett's excitement mounted. Could he really be looking at the route taken by the escaped dauphin so many years before?

CHAPTER 33

Every minute of Chibbett's free time was now devoted to writing his book. In early September 1959 he apologised to the Hitchings family for his recent absence from No. 63, advising them that he was due a Friday afternoon off work soon and so should be able to visit them then. In the meantime, would they ask Donald whether he could remember where the royal family had purchased their toys?

Chibbett was hoping for a success similar to that involving the Seugnot sweetshop. Unfortunately, Donald's answering letter of 7 September ignored his question about toys. Instead, it responded to some of Chibbett's other outstanding queries, including one about Hartwell House. A week earlier, Chibbett had told Donald that the dauphin's uncle, Louis XVIII, had not officially lived at Hartwell until 1807. This was several years too late for Donald's story: would Donald state unequivocally whether or not Hartwell had been home to royalist refugees before this date? Donald answered, 'HARTWELL HOUSE MON UNCLE LOUIS XVIII ESTABLISH RESDENCE CORRECT ABOUT 1807 – SOME OF THE REFUGÉE AFTER MON DIED WENT THERE INCLUDING MON SISTER MADAME ROYALE'. It wasn't exactly a straight answer but Donald's implication was that, yes, Hartwell had been used by French royalist refugees prior to 1807. This was something Chibbett would need to verify.

Inside No. 63, there were hints that trouble was imminent.

In the first place, Shirley had just broken up with a young man she had been dating. (According to Donald's letter of 7 September her boyfriend was 'JUST LIKE THE REST'.) Secondly, a prospective tenant – a Polish gentleman – had recently called to view the upstairs flat. Donald, who had taken over that flat after Mark moved out, was not happy, writing, 'A MAN AS BEEN TO VEIW THE HOUSE ET HE EST POLISH SO JE CALL MON MINESTER SOON ET JE DECIDE – IF HE MOVES IN JE WILL STRIKE'. If past behaviour was anything to go by, Donald did not intend 'strike' in the sense of industrial action.

At around the same time, there was some commotion at Shirley's place of work. The office kept two sets of keys for doors, safes, etc., and when one set disappeared, the cleaners were initially blamed. The keys reappeared the next day, but a few days later, both sets disappeared. Frantic searches failed to find them and in the end a locksmith had to be called to replace all the locks.

When Shirley woke up on Monday 14 September there were faint orange marks down the right side of her face. She went to work, but when the marks were still there that afternoon she was told to see a doctor. The doctor thought she might be allergic to something – he could not say what – and gave her some soothing ointment. When she woke up the next morning (the first anniversary of her starting her present job) the marks were worse.

Her boss sent her home at midday, to rest. The family telephoned Chibbett to let him know, and as soon as he put the phone down Chibbett rearranged his day's schedule and hurried to Battersea. The family, who had not expected him to visit, were delighted. Chibbett recorded:

> Shirley opened the door, and I saw at once that the markings on her face were not at all similar to the stigmata of 1956, which resembled long scratches. Now, the left side of her face was almost salmon-pink in colour, standing out in marked contrast to the other cheek. There were similar, but fainter, traces of the same colour on her left wrist. Shirley said that there was some discomfort when they first appeared, but no pain since. She felt well, but very tired. She was yawning all the time. Her mother said that when the previous stigmata occurred in 1956, there was similar tiredness.

While at the house Chibbett again looked around for any sign that Shirley had been researching French history. 'Since I had not been expected, there had been no opportunity to hide any evidence,' he noted afterwards. 'I [inspected] each room in turn, but could find nothing of any significance.'

There was little doubt a link existed between Shirley's marks and recent developments such as the prospect of a stranger moving into the upstairs flat. On that front, Donald was winning. The Polish gentleman who had been to see the flat had asked who was responsible for the marks drawn on the wall. His reaction on being told was not recorded but he had not returned. A mixed-race couple had also made enquiries about the rooms but had left hastily when the ever-honest Wally told them about Donald.

The morning after Chibbett's visit, while Shirley was in the kitchen putting on make-up in readiness for work, Wally brought her a cup of tea. When he turned around he spotted something on the sideboard. It was a silver-coloured Yale door key, similar to that which opened the front door to No. 63, although it did not fit that lock when Wally tested it. (Whether it might have been one of the missing keys from Shirley's office was apparently not ascertained.) Wally asked if Donald had left the key there and was answered with a single tap: 'YES'.

'Have you got any more keys?' Wally asked.

'YES.'

It was a worrying echo of the very first strange incident way back in early 1956, when Shirley had discovered a mystery key on her bed. Surely events were not going to start all over again?

On Saturday morning, 19 September, Chibbett's weekend was interrupted by a telegram from Wally, asking him to telephone urgently. He did so immediately and listened as an obviously upset Wally explained how two visitors – a man and a woman – had just been to view the upstairs flat. Thinking they were prospective tenants Wally had shown them the rooms, where the man asked about the markings on the walls.

'I told him it was the Ghost House and Donald wrote on the walls and ceiling,' wrote Wally later. The man replied that that was 'a lot of rot' and said the family must be mad.

'Well, I think *you're* mad!' retorted Wally angrily.

The couple scoffed when Wally explained that the attic door was kept locked because their resident ghost used that room. They demanded entry. Wally told them he didn't know where the key was. At that, the woman revealed she was the house owner's daughter and, with her permission, her companion kicked the door open. During the chaos a milk bottle smashed somewhere close by.

'Donald must have thrown a pint milk bottle up the stairs after Shirley,' wrote Wally. '[Shirley] by then was halfway up and when she came to us she was in a rage and covered in milk.'

'Look what you've made him do!' she yelled.

Shirley said afterwards that she had seen the bottle fly through the air from inside the downstairs kitchen, hit the kitchen wall or doorframe and bounce away towards the stair-case before disintegrating in mid-air, splashing milk over her.

The couple shouted that Shirley ought to be in a hospital. There was, in Chibbett's words, 'a heck of a row'.

The couple wanted the family removed from the house. Wally offered to buy the property from the owner for £650 but the couple demanded £800. They eventually stormed off, threatening to obtain an injunction for the family's eviction.

Five days later, when Chibbett visited No. 63, there had been no further word from the property's owner. Hoping to cheer everyone up with some good news, Chibbett announced that his article about Donald had finally been published and he showed everyone copies of the October issue of *Fate*. '"Donald" rapped a few times while I was there and expressed some excitement over the article,' noted Chibbett afterwards. Yet despite Donald's apparent enthusiasm, his letters to Chib-bett now stopped.

On 3 October, Chibbett wrote to remind Donald that the poltergeist had yet to reply to various important questions. This was not the time for him to fade away; they were on the verge of bringing Louis-Charles's story to the world! Chibbett felt certain his article would bring a good response from the magazine's readers, envisaging a small army of volunteers coming forward to help him. Together, they would be able to properly examine Donald's claims to be the spirit of history's long-lost Louis XVII. But one week later, not a single reader had contacted Chibbett. Even more disheartening was the continuing silence from Donald himself. It had now been three weeks since Donald's last letter to Chibbett. Was the polter-geist worried that an army of researchers would pick his story to pieces?

Chibbett eventually received a reply from Donald on 16 October: 'CHERI CHIBBETT – PLAIT PLAIT EXCEPT MOI APOLOGY FOR NOT EH WRITING – VOUS SEE JE AM TERREBLY WORRIED ABOUTE SOMEHTHING'.

Although he refused to explain what he was worried about, beyond hinting that it (once again) had something to do with Jeremy Spenser, Donald's letter replied to a number of Chibbett's most recent questions. For the next few days poltergeist and researcher exchanged further letters.

Regarding the key Wally had found on 16 September, Donald stated, 'THE YALE KEY EST A FLAT KEY OF ONE OF JEREMY AIM'S [i.e. 'amis', the French word for 'friends']'. When Chibbett asked for the friend's name and address so that he could corroborate Donald's claim, Donald replied, 'OF COURSE JE WILL ANSER VOUS QUESTIONS', but when Chibbett pressed him for a reply several days later there was no further response, and there that matter would rest.

Another of Chibbett's questions concerned the incident with the milk bottle: had Donald thrown it at the visitors and had he intended to hit them instead of Shirley? 'YES,' replied Donald. 'IT WAS JE WHO THROW THE MILK BOTTLE AT THOSE HORRIBLE PEOPLE ET JE WILL DO IT AGAIN IF THEY COME BACK.'

Chibbett also prompted Donald, twice, for a reply to his questions about the royal family's toys – who had made them, whether they had come from a particular shop, etc. – but when Donald eventually responded he merely stated that, 'MON ROYAL TOYS CAME FROM AIM'S [i.e. friends] … PEOPLE GAVE MOI THEM – MOSTLY SOLDIERS – JE DID NOT PLAY WIHT TOYS LIKE VOUS CHILDREN OF TODAY – IT WAS ALL LEARNING FROM BOOKS'. From the researcher's point of view this contained nothing useful, nothing he could potentially verify as evidence supporting Donald's claims of his past life.

There was, however, still the issue of the sweetshop. Hoping Donald could reveal more about this, Chibbett asked, 'Can you tell me in which part of Paris, or near which buildings, the shop of Mons Seugnot was situated, this to enable me to locate the Rue du Bac on a Paris map?'

'NEXT TIME VOUS COME OVER BRING A MAP OF PARIS RUE ET PLACE,' replied Donald, 'ET WE WILL HAVE FUN TELLING VOUS ALL ABOUT FRANCE.'

Reading Donald's latest letters, Chibbett noticed that the poltergeist had taken to interjecting the word 'EH' every now and again. Other characteristics of his messages remained unchanged, however, including his domineering personality. On Saturday 17 October Shirley and her friend Doreen stayed out late. Wally was at work until the early hours and, when he discovered that Kitty had been left in the house alone until after midnight, he scolded the two teenagers for their selfishness. Shortly after 11 a.m. on Sunday, Wally found the following note: 'WALT – PRAY TO CALM DOWN INSULTING MON RENIE FREINDS LIKE THAT – IT TIS NO WAY TO BEHAVE – VOUS VERY UNGENTLEMAN – IF JE HEAR ONE WORD BAD AGAIN THIS MORRING JE DO MY DUTY AS A GENTLEMAN ET BOP VOUS ONE RIGHT ON THE NOSE – PRAY SIR – JE NOT USED TO SUCH LAUGUAGE'.

In addition, certain old distractions had not completely vanished. In a letter received on 20 October Donald told Chibbett not to be cross with him but he wanted to get back in touch with the reporter Kirsch: 'PLAIT JE GOT TO SEE HIM – FOR WHAT JE CAN NOT TELL VOUS – NOT YET – BUT FIND HIM FOR MOI – THAT EST ET ORDER – PLAIT LIKE MON PERE ORDERD THE COMPAGNIE DE NOELLES'. Donald emphasised that, whatever his enigmatic reason might be, it had nothing whatsoever to do with Jeremy Spenser, and he ended with another plea for Kirsch: 'PLAIT TO FIND HIM FOR MOI – JE SO UPSET'.

Chibbett had no idea where the reporter might be now. He told Donald as much, explaining that reporters often moved from one job to another and suggesting that Donald try writing to one of the papers Kirsch had worked for. Donald probably did so but there is no indication that he ever managed to get back in contact with the reporter.

In any case, a different detail had caught Chibbett's attention, what exactly was this 'Compagnie de Noelles'?

CHAPTER 34

The 'Compagnie de Noelles', Donald answered Chibbett, had been a body of royal guard, somewhat similar to the British Household Cavalry, in pre-Revolutionary France. Chibbett pressed for further details but got no reply so, as he continued to scour historical records, he kept an eye out for any mention of these guards.

Meanwhile, he wrote to Donald to remind him of various unanswered questions regarding details of the poltergeist's alleged past life. When Chibbett visited No. 63 a fortnight later (on Saturday 14 November 1959), Wally handed him a letter. Although Donald had answered some of Chibbett's questions he had sidestepped others, avoiding them with comments such as that it was rude to ask a lady's age, or that he would answer some other time because he was tired.

Chibbett had also requested that the poltergeist provide a clear example of his apparent ability to predict the future, asking Donald to send him details of 'some national or international event which has not yet taken place,' signing and dating the letter 'so that the proof can be incontrovertible'. Donald ignored this.

Donald was, however, happy to look at the map (of the Paris Metropolitan Railways) Chibbett had brought along.

The researcher had perused this earlier but been unable to locate the Rue du Bac – the address of the Seugnot sweet-shop. Chibbett still had no idea whereabouts in Paris that address was. In fact, his only vague impression was that it was actually located outside the area shown on his map, somewhere close to the Palace of Versailles. With little expectation he asked Donald whether the shop's location appeared on his map and was surprised to be answered with a single emphatic tap: 'YES!'

Chibbett laid the map on the table so that it appeared upside-down from Shirley's viewpoint as she sat opposite him. He covered it with paper and exposed one quarter of the visible area at a time, asking Donald to tap to indicate when the correct part was exposed. By narrowing down the location in this manner Chibbett quickly arrived at a small area. There were the words 'R. du Bac'.

'This was quite remarkable,' recorded Chibbett. '"Donald" appeared to have an intimate knowledge of the locale. There was no hesitation in his direction.'

One week later, Chibbett again tried to force Donald to deal with a major inconsistency in the poltergeist's story. To recap, in August 1958, after Donald had claimed he was rescued from the Temple prison in January 1793, Chibbett tricked him into stating he had still been present in the Temple six months later, during an episode known to have occurred in July 1793. Donald had subsequently altered his story, changing the date of his rescue to January 1794. Now Chibbett wrote to the poltergeist again, pointing out that Donald had stated elsewhere that after his rescue his mother had remained in the prison accompanied by the young son of her best friend; Donald had said that that friend was Count Hensdorf, therefore the boy with his mother was presumably Hensdorf's son, Karl. This left Chibbett 'very perplexed'. If Donald had not been rescued until January 1794, as per the revised story, did this mean that the dauphin and Karl had *both* been in the cell with

Marie Antoinette in 1793? Had Karl later gone with Marie Antoinette when, as history recorded, she was transferred to another prison (the Conciergerie) in August 1793? And, if Karl were already in one of these prisons, how could he later have been substituted for the dauphin during the rescue if that had happened in January 1794?

Donald tried to blur the issue: 'NON NON – KARL TOOK MON PLACE IN LE TEMPLE JUST BEFORE SHE WENT TO THE CONCIEGERIE – KARL HENSDOFF DID NOT GO TO THE CONCIEGERIE PRISON WIHT MÉRE – THEY SAID A FREIDLY GUARD THAT MON MÉRE'. He left that sentence unfinished, continuing with, 'CELL IN THE CONCIERGIE TWAS NON WIDER THAN EIGHT SPACE ET 12 SPACE IN LENGH – JE ESCAPED THE DAY AFTER PÉRE DIED IN JANUARY OF 179[?]'. The last digit had seemingly been a 3 to begin with but had been deliberately written over to make it impossible to read. It was a blatant childish ploy to wriggle out of an impossible question. But the execution date of Louis XVI was a fact of history – he had been guillotined in January 1793. If Donald/Louis-Charles had been rescued the day after his father's death, he must, after all, have been rescued in January 1793.

'UNDERSTAND IT EST SO DIFFICULT TO REMEMBER,' pleaded Donald. 'IT SO CONFUSSING CHIB.'

Then, as if anxious to shift attention onto another matter, Donald's letter changed subject: 'NOW CAN JE ASK VOUS SOME THINGS[?]'

Donald gave Chibbett the number of a car registration plate. 'JE KNOW IT TIS A LOT TO ASK BUT PRAY COULD VOUS ASK ONE OF VOTRE OFFICE FREINDS TO HELP [...] JE WANT TO KNOW THE OWNERS NAME ET ADDRESS OF THIS NUMBRE'. He told Chibbett to keep this task secret from Shirley, not saying why he wanted the information but promising to answer more of the researcher's questions if Chibbett traced the details. Chibbett agreed to try, although he added that even if he found the information there might be some legal restriction to his disclosing it. He also warned that it would probably take some time, whereas the problems with the dates in Donald's story urgently needed resolution. Donald said he would reply later. Apparently, he was 'STUDING [studying]' the matter.

One question he did answer, though, was what he wanted for a Christmas present that year. More toy soldiers and a fort was the reply, and Chibbett and his wife brought these with them when they visited No. 63 in mid-December. While there, Chibbett broke the disappointing news to Donald that he had been unable to trace the car registration details. Shirley now revealed that the car belonged to a local newspaper photographer named David who had recently visited the house. Why on earth would Donald want to know David's surname and address, wondered Chibbett. It did not occur to him that someone was planning a spot of match-making between Shirley and a handsome young man.

Christmas 1959 came and went with little fuss (as before, Donald helped with the decorations, gave small gifts to the family and sent out Christmas cards) but at around 3.30 in the morning on 27 December Donald woke everyone by banging on the walls. Wally hurried into the 'front room' to see what was wrong and found a short note on Shirley's bed: 'SOMEONE ABOUT – DON'.

There was more banging at around 12.15 a.m. on the morning of 31 December. Again Wally was forced to get out of bed and he and Shirley thought they heard someone tap on the downstairs front bedroom window. Unable to see anybody outside, Wally went back to bed, but half an hour later Shirley complained that there had been more tapping, this time at her window in the 'front room'. Donald, recorded

Wally, was 'banging like mad' and threw several books at the window. He had also left a message on Shirley's bed: 'KITTY – THERES EST A MAN WALKING ABOUT OUTSIDE ET HE ARMED WITH A KNIFE ET HE VERY INTERESTED IN MON RENIE ROOM […] JE SURJEST RENIE GO IN WIHT BED IN VOUS ROOM'.

This time when Wally looked outside he saw a man and woman standing on the other side of Wycliffe Road. They were next to a car that had its doors open and they had probably simply returned home from a night out. Then again, he thought, 'Perhaps Don was right.'

Tapping from the 'front room' again forced Wally to investigate shortly before midnight on 6 January 1960. Shirley said someone had run past her window and tapped on it, but Wally saw nothing and went back to bed. Fifteen minutes later Donald resumed his tapping, softly this time. Then Wally heard what sounded like two pebbles hitting the 'front room' window. Again he looked outside and saw nothing, but Donald would not let him leave, tapping insistently until Wally told Shirley to share the double bed with her mother while he spent the rest of the night in Shirley's bed in the 'front room'. In the morning Wally looked for any trace of the pebbles he thought he had heard but found nothing. He now doubted there ever had been a prowler, commenting in his diary, 'Donald gets a bit bored at times & like to wake things up a bit.'

Just after midnight on 10 January, Donald again tapped until Wally went to investigate. Wally found a note on the 'front room' floor – 'MAN OUTSIDE – DON' – but once more there was nobody there.

Chibbett started 1960 with renewed vigour and a repeated attempt to get Donald to answer the discrepancies in his story. Unfortunately, the six-page reply Chibbett received on 7 January did not give those answers. Instead, it told him how delighted Donald was that he had discovered the surname of David the photographer. Donald had also used a telephone directory to find David's workplace address, but now he wanted more. He commanded Chibbett to discover David's home address and whether or not David was married. The poltergeist intended to 'PLAY CUPID', he announced, reminding Chibbett not to tell Shirley.

Chibbett tried to discourage this but a few days later Shirley telephoned David on some pretext or other. Unfortunately, whatever they spoke about failed to ignite any romance and over the next few weeks Donald tried to enlist Chibbett's help in finding a different potential boyfriend for his Renie. If Chibbett did this, he said, then Donald would answer his questions. Chibbett agreed to keep his eyes open, although he made clear his opinion that Shirley would have more success doing this herself.

While Donald wanted to expand Shirley's social life with the aid of the avuncular Chibbett, the latter just wanted to make progress with his research. On 9 January, Chibbett reminded Donald that he had now been waiting over a month for replies to his latest questions. On 18 January Chibbett received a lengthy response: Donald was finally addressing some of the outstanding issues – although, he reminded Chibbett, his further cooperation was to be conditional on Chibbett helping Shirley.

In an attempt to explain how Karl Hensdorf could have been substituted for Donald/Louis-Charles during the rescue from the Temple prison, yet also been in that prison with Marie Antoinette in mid-1793, Donald again changed the dates in his story, reverting to saying the rescue had happened in January 1793, not 1794. Moreover, his previous memory of being taken from his mother in July 1793 was forgotten: he now stated that the boy taken from Marie Antoinette then had been Karl Hensdorf, not him. 'JE ESCAPED WIHT HENSDOFF

JANUARY 1793 22ND DE JANUARY – JE CHANGED PLACES WIHT KARL,' he wrote. 'IT TWAS KARL NOT MOI' who had been in prison with his mother and later died there.

Despite (or perhaps because of) Chibbett's years of hard work, Donald had clearly lost interest in bringing his story to the world. When Chibbett urged him to reply to further questions quickly because his book was well underway, with 52,000 words already written, Donald nonchalantly replied, 'WELL – HAPPY WRITING – 52000 LOTS OF WORDS EH – WELL – HOPE TO SEE VOUS SOON – REMEMBER KEEP LOOK OUT [for a boyfriend for Shirley]'. It was clear which subject Donald considered most important.

Perhaps Shirley might find a boyfriend if she socialised more, suggested Chibbett. Donald replied that Shirley needed pushing: 'JE TRY TO SEND HER ART SCHOOL – EVENING CLASSES – YOUTH CLUB – BUT NON LUCK'. After some discussion, poltergeist and researcher agreed to encourage Shirley to take art classes, where she might meet someone who shared her interest in that subject. Chibbett happened to know somebody who worked at a London art school and was able to help find Shirley a place. Her employer generously allowed her to dedicate two days a week to her studies.

Shirley decided to study theatrical costuming; it was something she had acquired practice in thanks to helping dress Donald's dolls and she thought it might also offer a way into films. From what Shirley can recall Donald behaved himself at art school – although paints and brushes mysteriously went missing from time to time – but ultimately it was not Donald who proved to be the major problem here.

Part of Shirley's studies involved helping out at a theatre for several hours each week. The idea was to gain practical experience, yet she was only ever given menial chores such as making tea and sweeping the stage. After putting up with this for several months she complained to her tutor. He replied that she had to work her way up from the bottom, but the climb was frustratingly slow. There was also friction at home. Although Shirley easily made friends at the school, her parents (in particular, the staunchly working-class Wally) disapproved of them. They weren't his kind of people at all. Matters got worse when her employer told her she would need to start working four days a week, rather than three. Shirley couldn't leave her job because she needed the wages to cover her school fees, and after some discussion the school agreed to let her attend just one day per week. But this placed extra pressure on her studies and in the end it was just too much to cope with. Shirley dropped out of art school, abandoning her ambitions of a career working with theatrical costumes. It was a decision she has bitterly regretted ever since.

CHAPTER 35

Chibbett was preparing to enter retirement and he was looking forward to spending more time working on his book. The writing was going well but it was proving difficult to find an interested publisher; he had approached four so far and all had turned his manuscript down. On another front, though, things were looking up.

Examining Donald's story from London had always been problematic because so many of the sources Chibbett would have liked to consult were in France. Now, though, he informed Donald on 6 February 1960, 'I have at last secured a collaborator in France'. That 'collaborator' was actually a couple, Monsieur and Madame G—, who lived in Meudon, a couple of kilometres south-west of the centre of Paris. Their location was appropriate given that it had been in Meudon that Donald's supposed elder brother (Louis-Joseph) had died in 1789. The G—s (who had probably contacted Chibbett in response to his *Fate* article) were interested in psychical phenomena and experienced in library research. Madame G— in particular was familiar with the history of the French Revolution. Chibbett was delighted to accept their offer of assistance. His friend Mr Biddle was also able to help, not only by continuing to assist Chibbett with background research but also by translating English material into French for the G—s, and vice versa.

Almost immediately, the G—s helped resolve the issue of the enigmatic 'Compagnie de Noelles'. By the end of 1959, Chibbett had found no historical record of this body and had more or less decided that this line of enquiry was a dead end, yet he stubbornly continued to pursue it just in case. On 4 January 1960, Chibbett asked Donald if the poltergeist could remember any further details at all about the Company, even requesting that Donald sketch their uniform for him. 'COMPAGNIE DE NOELLES EST BODY GUARD TO PÉRE IN FRANCE WHEN EVER HE TRAVELED,' replied Donald. 'JE WILL ENDEVER TO SKETCH FOR VOUS.' A rough sketch was indeed enclosed and, around a week later, further questioning elicited the information that the soldiers were actually 'FOOT GAURDS' rather than cavalry. The Military Historical Society at London's Imperial War Museum did their best to answer Chibbett's enquiries regarding the Company but, because of the probably incorrect spelling and vague information, they had little idea what to look for. Now Chibbett sought help from the French couple. They replied a few weeks later: 'From 1755 to the end of the French kingdom, the company of Scottish Body Guard was commanded by Jean-Louis-Francois-Paul, duc DE NOAILLES, Field Marshal of France. So, all this is exact, except the spelling of the name…' Donald's sketch of a member of this Company, although very rough, also appeared to be broadly in keeping with what would have been expected. But, commented Chibbett in his book manuscript, '[the] question remains: Did "Donald" alias "Louis XVII" "remember" the Compagnie de Noailles? Or did Shirley spend long hours of research to seek this obscure piece of information? Or did she merely conjure it out of the air, so to speak? Your guess is as good as mine!'

The G—s also assisted in the matter of a curious phrase Donald had used two years earlier. In January 1958, when referring to the French Parliament, Donald had written, 'WE HAD ONE AT VERSAILLES YOU KNOW – AND I OR MY FATHER WOULD SIT ON THE BED OF JUSTICE'. Chibbett had never heard of a 'bed of justice' before and his researches turned up nothing, but thanks to Madame G— he learned that the expression – properly 'lit de justice' – referred to the seat occupied by the French king while attending the deliberations of his parliament. The last 'lit de justice' had been held by Donald's alleged father, Louis XVI, in 1787. Tracking down this information had taken weeks and searches through scores of volumes. 'Is it reasonable to suppose that … this adolescent Shirley deliberately sought out such data?' wondered Chibbett. 'Recollect, too, that this instance is only one of dozens of other statements by "Donald" which have been proved to be correct, or partially so.'

Chibbett also told the G—s about the *Nom de Nom Roi*, but not even they were able to trace this elusive volume, and Chibbett never did discover evidence that it had ever existed. Nevertheless, the other confirmations meant that Chibbett was once more growing confident that Donald really was the spirit of Louis-Charles.

The G—s were less willing to reach that conclusion. Monsieur G— wanted Chibbett to put Donald 'to the test' and sent six questions relating to Donald's/Louis-Charles's supposed brother. Chibbett promptly forwarded these to No. 63, urging Donald to reply as soon as possible. Donald did reply – to say he would only cooperate if Chibbett helped him first. Donald had enclosed several sketches by Shirley and he told Chibbett to show them to an artist to 'GET THEM CRITICSED SEE IF SHE EST ANY GOOD'. Chibbett took them to an artist friend, but his friend was unimpressed. In his opinion, they were simply tracings of pictures in magazines.

On 18 February, Chibbett received Donald's responses to Monsieur G—'s questions. The poltergeist began by pointedly commenting that 'MON BROTHER AFFAIRS WERE NOT MINE MONSEUIR' before writing (evidently riled by the artist's assessment), 'ABOUT SHIRLEY – HER SKETCHES ARE ALL HER "OWN. WORK." – TELL VOUS SO CALLED ARTIST – PRAY WHO EST HE! [...] OH PERHAPS VOUS WOULD CARE TO VISIT MOI SOMETIME ET BRING VOUS ARTIST FRIEND.'

As for Donald's answers, they were – unsurprisingly – less than clear-cut. The G—s' original questions are given below, together with Donald's responses:

Q. 1: 'While he was ill, who was Louis-Joseph's governor at Meudon Castle?'

A: 'MON BROTEHR TWAS ILL AT MEUDON CASTLE BUT JE WAS STILL IN MON CRADLE.'

Q. 2: 'Where did Louis-Joseph spend Christmas, 1788 (his last Xmas)?'

A: 'JE DID NOT SPEND CHRISTMAS IN 1788 WIHT MON BROTHER – JE WAS FIVE THAT YEAR BUT JE WAS NOT WIHT MON BROTHER.'

Q. 3: 'What was the meaning of a 'billiard' for Louis-Joseph?'

A: '——————?'

Q. 4: 'What was the last animal to be ridden by Louis-Joseph before he died?'

A: 'JOSEPH RODE NON ANIMAL – HE TWAS ILL – HE HAD RICKETS HAS A BABY ET FOR THAT HE COULD NOT WALK.'

Q. 5: 'What were the reactions of the 'Tiers-Etat' after Louis-Joseph's death?'

A: ''TIERS ETAT' TWAS AN ORDER OF THE ONE, LOWEST ESTATES OF THE REALM GIVEN TO NOBILITY ET MOI BROTHER.'

Q. 6: 'What were Louis XVI's feelings on this?'

A: 'VOUS MEAN MOI PÉRE – HE HAS NON FEELINGS AFTER JOSEPH DIED – ONLY HOPE IN MOI.'

Donald's answers were extremely evasive and in the case of the third question he had failed to reply at all. (The answer the G—s were probably looking for was along the lines of 'a bed'. At one point during his time at Meudon, Louis-Joseph expressed a desire to sleep on top of the new billiard table and a bed was duly made up for him there.) There was definitely an error in his answer to the second question – Louis-Charles had been born in March 1785 so would have been 3 years old in December 1788, not 5. And with regard to question five, Donald would have been expected to answer that the reaction of the French people was cold. Rather than the expected national mourning, the general population of France essentially ignored the boy's death, their attention instead concentrated on drastic food shortages and the forthcoming meeting of the Estates General. Despite such shortcomings, Donald seemed confident that his responses would convince Chibbett's French associates. 'PRAY DO SEND MORE QUES-TIONS,' he offered airily.

Chibbett, well accustomed to Donald's slipperiness, was already worried on the G—s' behalf. He commented to Biddle, 'I expect they will go grey in the end – or bald, like me.'

Apart from the tapping noises there were few instances of poltergeist-like phenomena anymore, but Donald's 'domestic notes' continued to appear in abundance. Space precludes looking at these in detail, but one strong theme was Donald's interest in his collection of dolls. In particular, he often returned to the subject of making clothes for them, ordering Wally, Kitty or Shirley to obtain wool, silk or whatever, and telling Shirley what outfits she should make from the material. Donald also wanted other treats for his dolls – items of furniture, for example, or a pram – and frequently left instructions for Wally to make specific items, sometimes sketching what he desired. If his commands were not obeyed swiftly he would leave further, impatient reminders. 'His instructions were always obeyed to the letter,' noted Chibbett.

Another regular theme was that Shirley should make more of an effort with her appearance. 'JE WANT VOUS TO LOOK BEAOUTIFUL,' Donald explained in late February. He left notes encouraging Wally and Kitty to let Shirley get her hair cut in particular styles – on 26 March, for example, Donald decided that Shirley should get her hair cut in the style of an actress the family had just been watching on television – or urging Shirley to buy particular clothes, even when doing so required Kitty to pay.

One note concerned the upstairs flat, which still awaited new tenants. On 27 February Donald wrote, 'ABOUT THE HOUSE – JE WILL NOT MAKE TROUBLE – JE LEARNT THAT BUT JE WILL NOT HAVE NO ONE UP STAIRS – JE HAVE MOI HAVE WAYS ET MEANS BUT VOUS WILL NOT BE HARMED – JE PROMISE VOUS THAT – DON.'

Other notes concerned the downstairs 'front room' (now Shirley's bedroom). To save money, the fire was not usually lit and during the winter the room could become uncomfortably cold. Donald repeatedly left notes asking for the fire to be lit and told Kitty she would be held responsible if his Renie died from pneumonia. He claimed that 'fierce spirits' lurked in that room and occasionally left further (unfounded) warnings of a man 'prowling' outside the window. Throughout February and March Donald worried that the room's chimney was unstable and would collapse. Even when he won permission for Shirley to light the fire, Donald continued to plead that she be allowed to sleep elsewhere: in her parents' room, in the kitchen, or even in the passageway. The fuss continued into April, until Wally finally ensured the room would be warmer in future. Chibbett recorded, 'On 3rd April [Donald wrote]: "CHIMNEY STILL FALL – LISTEN – I DO NOT LIKE IT – ITS STILL BROKEN UP THERE – I WILL REMOVE RENIES

BED INTO KITCHEN." "Donald" got so excited eventually that one night he moved Shirley and her bed right across her room and halfway into the hall. According to accounts, Shirley got out of bed, and tried to pull it back, with the poltergeist tugging furiously in the opposite direction. Anyway, soon after this, the Hitchings installed electric fires!'

CHAPTER 36

Donald had clearly grown bored of telling people about his previous existence as Louis-Charles, so Chibbett was surprised by a letter he received on 31 March 1960. Back in July 1957 Donald had said he thought Shirley resembled his (i.e. the dauphin's) sister, Madame Royale, and in November 1957 he had said that Jeremy Spenser was 'VERY LIKE NICKALOS'. Now he elaborated upon this theme. He implied that Shirley might be the reincarnation of Madame Royale, that Jeremy Spenser was the reincarnation of his best friend, Nickalos, and that their spirits – and his – were being drawn to one another across time! His tale had become even more fantastic.

The following week, Donald began adding fresh detail to the story of his rescue. In three letters throughout April he described how, after leaving the Temple prison, he and Count Hensdorf had hidden for two hours in a paper factory that had once been owned by a Monsieur 'REVALLAN'.

Chibbett immediately contacted Monsieur and Madame G—. At the time, they were trying (unsuccessfully as it would turn out) to find any historical mention of the 'CANDOR DE SERINE' decoration Donald had awarded Chibbett in mid-1958. Chibbett, encouraged by the recent confirmations that the 'Compagnie de Noailles' and 'lit de justice' were not mere fantasies, urged his associates to devote their energies to researching the paper factory instead. He was optimistic that the new details would withstand scrutiny and he eagerly awaited the G——s' reply.

His own attention he turned towards consolidating some details regarding Hartwell House, the property Donald claimed he (i.e. Louis-Charles) would have lived in had he survived the crossing to England. Having previously learned that Hartwell did not become the *official* residence of Louis-Charles's uncle (Louis XVIII) until 1807 at the earliest, Chibbett expected he would be able to find evidence the house had been *unofficially* used by French refugees before that date, as far back as 1795. In July Chibbett wrote again to the school at Hartwell. The principal, it transpired, was on holiday and the secretary suggested Chibbett write to Aylesbury Museum instead. The museum curator advised Chibbett that there was absolutely no evidence for French refugees at Hartwell during the period in question.

This dealt a serious blow to Donald's story and there was more bad news to come. Donald again stopped replying to Chibbett's letters. Worse, the G——s withdrew their assistance, the likely reason being Donald's unwillingness to give direct answers to their questions.

With little else to go on for the moment, Chibbett looked more closely into the history of Hartwell House. He knew that before Louis XVIII had taken up residence there the property had been leased to Sir William Young. In August, Chibbett contacted another Sir William Young – the descendant of the one who had lived at Hartwell – to ask whether the Young family archives contained anything that might suggest his ancestor 'gave shelter to French aristocrats at any time during the years 1795 to 1810'. Sir William helpfully delved through his family documents but his reply on 1 September unequivocally stated that no refugees had been entertained or sheltered at Hartwell before Louis XVIII's occupation.

Then J.B. Morton, author of *The Dauphin* (1937), sent a short and sharp response to a query from Chibbett, stating, 'I am convinced that the Dauphin died in the Temple prison on 8th June, 1795. [...] The claim of a rescue in January 1793 is preposterous...'

Despite the setbacks, Chibbett persevered. In September he wrote to inform Donald of Morton's reply, entreating the poltergeist to respond. Chibbett also asked further questions regarding the possibly pseudonymous 'Count Hensdorf'. His enquiries had by now led him to wonder whether the count might have been a Baron Von Ense. Chibbett had found mention of a Carl August Ludwig Philippe Ense who had been born in 1785, the same year as the dauphin: could this be the 'Karl' Donald claimed had taken his place in the Temple? Had Donald ever overheard someone mention the count's Christian name, or where he had been born?

Chibbett was also still searching for the *Royal Ark*. Now he consulted Privy Council and Home Office Records containing, in his words, 'the complete record of all the naval and private operations conducted on behalf of the French emigrants, also a list of all the vessels used, including the names of persons carried.' He found that, 'Many scores of different ships were used for the purpose, but there is no mention of a ship called the "Royal Ark".' Why not? Chibbett wondered again whether Donald was mistaken regarding the ship's name. He had found records of a vessel named *Royalist* but this had been commanded not by a 'Captain Stuart' as in Donald's story but by 'Lieutenant Dowsing'. Chibbett sent yet more questions to No. 63. Could Donald remember the name of a lieutenant on board the ship? Could he remember the name of the port for which the *Royal Ark* was destined? Would he state again the name of everybody aboard? And so on.

Another fortnight passed without response. On 27 September Chibbett received a letter from Donald – but no answers. Donald claimed to have lost the questions! Exasperated, Chibbett re-typed his letters. Another month went by.

On 28 October two letters from Donald were found in No. 63. Both had been typed and both were intended for Chibbett. In the first, which began with an attempt at French, Donald again blamed his difficulty with that language on being more familiar with 'old French' before repeating that he had come to Battersea because Shirley resembled his sister. The second gave partial responses to a few of Chibbett's queries. In answer to Chibbett's continued concern over the dates in his account, Donald simply insisted that he was correct and the history books were wrong. As for the identities of those aboard the *Royal Ark*, there had apparently been a total of ten people: Lord Arverington, Count Hensdorf, Nickalos, the Duke of Bedford, 'the Stuart' (i.e. Captain Stuart), 'et moi et four sailors'. There was no mention of any Lieutenant Dowsing and most of Chibbett's questions were simply ignored. It was hugely frustrating. In the meantime the school principal at Hartwell House, having returned from her travels, had replied to Chibbett confirming what others had said: there was no evidence that French exiles had stayed at Hartwell in 1795.

Still Chibbett persisted. As he perused a recently published book – *The French Exiles, 1789 – 1815* by Margery Weiner – he stumbled upon the answer to a minor question that had arisen three years earlier. In October 1957 Donald had tapped out a message consisting of the words 'COMTE DE PROVENCE' followed by 'ENGLAND NO MORE VOUS FOE WILL BRING YOU OVER – WHEN FRANCE SHALL WELCOME HOME THE WHITE COCKADE'. It had meant nothing to Chibbett then but he now spotted that one chapter of Weiner's book 'was about the return to France from Hartwell House in 1814 of Louis XVIII; and before his departure in April of that year, the Bourbon supporters in Piccadilly were humming the tune which was then all the rage – the "White Cockade". The words were, "England, no more your foe, will bring you aid, When France shall welcome home the White Cockade".' The discovery lifted Chibbett's spirits a little.

Then on 1 November Weiner herself wrote to Chibbett, replying to a letter he had sent her in August. She knew nothing about any ship called *Royal Ark* but suggested that, 'Since so many people in those days crossed the Channel in open boats, it may well have been a mere fishing smack.' If the *Royal Ark* had been a simple fishing smack, it was unlikely Chibbett would ever find documentary proof that it had existed. On the other hand, reasoned Chibbett, the absence of such a vessel in the historical record should not then be counted as a point against Donald's story. It was something to consider, but later, for there had been another development that might yet bolster Donald's flagging claims.

On 15 October Chibbett was visited by an Austrian acquaintance named Fritz Weiss, and Chibbett showed him the small metal crown that was still in his possession. This was the object Donald claimed had come from the hilt of 'a sword of France' but which, Chibbett had learned, had almost certainly been manufactured within the previous thirty years. Weiss immediately remarked that it resembled one of the Austrian crowns. This was interesting because even if the crown were not an authentic object from Donald's own time, a resemblance to an Austrian crown suggested a *symbolic* connection to Donald's story – Marie Antoinette had been the daughter of Empress Maria Theresa of Austria. At around this time, the BBC broadcast a television interview with Lord Twining, author of *A History of the Crown Jewels of Europe*. If anyone had the expertise to help Chibbett definitively identify the crown it was Twining, so Chibbett wrote to him seeking his expert opinion. Chibbett enclosed both the small metal crown and either a drawing or a wax impression of one of Donald's seals (the nine-pointed design Chibbett had been told resembled the coat of arms of the French kingdom of Navarre). His lordship replied a few days later. In his view, the seal resembled 'the heraldic form of Catherine Wheel' rather than the Navarre coat of arms. Better known today as a type of firework, the original Catherine Wheel was an execution device used from the Middle Ages onwards, on which the condemned man or woman would be spread-eagled before their limbs were broken. The Catherine Wheel featured on various coats of arms, but there did not after all appear to be any connection between the design on this seal and Donald's tale. As for the crown, Twining positively identified this as a representation of the English Imperial State Crown, remarking, 'A number of objects of this nature were made for the Coronation of King George V in 1937.' Far from being a valuable relic of the dauphins's sword, or even a symbolic reference to his mother, the crown was simply part of an old English souvenir.

Wally's diary for 1960 is the latest that survives and it ends with the following summary:

> Donald has not been a very bad boy this year but always wanted something. I hope we have a better time next year & also hope he leaves us for good so has [*sic*] we can get back to normal again. If he does we should miss him. But still while he his [*sic*] with us he don't do any good for us. Only cost money to us in one way & another. So with all blessing & hope he might leave us for good in the year of 1961.
> God rest his soul.

Donald did not leave. His 'domestic notes' stayed as prolific as ever and his continuing presence was again creating friction between the Hitchings family and the owner of No. 63. The upstairs rooms were still vacant because prospective tenants who called to view them quickly changed their minds when they learned about Donald, and Wally thought it only fair to warn them. By March 1961 the owner wanted to pass the headache to someone else by letting the upstairs rooms to someone who would act as his agent and assume responsibility for collecting the Hitchings family's rent. This worried Wally, who wrote to a newspaper's advice column for guidance and was told there was nothing he could do. He could only hope Donald would approve of the new tenants when they arrived.

Although his 'domestic notes' continued to appear inside No. 63, Donald was ignoring Chibbett's letters. 'Perhaps the difficult questions I have asked him are beyond his capacity to answer,' mused the researcher in May, 'or he has lost interest, or the ability to reply.' The results of Chibbett's investigations into Hartwell House, the *Royal Ark* and the metal crown, coupled with Donald's silence over the problems with some of his claims, were disheartening, but Chibbett's research still occasionally yielded encouraging results. In May Chibbett was reading a book about Paris when he chanced upon a comment that visitors to 'the Forney library', which held a collection of wallpapers, should remember 'that it was over fair wages in the Réveillon wallpaper manufactory that, on 28th April, 1789, the first troops … fired on the first victims of this Revolution.' This had to be the Parisian paper factory 'ONCE OWNED BY M. REVALLAN' that Donald had referred to the previous April. The discovery led Chibbett to remark, 'After this incident … and the scores of other verifications, I am more optimistic that eventually the "Royal Ark" will be traced.'

The 'scores of other verifications' referred to the multitude of incidental details that had cropped up in Donald's communications over the years and which seemed to fit historical facts. A very few of these, such as Donald's reference to a 'bed of justice', have been mentioned already, but the majority – numerous instances involving the names of people Donald claimed to remember, passing references to life at the royal court and so on, where Donald's details had proved to be consistent with historical records – have been omitted here for reasons of space. Ultimately, however, such 'verifications' proved nothing. Any reference book, novel, radio or television play, film, etc. that dealt with France at around the time of the Revolution was a potential source of such information. Yet, although he accepted that any of these details alone constituted poor proof, Chibbett believed (rightly or wrongly) that the cumulative effect of such circumstantial evidence counted for something.

Seeking information about the Réveillon factory, Chibbett contacted the Bibliothêque Forney in Paris. He learned that by 1793 the factory had no longer been owned by M. Réveillon but by Messrs Pierre-Jacquemart and Eugene Bénard. This was consistent with what Donald had written, but the Forney also stated that Bénard had been an ardent republican, a detail that dampened Chibbett's enthusiasm. Why would a republican have helped the dauphin escape? Had Bénard, perhaps, been a secret royalist? Chibbett considered this a possibility, but the evidence concerning the factory was at best ambiguous.

In mid-1961 Chibbett looked back over five years' worth of research notes concerning Donald's evolving story, his frequent evasiveness and his apparently paranormal abilities, and declared himself reasonably certain that Donald was an 'earthbound' spirit. But was he really the spirit of Louis-Charles, wondered Chibbett, or the spirit of someone or something else?

Long months passed with Donald continuing to ignore Chibbett while leaving endless 'domestic notes' bossing around the Hitchings family. Then Chibbett heard about a new witness to Donald's activity. Because of her poor health, Kitty had for some time been receiving help from a W.V.S. (Women's Voluntary Service) visitor. During her visits to No. 63 the lady in question had come to share the family's belief that Donald was a genuine supernatural presence in their house

and in March 1962 she handed Kitty a copy of a letter she
had written to a friend, giving Kitty permission to pass it on to
Chibbett as a testimonial:

[Copy of letter from Miss Barlow-Poole, dated 19 March 1962]

My dear Molly,

It is strange you should again tell me you cannot believe that there
are such spirits as Poltergeists: a few years ago I should have said
the same, but after coming in contact so much with a family who
have one in their home, I have changed my mind.

And about a fortnight ago, I was talking with the mother in the
family – all at once I felt we were no longer alone. Also heavy things
[this referred to the tubing of a vacuum cleaner] started to move as
though there was a draught from an open door or window, though
none had been opened: my companion saw I had noticed & just
said 'it's Don' for that is the name – or one of them – by which the
poltergeist is known.

I have seen his letters, that he has written, and the many things
that he has asked of his adopted family, all laid out by him. I know
he exists there.

Kitty forwarded Miss Barlow-Poole's testimony to Chibbett,
and at the same time she enclosed an apologetic note to the
researcher, 'I've told Don to hurry up and write to you [but] all
he says is yes. That's as far as it gets just lately.'

CHAPTER 37

By mid-June 1963, Chibbett had finished writing his book. To celebrate, he arranged a short holiday in Paris for himself and Lily. On a drizzly Tuesday afternoon they set off in search of the Seugnot sweetshop and, in the Rue du Bac, close to the intersection with the Rue de l'Université, Chibbett found the old building – but the sweetshop was gone.

It was now a library, and an assistant inside informed Chibbett that the Seugnot family had departed some two years before, leaving no contact details. It was desperately disappointing because Chibbett had never received the hoped-for follow-up letter from Monsieur Seugnot and had been looking forward to discussing Donald's story with the *confiseur/chocolatier* in person. But there was nothing that could be done so Chibbett thanked the assistant and headed back to his hotel.

In between sightseeing that week, Chibbett made time to visit the Bibliothèque Forney and he spent some hours there searching through old records. He hoped to discover more about the Réveillon paper factory but learned little he did not already know.

Before leaving Paris, he took a photograph of the building in the Rue du Bac. He later sent a print to Donald, who replied, 'THANK YOU FOR THE VIEW OF THE SWEETSHOP – I THINK IT HAS CHANGED A LITTLE'.

Chibbett's journey to Paris took him no closer to deciding whether or not to believe Donald's claims to be the spirit of Louis-Charles. Over the years Donald had given plenty of general information about his alleged life, much of which had turned out to be accurate but ultimately proved nothing because it could have come from plays, films, books, etc. The final test of his supposed identity, decided Chibbett, had to be whether his story of an escape from the Temple prison stood up to scrutiny – had Louis-Charles truly been rescued as Donald claimed or had he died in misery in his cell as the history books maintained?

Those books left no doubt that there had genuinely been plots to rescue the young prisoner, and various other authors had published books proclaiming their belief that such a rescue had actually occurred, with another boy being substituted for, and later dying in place of, the dauphin. Chibbett had come to accept that the rescue *might* have happened, but in the end had found no compelling proof that it really had.

What about events that supposedly followed the rescue? According to Donald, he and Count Hensdorf had hidden in the paper factory and, during his visit to the Bibliothèque Forney, the staff advised Chibbett on how he might be able to trace the descendants of the factory's owners. Chibbett did his best but never found anything to prove or disprove this aspect of Donald's story. Neither did he ever find any evidence that the sheep farm described by Donald had existed.

To a large extent, Chibbett realised, Donald's story rested on the historical existence or otherwise of the *Royal Ark*. If Chibbett could find documentary evidence that a ship of that name had been lost in the Channel in 1795, it would go some way towards bolstering Donald's story. On the face of it, it should have been a straightforward matter to confirm this in the appropriate historical records, but despite his best efforts Chibbett was unable ever to find any trace of the *Royal Ark*, or of Captain Stuart, or of the vessel's alleged owner, Lord Arverington. This did not necessarily mean the ship had never existed. Perhaps Donald had got the name wrong, for example, and although Chibbett had also searched without success for variants such as *Ark Royale*, it remained possible that the correct name was out there somewhere. Even if the name were correct there were ways of explaining its absence from the records. One possibility was that a covert mission to rescue Louis-Charles might have been covered up, especially if it had ended in tragedy. Another was that a small, privately owned vessel such as a brig or a fishing smack might have been lost beneath the waves without ever warranting mention in public records.

The lack of evidence for the *Royal Ark* did not demolish Donald's story. More damning, however, was the apparent survival of the Duke of Bedford. According to Donald's account, the duke had been aboard the *Royal Ark* when the ship was lost with all hands, so he should have drowned, yet this significant detail did not appear in any historical records.

Hartwell House presented further problems. Despite early encouraging results, Chibbett's investigations had in the end found no reason to believe that French refugees stayed at Hartwell during the period in Donald's story.

Most disheartening of all, acknowledged Chibbett, was that even if every one of Donald's claims were eventually to be verified – a possibility that seemed increasingly unlikely – 'it still would not confirm beyond doubt that "Donald" was the ill-fated Louis XVII; only that the information – wherever and however derived – was correct.'

After coming so far, Chibbett truly wanted to believe that Donald was Louis-Charles, but he had turned up nothing solid to which he could pin his hopes.

On 25 August 1963 Chibbett received a letter from Donald. The poltergeist had apparently been to Basel and found

the location of the sheep farm where he had been hidden. He wanted Chibbett to know that the farm no longer existed. Chibbett wrote back for more details. Where exactly was the farm? Could Donald pinpoint it on a map? Donald does not seem to have replied.

Donald's letter also revealed that Shirley – now 22 – was in love. She had starting seeing a young man named Derek and Donald said he wished the couple well. Derek lived in Carshalton Beeches – a 15-or-so-mile-journey from No. 63 – and when he first met Shirley he had no idea of the stories about her and her poltergeist. They met by accident. Derek was working at the Decca Radio and TV factory in Battersea, where one of his female colleagues lived in Wycliffe Road. After driving her home one night Derek met her daughter. They got chatting and arranged to go out together one evening as a foursome with a friend of Derek and one of the daughter's friends; the daughter's friend turned out to be Shirley. From the start it was clear that Derek and Shirley were more suited to each other than to their intended partners, and they soon started dating.

Donald, naturally, felt obliged to comment on their relationship. Shirley recalls one occasion when she returned home from a date with Derek to find her mother holding a note from Donald. 'Good night was it?' asked Kitty archly. Kitty had found the note earlier that evening and it informed her (correctly) that the young couple had been kissing in the back of Derek's car.

Derek dated Shirley for several months before the family mentioned Donald to him. It was only when Shirley's parents realised the relationship was becoming serious that Wally decided the young man should be warned. When he was told, Derek had no idea how to react. Very quickly, however, he realised that he was not the butt of some bizarre joke and he made his choice. The situation bewildered him but if staying with Shirley meant accepting her poltergeist then so be it.

Although now a frequent visitor to No. 63, Derek arrived on the scene too late to witness any of the dramatic poltergeist phenomena that had marked the early months. As such he never saw anything that incontrovertibly proved to him that a supernatural entity resided in the house. Even so, he soon experienced enough to give him pause for thought. He still recalls how Donald sometimes seemed to know when he and Shirley were arguing, no matter where they were. More than once they returned from a date to find, waiting for them on the 'front room' coffee table, a note along the lines of, 'DON'T ARGUE CHILDREN'.

'Well,' recalls Derek, 'that proved to me that either Shirley had written that before we went out and somehow engineered the argument … or she'd told the family to write it because she was going to engineer an argument. But I like to think that I'm practically minded enough to know that [such an] argument couldn't possibly have been foreseen.'

Although Donald rarely wrote to Chibbett any longer, his 'domestic notes' still appeared frequently inside No. 63. His requests – for new dolls, for Shirley to make clothing for his dolls, etc. – were more courteous than his earlier imperious commands had been (often, he even remembered to leave thank you notes afterwards) and, as well as offering general comments on events inside the house, he continued to look out for his Renie's wellbeing. He cautioned her not to work too hard, suggested she buy new clothes, offered relationship advice, and so forth. On 7 January 1964, the following note was discovered after Shirley and Kitty argued: 'KITTY WITTY – JE DO NOT LIKE THE WAY VOUS SPOKE TO MOI RENIE – IT EST NOT NESSARSSY KITTY WITTY […] WE ALL KNOW WHAT YOUNGSTERS ARE LIKE – JE KNOW RENIE GOT A LOT TO LEARN ET SO DEREK TO [too] – THEY NOT BE GROWN UP A [as] THEY THINK BUT THEY WILL FIND OUT TOGETHER […] DON'.

A second note found at the same time was addressed, 'TO RENIE ET DEREK': 'RENIE – BE A GOOD GIRL TO KITTY WITTY – SHE MAY BE ANY OLD MOANER BUT SHE

EST VOTRE MERE ET A DARN GOOD ONE – VOUS ARE A
VERY LUCKY GIRL – RENIE – DEREK – BE GOOD CHIL-
DREN – VOUS BOTH GOT A LOT TO LEARN – TAKE THE
ROUGH WIHT THE SOOMTH ET DO NOT LET MON
RENIE GET ALL HER OWN WAY – YES RENIE VOUS
MAY PULL A FACE BUT VOUS KNOW THIS EST TRUE –
REMEMBER DEREK SHE NEEDS A LOT OF PUSHING ET
VOUS STAND UP FOR VOTRE SELFS […] BE HAPPY ET
STAY SMILING – JE LIKE VOUS BOTH – DON'.

That March, Donald 'redecorated' the downstairs front
bedroom, painting black lines across the ceiling, and the
phrases 'VIVA FRANCE' and '[JE?] ROI LOUIS' on the walls.
Chibbett photographed the results. There was little need to
worry about the mess because the family was getting ready
to move out. It was something they had been discussing
at least as early as 5 February, on which date Donald had
left a note announcing his willingness to leave with them:
'KITTY WITTY – OF COURSE JE GO WIHT VOUS WHEN
VOUS MOVE – IT A NICE HOUSE WE GO – DON'. No doubt
the family was delighted.

Wally had probably learned that this part of Battersea was
likely to be redeveloped in the near future and that their house
stood in a part of Wycliffe Road that was to be demolished.
If so, this was certainly a factor in his decision to move. In any
case, the family home was very different now to how it had
been. Ethel had died, Mark had moved abroad and Shirley
herself would most likely be leaving soon. Moreover, the owner
had finally rented out the upstairs flat, a move that – thankfully
– Donald had come to accept. Shirley remembers that the new
occupants were 'a young couple with two little kiddies and two
giant bulldogs.' The dogs seemed able to sense Donald and
would stand and growl when the husband brought them down
through the passageway to go outside. The Hitchings family
and the newcomers got on well enough, but home just didn't
feel the same any longer. The final factor was that Wally was

coming up to retirement age and had managed to save enough money to move the family out of rented accommodation and into a house of their own. All in all, the time had come to bid farewell to No. 63.

In 1964 the family moved into their new home only a few streets away, in Latchmere Road, Battersea. Donald went with them, although he seemed to be slipping away a little now and his notes appeared increasingly less frequently. Shirley moved into Latchmere Road with her parents but everyone knew she wouldn't be staying long. Derek had proposed to her.

Shirley and Derek were married in March 1965 and among the wedding guests were Harold and Lily Chibbett. After the happy couple returned from a week's honeymoon in Devon, Derek moved into the Latchmere Road house for a month or so before the couple left to live briefly with his parents. For almost two years they spent no more than a few months living in any one place as they pooled their finances and built a life together. In late 1966, while they were sharing a house with Derek's brother in Worcester Park, south London, they had their first child. Shirley remembers learning she was pregnant via a note from Donald informing her (correctly) that she was to have a son, but although Donald's notes did still occasionally appear there was really very little sign of him anymore.

In early 1967, Shirley and Derek left London to live in a town on England's south coast. Donald was barely evident any longer but every now and then a note was found, usually commenting about Wally or Kitty. Derek vaguely recollects that Donald once asked him to build a dolls' house or theatre stage. Derek refused.

If anything, Donald appeared to be more active back in Latchmere Road. Kitty certainly felt Donald was still around there and whenever any object or item of furniture seemed a little out of place her first instinct was to blame the poltergeist. Shirley remembers her mother saying that the television set was affected most, that it would occasionally switch on or off of its own accord (possibly even while unplugged, she thinks) and that Kitty would take that as a sign of Donald's presence. In Derek's more sceptical opinion, however, 'Anything that was slightly out of the everyday [Kitty] could put down as being Donald. The house could creak by cooling down at night or whatever and [she would say], "Oh, that's Donald".'

'"Donald" departed from this life a second time during 1968,' recorded Chibbett, and Shirley and Derek agree that 1968 was probably when they realised there were no longer any signs of the poltergeist. The increasingly lengthy gaps between events make it impossible to pin his departure down to a particular date but as the weeks, months and then years passed Shirley and Derek grew to understand that he really was gone. Some twelve years after Donald's first arrival the haunting was finally over.

Things were over for No. 63 too. By the summer of 1967 Wandsworth Borough Council had arranged to move many of Wycliffe Road's occupants into new accommodation so that houses could be demolished. As the 1960s rolled into the 1970s the area was redeveloped and the Hitchings family's old home vanished forever.

Harold Chibbett never found a publisher for his book. By the end of the 1960s, after two good quality typescripts had been circulating around publishing companies for years only to be lost either in offices or in the postal system, he could not face the cost and effort of preparing a new typescript from his increasingly dog-eared original. But despite this disappointment and despite his deteriorating health he remained passionately interested in esoteric subjects, setting up a postal chain-newsletter (a forerunner of modern-day internet discussion groups), which he ran and funded himself. And still he continued to pursue Donald's story, remaining undecided as to whether or not to believe the poltergeist's claim to be the spirit of Louis-Charles, but hoping to find something one day to prove the matter one way or the other. Yet although

Chibbett followed trails through countless museums, archives, and other sources, he never found the conclusion he sought. It was, perhaps appropriately, like trying to grasp a ghost.

Harold Chibbett died of a heart attack on 23 February 1978, four days after his 78th birthday. His passing was marked by *Fortean Times*, the long-running journal of strange phenomena. In one of two obituaries to the researcher published in their spring 1978 issue, Sid L. Birchby remembered that Chibbett had 'encouraged everyone to think for themselves and not to reject any possibility until they had done so. All who knew him were never quite the same again.'

Kitty died on 6 June 1980, from cancer of the throat. Wally died eight months later, on 6 February 1981, after suffering a heart attack.

Shirley and Derek are still happily married, enjoying life together in the south of England.

Donald, thankfully, has not returned.

DISCUSSION

Three years before Donald's arrival in Battersea, scientists at Cambridge University made a major scientific breakthrough. In 1953 James Watson and Francis Crick deduced the structure of deoxyribonucleic acid (DNA), and one of the many fruits of their insight has been the development of techniques for comparing the DNA of different people to see how closely those people are related. As the twentieth century came to an end, work began to use this new knowledge to answer an old mystery: had the boy who died in Paris's Temple prison in 1795 been a substitute as so many rumours claimed, or had he truly been Louis-Charles, aka Louis XVII?

After the prisoner's death – and before his body was buried in an unmarked grave and lost to history – his heart was removed by Dr Philippe Jean Pelletan. It would eventually be kept as a relic in a crypt in the Basilique Saint-Denis in Paris. Over two centuries later scientists from the Center for Human Genetics at Belgium's University of Leuven and the Institüt für Rechtsmedizin at Germany's Universität Münster looked at the mitochondrial DNA (mtDNA – genetic material passed from mother to child) preserved within the heart and compared this with mtDNA samples from surviving maternal relatives of Marie Antoinette. Their findings, published in the

European Journal of Human Genetics in 2001, showed that the boy who died in the Temple in 1795 was highly likely to have been Louis XVII, not a substitute. This means that Donald's account of his rescue and his eventual drowning in the English Channel are highly unlikely to be true.

One person who would have been unsurprised by this was Mr O. Malthouse. In August 1967, Chibbett submitted an article about Donald to Malthouse, who was then editor of *Prediction* ('The Leading Journal of the Occult Sciences'). After examining one of Donald's letters, with its poor grasp of the French language, Malthouse declined the article, saying, 'To ask one to accept that such a person was the Dauphin of France is surely to stretch credulity beyond reasonable bounds.' Yet his conclusion that the story would, therefore, not interest his readers was surely a mistake. Regardless of how they are interpreted, and whether their origin was human or spectral, the events Chibbett chronicled had certainly happened. Rather than ignore them the question should be asked: if Donald was *not* the spirit of Louis XVII then who or what was he?

For the sake of argument, assume for a moment that the poltergeist phenomena were caused by something genuinely 'supernatural' or 'paranormal'. In this case, there are two general possibilities. The first is that they were caused by one or more discarnate 'entities' ('spirits' or 'intelligences'). *If* such entities exist then why should they also be assumed to be truthful? Might not such an entity have masqueraded as Louis-Charles, 'James Dean', etc. for reasons known best to itself? The other broad 'paranormal' possibility is that poltergeist phenomena are created by some as-yet unknown ability of the human mind. If this is so then we cannot say we fully understand what the human mind in question should be like. Perhaps, for example, a mind experiencing some sort of psychological disorder (see below for further thoughts regarding this) is an important component of what causes such phenomena. Either (or a combination) of these two general possibilities is surely of interest.

Now assume instead, again for the sake of argument, that all of the events described in this book were deliberately hoaxed and/or emerged from an extraordinary interplay of human frailties, as the collective common sense of numerous people was overpowered by the desire to believe in something outside ordinary experience. Again, such a scenario cries out for attention.

Chibbett, for all his personal eagerness to believe Donald's story, understood this. In February 1960 he wrote, 'even if "Donald" is not the personage he claims to be, the case still remains immensely interesting from a psychological point of view, or from any other angle.'

So we come back to the question: who or what was Donald?

One possibility that can be swiftly dismissed is that all the events were faked by somebody other than Shirley. There is no doubt that Shirley was at the centre of this story. In fact, it needs to be acknowledged that there appeared to be deep connections between Shirley and Donald, the clearest evidence of which is visible in the spelling difficulties they both exhibited. Donald's spelling was always unreliable, and when she was in her thirties Shirley was diagnosed as mildly dyslexic. There is also at least one example of what Chibbett termed the 'reversal phenomenon' appearing in Shirley's own writing: the family kept several newspaper clippings relating to their story, including one from the *South London Advertiser* dated 28 March 1956 and on this Shirley recorded the source as 'Avdertiser', with the 'd' and 'v' reversed.

Some have claimed to see similarities between Shirley's and Donald's handwriting. Andrew Green had samples of their handwriting compared and concluded that, despite surface differences, the two styles were similar enough to suggest that Shirley was the true author of Donald's letters. If correct then this might be considered evidence against the idea of

Donald as an independent entity. On the other hand, it could be argued that Donald was communicating *through* Shirley, using her hands to write the letters just as spiritualists believe spirits can temporarily possess the body of a medium to write or paint through them. If so then any vestige of Shirley's own handwriting in the resulting letters might be unsurprising. That said, Shirley herself is adamant that Donald did *not* write using her hands but that his letters and notes simply appeared inside the house, awaiting discovery.

Fig. 31 depicts letters written by Shirley (left) and Donald (right) on the same day (7 September 1959) to show how similar – or different – the two styles of handwriting were. The same illustration contains another detail worth commenting on, which is Donald's erroneous use of the word 'AS' to mean 'HAS'. This is a mistake that Shirley herself also occasionally made (and still makes) in her writing. It is one that Wally also sometimes made in his diary entries. This is not to suggest that Wally (who was usually out of the house when Donald's letters would have been written) was the author of Donald's writings; rather, that Donald's spelling reflected patterns of speech and literacy within the Hitchings household.

Another connection between Shirley and Donald appears in their shared interests in matters such as dressing dolls (remember Shirley's interest in theatrical costuming) and in historical dramas featuring characters such as Robin Hood and Sir Lancelot. A connection can also be sensed in a particular incident that happened in May 1956. Commenting on two messages Donald wrote that day, Chibbett noted that they seemed 'rather disjointed … and sound as though [Donald] had been indulging in strong drink'. When he visited No. 63 a few days later Chibbett learned that Shirley had been suffering from chickenpox at the time.

Given such indications, an inevitable question is: did Shirley deliberately hoax the happenings?

There were occasional signs of hoaxing. One example involved the small metal crown Shirley discovered in the passageway in August 1956. According to Donald this came from the hilt of 'a sword of France' but it was later identified as a representation of the English Imperial State Crown, probably a common souvenir made for the Coronation of King George V in 1937. Another example concerned the wax seals Donald sometimes attached to his envelopes, and here the information suggesting a hoax comes from Shirley herself. Any notes Chibbett made concerning this have been lost but Shirley remembers that Chibbett eventually decided that at least one of the seal designs (that featuring a crown) had probably been made using an embossed button from a British army uniform.

Then there was the 'sealed envelope' experiment of February 1959. At first it appeared that Donald had successfully removed the letter from the envelope without breaking Chibbett's seals, but closer examination suggested that somebody had actually lifted a section of the sticky tape and inserted a thin metal tool through a slit to remove the letter before replacing the tape.

When it comes to the information Donald provided regarding his life as Louis-Charles, Chibbett placed great value on the fact that Shirley did not belong to a public library, citing this as evidence she could not readily obtain historical details. Likewise, Chibbett emphasised that the family kept very little reading material of any kind in No. 63, and in particular no books about French history (although Andrew Green claimed to have seen books about this very subject in Shirley's bedroom). But – *if* Shirley were perpetrating a hoax – she could have obtained historical details in other ways. One does not need to be a member of a public library to walk inside and consult books, for example. Information could have come from various television and radio plays, cinema films, novels, magazine articles, etc. In short, there is no way to be certain that Shirley did not obtain any of the information by normal means.

Sometimes, Chibbett seems to have been overly willing to be persuaded by Donald's claims. In November 1959, for example, Chibbett took a map of Paris to No. 63 and was impressed when Donald indicated the location of the Seugnot sweetshop. Yet Chibbett seemed unconcerned that he had given plenty of warning that he would be bringing a map with him. In fact, the map had been Donald's idea! There would have been more than enough time for Shirley to study another map beforehand and locate the Rue du Bac. On that subject, the earlier discovery that Donald's sweetshop had truly existed was, for Chibbett, a major turning point in his investigation. He considered it such an obscure detail that Donald's knowledge of it was persuasive evidence that the poltergeist really was the spirit of Louis-Charles. But was this fact really so obscure? Seemingly not because when the author Margery Weiner wrote to Chibbett regarding the *Royal Ark* in November 1960 she commented in a postscript, 'Incidentally, I know the Seugnot shop well in the Rue du Bac.' This suggests that the shop may have been well known to those interested in the history of Louis XVII, and thus might have appeared in fictional or non-fictional accounts of his life that were potentially available to Shirley.

If (yet again for the sake of argument) Shirley did deliberately fake all or some of the phenomena, why might she have done this? Evidently not for financial gain because, apart from a fee of three guineas for an appearance on the BBC in February 1956, she neither earned nor asked for any money. Perhaps her motive was partly to do with asserting her will. For instance, thanks to Donald, she was allowed to play with dolls rather than take jobs she did not want. Alternatively, many hoaxers simply desire attention and/or fame. If this was what Shirley wanted she certainly got it, with stories about her in the newspapers, an appearance on television, countless strangers travelling to meet her and, most of all, years of attention from Chibbett. Finally, Chibbett suggested another possible motive, 'perhaps the desire to make people believe she was telling the truth about [genuine phenomena] pushed her into faking some things in order to try to convince people.'

However, Shirley has always denied perpetrating any hoax and Chibbett did not seriously believe that she was hoaxing. In around 1961, he wrote, 'although Shirley is a likeable [young woman] I doubt whether she has the powers of application at her age which would be essential to put over a deliberate and calculated deception of this kind for more than five years.' He drew attention to the fact that Shirley had been 'under considerable if not perpetual observation during the whole period' and not once had anybody caught her actually in the act.

In fact, it seems that nobody who seriously investigated these events while they were happening concluded that Shirley hoaxed everything that happened. The researcher Andrew Green did consider it possible that there had been 'some instances of deliberate deception by Shirley' but not that the whole affair was simply some gigantic trick. Green came to believe that much of what took place was the result of hysteria spread by the excitable and 'highly imaginative' Shirley but also that some of the phenomena (in particular Donald's tapping sounds, of which more below) were truly paranormal. And although he believed that Shirley physically wrote the notes and letters attributed to Donald, Green felt that she was probably unaware that she was doing so.

Most of the many newspaper reporters who visited No. 63 wrote afterwards that they believed inexplicable things were happening, although it should be acknowledged that in some cases the desire for a good story might have encouraged them to suspend scepticism. Not all journalists were convinced, though, a notable exception being Michael Kirsch. In early May 1956 Kirsch was present when the medium Eric Davey made one of several unsuccessful attempts to drive Donald away. Throughout the attempted exorcism Donald made

tapping noises and it seemed to Kirsch that the tapping originated in the vicinity of Shirley's feet. Afterwards, Kirsch stated
that Shirley's foot appeared to 'throb slightly' in time with the
sounds. Moreover, he claimed that when Shirley spotted him
looking at her foot the tapping stopped for a time and only
resumed when he looked away.

As for the other reported phenomena, Kirsch seemed to
think that Shirley was encouraged to play tricks by the general
air of chaos in the house and the attention she received.
Rather than blame Shirley, though, Kirsch laid most of the
blame on the 'dozens of spiritualists who descend on the
Hitchings', believing they added to the hysteria. Kirsch did not
believe there was a poltergeist in the house, yet even though he
felt Shirley was driven to fake some of the happenings he did
not think she was doing so *deliberately*. Kirsch felt that Shirley
truly believed a poltergeist was responsible.

Two other journalists with similar views were John Knight
and Ronald Maxwell, authors of the article that appeared at
the beginning of March 1956 claiming that Donald's tapping
was caused by Shirley unconsciously cracking the joint of her
right big toe. Knight and Maxwell took Shirley to see a doctor,
in whose opinion she might have been responsible for the
other phenomena which had happened by that time (such as
small objects being thrown through the air) without realising
she was doing it. 'In her present condition,' stated the doctor,
'she would be quite capable of moving something and forgetting that she had done so.'

In around mid-April 1957, W.E. Manning, the psychologist
who accompanied Chibbett to No. 63 on a few occasions early
that year, told Chibbett that the case should be considered
one of dissociation. (Chibbett's response was that he had 'no
doubt that the reaction of most psychologists and psychiatrists
would be similar' but in his opinion this diagnosis merely
gave a name to the phenomena and failed to address the
underlying cause.) The psychological term 'dissociation' refers

to a condition that exists along a spectrum that, at one end, includes many common experiences such as daydreaming, or the experience of walking down a street lost in your own thoughts and arriving somewhere without having been fully aware of your journey. More severe forms of dissociation can include carrying out conversations or actions without later remembering doing so. The most severe manifestation is what is called Dissociative Identity Disorder (DID – previously known as Multiple Personality Disorder). The International Society for the Study of Trauma and Dissociation describes DID as being 'characterized by the presence of two or more distinct identities or personality states that recurrently take control of the individual's behavior [sic], accompanied by an inability to recall important personal information that is too extensive to be explained by ordinary forgetfulness.' Such a diagnosis would appear to fit with much of what took place within No. 63.

When considering a psychological viewpoint, it is interesting to examine how this story developed. For the first three weeks events were restricted to strange noises. It was not until 18 February 1956, by which time the idea of a poltergeist – and hence the expectation that objects might be moved – had become established, that the first 'physical phenomenon' was reported. (Shirley accidentally dropped a pair of gloves and when she bent down to pick them up they flew up and hit her father.) As for the poltergeist's identity, the story told about that began to change after Chibbett became involved. By early April 1956, Chibbett was becoming a trusted and frequent visitor to No. 63 and this coincided with the first emerging signs of the personification that would evolve into Louis. And Louis did not emerge fully formed – far from it. In early communications he claimed to be the first-born son (who would have been Louis-Joseph) of Louis XVI and Marie Antoinette but later, in response to Chibbett's questioning, he became his own brother (Louis-Charles). Tangled up in the changing story of which son he had been was the confusing issue of his claim to be named 'Philippe'. In the face of Chibbett's questions, the only way this element could be retained was to insist that both he and his brother had been known by multiple names. Then there were the dates. Originally, Donald claimed to have been born in 1798 and to have drowned at the age of 15 (the same age as Shirley), although this had somehow happened 'before the Revolution' of 1789. Later Donald stated that he had actually been born in either 1771 or 1772 and had died in either 1788 or 1789, but once it had been established that, of the two sons, he must have been Louis-Charles, historical records showed that his date of birth needed to be 1785. After it became clear that Louis-Charles had not died in 1789, Donald changed the year of his alleged drowning to 1795 (at which time he would have been 10 years old rather than 15 as he had claimed earlier). Of course, before he drowned he had to have escaped from the Temple prison, which Donald stated he had done in January 1793. Then Chibbett tricked him into confirming he had still been in the prison in July 1793 and Donald pushed the escape back to January 1794. Chibbett pointed out problems this new date posed for other claims in Donald's story, and Donald reverted to January 1793.

Seen in this drastically summarised form, it appears less as if Chibbett's questioning was homing in on Donald's true identity and more as if that identity was an evolving fantasy, developing in and being moulded by the details shared between Chibbett and Donald.

A psychological interpretation can also be placed on the methods by which Donald (and the 'James Dean' personification) communicated, which were similar to phenomena known as channelling and automatic writing. The *Chambers Dictionary of the Unexplained* defines the former as 'the process whereby a spirit apparently communicates through a human medium' and the latter as 'the production of written material, supposedly without the conscious control of the person who is writing it down ... [This] is normally carried out by a medium, who may enter a trance – the pen or pencil [held by the medium] is then supposedly directed by spirits.' To psychologists, channelling and automatic writing are examples of dissociative activity, the belief being that the content of the communications comes from the medium's unconscious mind. Shirley insists that (unlike 'normal' channelling or automatic writing) the written communications here were supposedly produced directly by the entity or entities concerned (i.e. not through Shirley's hands). However, if Shirley were producing the writing herself in a dissociative condition then she would later have no conscious recollection of having done so and, when the letters and notes were later discovered, it would have seemed to her that they must simply have materialised.

The nature of Donald's story could be viewed as a form of escapism. A teenage girl trapped within her claustrophobic working-class life in the greyness of 1950s south London is chosen by the supernatural Donald/Louis, who gives her the title 'Princess' and sets about changing her home into the royal court of romantic late eighteenth-century France. The whole story was coloured further by the doom hanging over the French aristocracy and tales of heroic exploits *à la* the adventures of the Scarlet Pimpernel.

On a more prosaic level, Donald's existence helped Shirley in a number of practical ways. For example, although she was a teenager in 1956 she was still sharing a bedroom with her parents on account of her sleepwalking. In the early weeks and months of this story, Donald often demanded that Shirley be allowed to sleep upstairs instead, and it wasn't until Donald took over the 'front room' that Shirley was allowed to move her bed into there. Likewise, elements such as Donald's insistence that Shirley restyle her hair in a more fashionable cut and buy better quality clothes, along with Donald's pleas to light the fire in his/Shirley's room, could be seen as Shirley unconsciously using Donald to impose her will on the household.

If Donald was indeed an unconscious fantasy created by the teenage Shirley then this could also shed light on his otherwise surprising interest in handsome young actors such as Jeremy and David Spenser, James Dean and the stars of the *Robin Hood*, *Sir Lancelot* and *Scarlet Pimpernel* television serials. Furthermore, from this perspective Donald's odd fixation on the sceptical but handsome young reporter Kirsch could be viewed as an expression of Shirley's confused feelings towards him, and Donald's keen interest in 'playing Cupid' between Shirley and the photographer David becomes easier to understand.

Chibbett accepted the possibility that Donald was actually a product of Shirley's unconscious fantasising, but considered this explanation unlikely. To him, Donald and Shirley seemed too dissimilar in personality. Sometime between December 1961 and December 1962 Chibbett wrote, 'I have now "corresponded" with "Donald" for more than five years, and "he" shows so much of an individuality of his own as entirely distinct from that of Shirley, that if I did not know he had no real existence as a normal human being, I would be prepared to accept him as a real person with opinions and a strong will.'

Arguing against a purely psychological interpretation is that when Shirley was actually examined by specialists in psychiatry (and also given a thorough medical examination) in March 1956, doctors at London's Maudsley Hospital found no mental or physical abnormalities. A sceptic, however, might point out that the only available source for the results of Shirley's examination (a local newspaper article) is not necessarily reliable because the journalist responsible could only report what he or she had been told by Wally and Kitty, who may either have rejected what the doctors were trying to tell them or else felt unwilling to make the real results public. Shirley does remember that the hospital prescribed her some large blue pills to calm her down (Donald promptly got rid of the entire supply by dissolving them in water) and it would be interesting to know what the pills were, but the medical records no longer exist.

Then there were those occasions where Donald was seemingly present when Shirley was not. There were numerous instances of notes being discovered inside No. 63 when Shirley was not at home. Obviously, these could have been left by Shirley beforehand, to be found later, but Shirley's future husband Derek remembers how he and Shirley sometimes argued while out on dates, and would return to No. 63 to find that Donald had left a note referring to their arguing. In Derek's opinion, it is unlikely Shirley would have been able to plan such arguments in advance and engineer the notes' discovery accordingly. There were also times when Shirley's parents heard noises they thought were made by Donald at times when Shirley was not home, although it is possible that they only ascribed these noises to Donald because they were primed to do so. Occasionally, visitors to No. 63 experienced phenomena that could not have been directly caused by Shirley. On 30 April 1956, for example, the journalist Elizabeth Few claimed that Donald gave a message to her and her photographer while Shirley was not with them. Had the pair been so caught up in the drama that they unconsciously created this message themselves? A particularly cynical sceptic might even suggest that a journalist would have an ulterior motive for inventing such a message. Yet Few and her photographer were not the only people affected. At the end of April two unnamed visitors to No. 63 were reportedly 'followed by mysterious rappings' after they left the house and, in mid-1956, a friend of Mark gave Chibbett signed statements that he had heard Donald tapping in his own house on multiple occasions. But again such incidents might only illustrate how some visitors became caught up in the story and mistakenly attributed quite natural happenings to Donald.

The strongest argument against a purely psychological interpretation would be if phenomena occurred that demonstrably defied scientific explanation. What evidence is there of this?

The major defining characteristic of a poltergeist outbreak is the apparently inexplicable movement of objects and there were numerous recorded instances of this. Unfortunately, there are none where it can be stated beyond doubt that the records provide proof of paranormal activity. Most of the records made at the time simply describe very briefly what the family *believed* had happened, taking it as read that Donald was real and was responsible, and they do not contain enough detailed information (e.g. precisely who was where and when) to allow assessment of the likelihood of other possible interpretations.

Chibbett did report occasional indications that Donald was aware of things that Shirley could not know. For example, in April 1956 Chibbett was recording words being spelled out by Donald's tapping when he 'became aware that replies were being made to my (as yet) unspoken questions.' Chibbett made Shirley secretly write down a word of her own choosing. Then, sitting opposite her, he held a card (on which was written the alphabet) in such a way as to prevent Shirley from seeing which letters he was pointing to. Even so, Donald's tapping spelled out the same word Shirley had written. Another example took place shortly before Christmas 1958, when Lily Chibbett noticed how Donald's tapping (warning people away from the unwrapped presents) did not rely on Shirley being able to see what was happening.

A particularly dramatic example of a seemingly inexplicable happening was the 'levitation' of Shirley in February 1956. After she complained of something pulling her bedclothes, Wally and Mark grabbed hold of them – and also felt something apparently tugging at them. The report that subsequently appeared in *Psychic News* quoted Wally as saying, 'While this was going on we saw that Shirley was being lifted out of her bed. She was rigid and about six inches above the bed when we lifted her out and stood her on the floor.' It sounds remarkable, yet there is a possible explanation. Ten days after the 'levitation', Wally was interviewed by

John Langdon-Davies, and the latter's account of what he was told described how Shirley 'involuntarily arched herself into a bow' that night, following which 'it was just as if her head was raised'. Shirley then complained of feeling 'stiff' and unable to sit up and Wally and Mark found that her body had frozen into position. When they pulled her up by her arms she maintained her posture until she was vertical, before the rigidity left and she collapsed. This more detailed description resembles what is known as a 'psychogenic non-epileptic seizure', a phenomenon that superficially resembles an epileptic seizure but is a manifestation of psychological distress rather than an effect of abnormal electrical discharges in the brain. Shocked onlookers might easily interpret a sufferer's rigidity and the violent upward arching of their spine as being caused by something suddenly lifting that person into the air, and the medical phenomenon has been proposed as an explanation for the violent physical contortions that can occur during instances of supposed 'demonic possession'. This, then, might explain the reported 'levitation', although perhaps not the invisible something that three people felt pulling at the bedclothes.

Then there was Donald's apparent ability to predict the future, occasionally accurately. On 29 September 1956 Donald tapped out the first of a series of warnings that Jeremy Spenser would have a car accident on 2 October. That date passed safely but Donald continued to deliver worried messages, eventually leaving one found on 25 November. It was a long time after the originally predicted date but Spenser was indeed involved in a (minor) car accident that evening. On 9 December, Donald again predicted a car accident. Assuming the timing details given to Chibbett by the family were correct, at around 11 a.m. Donald predicted that someone named Paula would have an accident. That evening, the television news reported that Paula Marshall, wife of David Nixon, had been killed that morning when her car overturned. Chibbett was convinced that the family could not have known about the accident before that evening. The strongest evidence for a successful prediction was recorded by Wally on 23 February 1957, at (according to his diary) just before 11 p.m. Donald stated that the film star John Wayne would have an accident and the following day Wayne tore ligaments in his left foot. One further example concerns Donald's warning of 25 February 1958 that there would be a plane crash. On 27 February a plane did crash in Lancashire, killing thirty-five people, but this may have been coincidence. At around this time Donald was leaving multiple warnings that a plane might crash *onto No. 63*, and this apparent prediction might actually have been just another of those.

Of all the apparently paranormal phenomena, that which impressed people more than any other also happened to be the most frequent: the tapping sounds, initially described by Wally at the end of January 1956 as 'tapping as though water pipes bubbling'.

Ross Werge, one of the reporters who visited No. 63 in February that year, noted that the sound appeared to come from inside the object affected. In his case the object was initially a wooden chair on which Shirley had placed her foot. Later, Shirley moved across the room and leaned against a cupboard, whereupon the tapping seemed to come from the cupboard instead. Werge paid careful attention to Shirley's foot while it was on the chair and was convinced Shirley was not making the tapping sounds herself. Others were less certain, suspecting that Shirley was clicking the joint of her big toe. Chibbett found this proposed explanation preposterous, based in large part it seems on reports that the sounds could be so loud they woke everybody in the house and could sometimes be heard from the street outside. Possibly, though, Chibbett was confusing reports of different phenomena here, because in addition to the aforementioned tapping sounds Donald often banged loudly on the walls, and a possible explanation for the latter noises is that somebody was simply hitting those walls. It is not always clear from Chibbett's or the family's reports exactly which type of sound was meant when they recorded that Donald 'tapped'.

The most interesting comments regarding Donald's tapping were made by the psychical researcher Andrew Green. Green's testimony is particularly valuable because he retained a cool scepticism towards the happenings (something that did little to endear him to the Hitchings family). Despite his eventual conclusion that much of what happened could be explained by hysteria, possible psychological disturbance and perhaps even instances of deliberate deception by Shirley, Green was profoundly impressed by the tapping sounds and he remained intrigued by them for the rest of his life. Before he visited No. 63 he believed that Shirley might be making the sounds herself by 'cracking her bones', but his direct experience of hearing the sounds convinced him otherwise. During his first visit Green was talking to Shirley and her family in the kitchen. Donald was supposedly upstairs. Green asked him to walk down the stairs, and was surprised to hear what sounded like footsteps doing just that and stopping in the clearly empty pas-sageway. A little later, while talking to Shirley in the downstairs front bedroom, Green asked Donald to knock on the ceiling, and two knocks duly sounded. He then asked Donald to knock on the wardrobe, several feet away from him and Shirley, and Donald apparently did so. It left Green at a loss to think of a non-paranormal explanation.

Recent research has analysed recordings of what might be similar tapping sounds from other reported poltergeist cases. (Interested readers are directed to Barrie Colvin's April 2010 paper in the *Journal of the Society for Psychical Research*, which suggests that these sounds possess an unusual acous-tic signature.) It is a shame that we cannot analyse Donald's tapping to determine how similar it was to sounds recorded during other cases, but unfortunately no known recordings of Donald's tapping exist. Neither the Hitchings family nor

Chibbett could afford a tape recorder and Shirley recalls that on the one occasion Chibbett borrowed a recorder from an acquaintance and tried to record the sounds, the tapping could not be heard upon playback.

If (once more for the sake of argument) at least some of the events described in this book were indeed 'paranormal', what would this imply? There would seem to be two possibilities: either they were caused by Shirley herself or else some outside force was responsible.

Andrew Green's final conclusions regarding Donald tended towards the first option. His decades of research into ghosts and poltergeists would lead him to believe that genuine cases of poltergeist activity are due to psychokinesis, the purported ability of the human mind to exert a direct influence on the physical world. Psychokinetic effects, Green felt, originate with the person at the centre of the reported poltergeist phenomena, usually a child or teenager, frequently living in stressful conditions and unaware that they are responsible. In the sort of scenario Green favoured, Donald's poltergeist phenomena were some form of external manifestation of Shirley's psyche, the Louis story was a product of Shirley's fantasising, and all of the notes and letters were written by Shirley (probably without her knowing she was doing so). This type of explanation is currently favoured by many of those researchers who feel there is a paranormal element to poltergeists, and it has to an extent replaced theories that hold spirit entities responsible.

Chibbett, on the other hand, was more of the opinion that the poltergeist phenomena around Shirley were caused by at least one spirit entity. In this scenario, Donald's writings were either written directly by the spirit(s) involved – assuming an ability to physically manipulate paper, pens, pencils, etc. as required – or else written by Shirley acting as a medium (as the spiritualist Hanks originally suggested). And if Shirley were acting as an unconscious medium, with the spirit(s) communicating via her mind and/or body, then this could explain the evident connections between Shirley and Donald. Investigation should be directed towards the spirit(s) involved. Was 'Donald' some sort of discarnate intelligence – perhaps a deceased human, perhaps something else, and perhaps more than one entity – who enjoyed playing games, masquerading as 'Louis', 'James Dean', and so on? This was the type of idea Chibbett originally favoured before he was pulled into the supernatural wild goose chase of trying to establish whether or not Donald truly was Louis-Charles. Almost four years into Chibbett's investigation, in February 1960, Chibbett's French correspondent, Monsieur G—, offered the wonderful suggestion that Donald might be the spirit not of Louis-Charles himself but rather of one of the numerous 'pretenders' who had claimed to be Louis-Charles in the years following the Revolution, thus neatly 'explaining' both the entity's awareness of general French history and lack of knowledge concerning precise details of Louis-Charles's life! But what if Donald truly had been the spirit of Louis-Charles after all?

The mtDNA analysis of the prisoner's heart argues against this, strongly but not entirely conclusively. For instance, although Chibbett's surviving notes do not contain the details, Shirley remembers Donald hinting on at least one occasion that the mysterious Count Hensdorf was a cousin of Marie Antoinette. If Hensdorf and Marie Antoinette had shared a recent maternal ancestor – and if the boy who died in the Temple prison was actually Hensdorf's son, Karl, as Donald claimed – then this might explain the mtDNA similarities. Alternatively, as the researchers who carried out the analysis admitted themselves in their report, it is conceivable that the heart taken from the boy who died in the Temple was later switched for that of someone else, someone who really was a maternal relative of Marie Antoinette. Such possibilities – no matter how slight – will always leave the door slightly ajar for those who wish to believe.

As for why Louis-Charles's spirit would have such difficulty confirming his identity, Chibbett had some ideas about this. In October 1957 he mused, 'It has been suggested that if "Donald" is – as he alleges – [the spirit of Louis-Charles] he seems to be incarcerated in a strange sort of "dream world" … His evasiveness can be attributed to a dream-like inability to rationalise, and some of the senseless poltergeist activity can be explained by the unmoral nature of the dreaming mind.'

By around 1962, Chibbett had thought further about this, suggesting that Donald's memories of his life as Louis-Charles were locked into an '"earth-bound" condition … in which state he is still a little boy […] So perhaps the explanation here is that it is not so much deliberate evasiveness as child-like forgetfulness.'

Chibbett never fully made up his mind as to who or what Donald was but this did not worry him unduly. As he saw it, his major role was simply to record what happened: 'As the chronicler of Donald's Doings I have faithfully recorded many of his rapped and written communications in an attempt to show that "he" may be an intelligent entity distinct from his hostess – Shirley Hitchings […] I do not profess to be an expert in these matters, but merely an observer who has by chance encountered something which appears to deserve further study.'

As for Shirley herself, all she knows for certain is that the events described in this book happened: they were real, she and her family lived through them for many years, and they were sometimes very frightening indeed. To the best of her memory, Shirley knows that she did not deliberately hoax any of the incidents that were ascribed to Donald, and while she is to some extent prepared to consider the idea that she was unknowingly responsible for the events (whether in a psychological or psychokinetic sense) she has always been more drawn to the view that Donald was a spirit and that she was a medium through which that spirit was able to manifest.

More than half a century has passed since Donald made his presence known in No. 63 and as the years have gone by Shirley has sometimes doubted his claim to have been the lost spirit of Louis-Charles. But she remains personally impressed by the numerous details Donald provided regarding his alleged life in France at the end of the eighteenth century, as well as by the personality that emerged through Donald's actions and communications, a personality she feels was better suited to the dauphin than to herself.

Who was Donald? Shirley doesn't know, and the question still keeps her awake some nights.

EPILOGUE

During the latter half of the 1980s, Shirley and Derek were living in a small town in the south of England. The people there knew nothing of Shirley's connection with the strange events that had started in 1956. Donald was in her past – and that was how she and Derek wanted it to stay. Occasionally over the years they had noticed articles, etc. that they felt misrepresented what had happened in No. 63 Wycliffe Road, but for the sake of their children (a daughter had come along a few years after their son) they had always declined to come forward and challenge the various authors. It hadn't only been to protect their family from unwelcome publicity and ridicule, but also because of a vague fear that susceptibility to 'poltergeist phenomena' – whatever that phrase meant – could be passed on from one generation to the next, and that talking about it might accidentally encourage something to happen. Although their children were grown up now, Shirley felt no desire to rake over old history.

With Derek out at work all day, Shirley felt a little lonely sometimes. A friend suggested she join the local Women's Institute, and for a brief period Shirley became a member. Using the embroidery skills her grandmother Ethel had taught her, Shirley made and contributed items for the W.I. to sell. Each Thursday morning, the women met in the town's church hall and

Shirley helped out at their craft table. She welcomed her newly expanded social life, yet she could not help finding some of her new companions a little fussy for her taste, and some of their rules – such as their strict instructions on how many stitches she should include per inch – were almost too much to bear.

Shirley was in her mid- to late forties, and younger than the two senior ladies who staffed the craft table with her. One of them, 'Doris' (pseudonym), was 'a stuffy old thing' in Shirley's opinion, with a tendency to order Shirley to 'come along now' in a snooty tone. It was not only Shirley who found Doris difficult at times, for the older woman had a bit of a reputation among the other W.I. ladies. Doris believed she had a gift as a medium that sometimes enabled her to sense those who had passed over to the 'Other Side', and most of her colleagues considered Doris to be a little 'weird'.

One Thursday, Doris waved Shirley over. It was an unusually quiet morning, with none of the few visitors showing any interest in the craft stall, and Doris invited Shirley to have a cup of tea with her. As they sat down together Doris turned to Shirley and said, 'Now, don't take this the wrong way.'

Instantly, Shirley was on the defensive, fearing she had once again fallen foul of the proscriptive W.I. procedures and was in for another telling off. But Doris had something else on her mind. Leaning forward confidentially, she asked, 'Have you got a little brother who's passed over?'

With a sudden horrible certainty Shirley knew what was coming. Struggling to keep her composure she quietly replied, 'No, I haven't got a brother.'

'No, no, don't get upset,' said Doris. 'I'm a medium. I've been watching you for weeks now and as you walk across the hall you've got a little boy following you about.'

'Really?' replied Shirley. 'What does he look like?'

'He's got a mass of reddish-brown curls. He's dressed in fancy-dress.'

'Is he?'

'Yes. He's got a little blue satin suit on, he's got loads of lace and he's got these lovely red curls and beautiful blue eyes. Are you sure you haven't got a relation or a brother? He's with you. He's behind you. He's there with you all the time. I see him.'

'I'm sorry, Doris,' answered Shirley firmly. 'I don't have any brothers and that doesn't mean anything to me. You must be wrong.'

Nothing further ever came of this episode, and Shirley never told anyone in the W.I. what she really felt – that while the description may not have matched any of her relatives Doris could very easily have been talking about a certain young French boy from her past, a boy named Louis-Charles.

APPENDIX

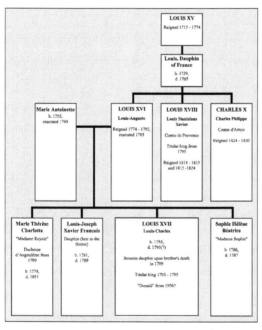

The French royal family: a simplified tree. (© James Clark)

BIBLIOGRAPHY

Books

Chambers Dictionary of the Unexplained, Chambers Harrap Publishers Ltd, 2007

Clark, James, *Haunted Wandsworth*, The History Press, Stroud, Gloucestershire, 2006

Green, Andrew, *Ghost Hunting: A Practical Guide*, Mayflower Books Ltd, Hertfordshire, 1976

Green, Andrew, *Our Haunted Kingdom*, Wolfe Publishing Ltd, London, 1973

Newspapers

'Mystery noises that haunt Shirley', *Daily Mirror*, 20 February 1956

'Poltergeist follows me, says Shirley', *Daily Express*, 20 February 1956

'Shirley's private spook gets rough', *Daily Herald*, 20 February 1956

'KNOCK, KNOCK! It's Shirley's poltergeist ...', Elizabeth Few, *Daily Express*, 21 February 1956

'Shirley talks on TV about her ghost', Marion Slater, *Daily Sketch*, 22 February 1956

'The diary of a girl with a poltergeist following her', Elizabeth Few, *Daily Express*, 22 February 1956

'"Black magic" said radio message, Police call on "Donald" séance', Elizabeth Few, *Daily Express*, 23 February 1956

'Police interrupt Shirley's séance for Donald', Jack Lewis and Thomas Halfpenny, *Daily Sketch*, 23 February 1956

'Séance, not black magic', *News Chronicle*, 23 February 1956

'Shirley is "freed" from poltergeist', *The Star*, 23 February 1956

'Shirley's ghost has too much publicity', *Daily Sketch*, 23 February 1956

'Turned down by a ghost!', *South London Advertiser*, 23 February 1956

'Who sent police to séance?', *Daily Mail*, 23 February 1956

'A spirit interviewed in Battersea', Ross Werge, *South Western Star*,
     24 February 1956

'Poltergeist follows her around', *The Two Worlds*, 25 February 1956, p. 2

'Poltergeist levitates girl?', *Psychic News*, 25 February 1956

'Spook was in girl's big toe!', John Knight and Ronald Maxwell,
     Weekend Mail, March 1-5 1956

'South London poltergeist gets phenomenal publicity', *Psychic News*,
     3 March 1956

'The press barred from dramatic secret séance with poltergeist girl',
     W.F. Neech, *The Two Worlds*, 3 March 1956

'Home Secretary questioned on police visit to séance', *Psychic News*,
     10 March 1956

'MP questions police visit to séance', *The Two Worlds*, 10 March 1956

'They can't sleep for Spookie Willie', *The People*, 11 March 1956

'Police called to "haunted house" blaze', *Evening Standard*, 12 March 1956

'Detectives call on a ghost: Shirley's own poltergeist sends a warning,
     then a fire starts', Elizabeth Few, *Daily Express*, 13 March 1956

'Poltergeist Donald getting spiteful: attempt to burn Shirley's home?',
     South Western Star, 16 March 1956

'Just what is going on in Battersea?', 'The other Battersea Poltergeist'
     and 'A night with a poltergeist', *South London Advertiser*, 17 March 1956

'Poltergeist still on the job', *The Two Worlds*, 17 March 1956

'Exit a ghost', *The People*, 18 March 1956

'Poltergeist failed to keep promise', Christopher Riche-Evans,
     Psychic News, 24 March 1956

'"Knockings girl" in hospital for test', *South London Press*, 27 March 1956

'Well, what do you know!', *South London Advertiser*, 28 March 1956

'Tapper Donald has learned to write', *South London Press*, 30 March 1956

'Poltergeist speaks colloquial French?', C. Riche-Evans, *Psychic News*,
     31 March 1956

'There's a knock! It's only a ghost', *Clapham Observer*, 6 April 1956

'Spend a night with "spook" offer made', *South London Press*, 10 April 1956

'Granny goes', *Psychic News*, 28 April 1956

'Fire riddle at "ghost" house', Elizabeth Few, *Daily Express*, 1 May 1956

'Haunted Hitchings get fire handout – then another fire',
     South London Advertiser, 3 May 1956

'Donald the ghost is busy again', *Clapham Observer*, 4 May 1956

'Don't look down on Shirley's "ghost"', Michael Kirsch,
     South London Press, 4 May 1956

'Poltergeist "Donald" is still at it', *South Western Star*, 4 May 1956
'b-a-f-f-l-e-d', *Psychic News*, 5 May 1956
'Donald intervenes', *South London Advertiser*, 7 June 1956
'Blue-blooded poltergeist likes TV', *Clapham Observer*, 31 August 1956
'Haunted out of house and home', *Clapham Observer*, 26 October 1956
'Poltergeists are in the news', *The Two Worlds*, 10 November 1956
'Thanks, folks', Edgar Bulstrode, *South London Advertiser*, 20 December 1956
'The ghost goes home – it says – when Easter's here …',
      South London Advertiser, 3 January 1957
'Writer of poison pen letters a "crank" – Police', *South Western Star*,
      28 June 1957

Magazines, Journals

Chibbett, H.S.W., 'The Poltergeist that can Write', *Fate* (US edition),
      Vol. 12, No. 10, October 1959, pp. 68-78
Colvin, B.G., 'The Acoustic Properties of Unexplained Rapping
      Sounds', *Journal of the Society for Psychical Research*, Vol. 74, No. 899,
      2010, pp. 65-93
Green, Andrew, Correspondence, *Journal of the Society for Psychical
      Research*, Vol. 66, No. 868, 2002, p. 192
Jehaes E., Pfeiffer H., Toprak K., Decorte R., Brinkmann B.,
      Cassiman J-J., Mitochondrial DNA analysis of the putative heart
      of Louis XVII, son of Louis XVI and Marie-Antoinette, *European
      Journal of Human Genetics*. 9, 2001, 185-90, Center for Human
      Genetics, University of Leuven, Belgium
Obituaries, *Fortean Times* 25, Spring 1978, pp. 32, 43
The Inexplicable Force, *The X Factor* issue 7, Marshall Cavendish,
      1996, pp. 171-72

Online

The International Society for the Study of Trauma and Dissociation:
      www.isst-d.org – accessed March 2011

Other

Chibbett, Harold: assorted papers
Green, Andrew: personal communication with James Clark,
      November 2003
The Hitchings family: diaries/journals, 1956–1960

INDEX

Made in the USA
Middletown, DE
13 October 2021